Corporations and Partnerships in Argentina

Corporations and Partnerships in Argentina

Second Edition

José Pablo Sala Mercado

This book was originally published as a monograph in the International Encyclopaedia of Laws/Corporations and Partnerships.

Founding Editor: Roger Blanpain
General Editor: Frank Hendrickx
Volume Editors: Koen Geens

Wolters Kluwer

Published by:
Kluwer Law International B.V.
PO Box 316
2400 AH Alphen aan den Rijn
The Netherlands
E-mail: lrs-sales@wolterskluwer.com
Website: www.wolterskluwer.com/en/solutions/kluwerlawinternational

Sold and distributed by:
Wolters Kluwer Legal & Regulatory U.S.
920 Links Avenue
Landisville, PA 17538
United States of America
E-mail: customer.service@wolterskluwer.com

ISBN 978-94-035-3278-3

e-Book: ISBN 978-94-035-3288-2
web-PDF: ISBN 978-94-035-3298-1

The Author

José Pablo Sala Mercado is a Professor of Corporate Law and Intellectual Property Law at the universities Nacional of Córdoba and Blas Pascal in Argentina. He is a lawyer and notary who graduated from the Blas Pascal University, graduated in law from the La Rioja University of Spain, and he graduated with Doctor in Law and Social Sciences from the National University of Córdoba, Master's in International Business Law from the Complutense University of Madrid, Master's in Business Law from the Austral University (Argentina), and Master's in Business Administration from the International University of La Rioja (Spain), among other postgraduate degrees. In turn, he is a practicing lawyer, a member of the firm "SALA MERCADO," in charge of the corporate advisory area; he is also a member of the list of arbitrators of the World Intellectual Property Organization, as well as the General Coordinator of the Graduate Secretariat of the National University of Córdoba and coordinator of the Master's Corporate Law program at the Blas Pascal University. Also he is the pressident of the Arbitration Court Specialized in Intellectual Property and New Technologies of the Córdoba's Lawyers College. Finally, he is the author of books and publications on topics of his specialties.

The Author

Table of Contents

List of Abbreviations

AFIP	Federal Administration of Public Revenues
CC	Civil Code
CCCN	Civil and Commercial Code of the Nation
CIDIP II	Second Specialized Inter-American Conference on Private International Law
CNV	National Exchange Commission
CSJN	High Court of Justice
CUIT	Individual Taxpayer Identification Number
EBAB\EBBA	Bi-National Argentine-Brazilian Company
EC	European Community
IGJ	General Inspection of Justice
INAES	National Institute of Associativity and Social Economy
IPJ	Inspection of Legal Entities of Cordoba (Inspección de Persona Jurídica)
LGS	General Companies Act
LMC	Capital Market Law (Ley de Mercado de Capitales)
NC	National Constitution
OPA	Public Offer
R.P	Public Registry
S.C	Collective Partnership
SA	Stock Corporation
SAE	European Limited Company
SAS	Joint-Stock Company
SAU	Public Limited Company (Sociedad Anónima Unipersonal)
SFC	Collective Financing System
SL	Limited Company
SRL	Limited Liability Company

List of Abbreviations

TFEU	Treaty on the Functioning of the European Union
TJEU	European Union Court of Justice
YPF	Fiscal Oil Deposits

Conversion Rate ARS-EUR
ARS 965 = 1 EUR (Argentinian National Bank as at March 14, 2024).
Every Law or act referred to in this work can be found at http//:www.infoleg.gob.ar

Preface

The personified organizational relations pose a complex legal system in Argentine law, with a strong imprint of continental law but with some influences from Anglo-Saxon law.

The simplification of corporate law, the result of a global market that seeks common regulatory standards to provide security to operators, poses the challenge of building a regulatory system that makes corporate types more flexible so that constituents can adapt them to measure and that this does not generate insecurity or transfer risks to third parties.

Throughout the present, we develop the fundamental aspects of Argentine corporate law, so that its characteristic notes, its evolution and its near future can be noted. Thus, we will develop the regulatory compendium focusing on the general system of the common fund for all private legal entities, the general part of the micro system common to all companies and, finally, the characteristic elements of each type of company.

General Introduction

§1. General Context of the Country

1. Argentina is formed by twenty-three federal states, called provinces, and an autonomous city that is the capital of the country. The division of the country into federal states has been the result of a long process from the revolution of May 25, 1810, up to the present, through the independence declared on July 9, 1816. In this way, during the time elapsed, the structure of the countries was established from important events such as the ratification of the National Constitution (NC) in 1853, a time in which the Argentine Republic was constituted by thirteen provinces without the province of Buenos Aires; the latter being then reinstated in 1960. With the passing of time, new provinces were created until reaching the number of twenty-three that today make up Argentina. According to the provinces, the country is subdivided into five regions: Cuyo, Northeast, Northwest, Pampeana and Patagonia.

I. Geography

2. According to the data provided by the National Geographic Institute,[1] the country has a territorial extension of 3,761,274 km^2, of which 74% corresponds to the continental area and the remaining 26% to the Antarctic continent and the Southern Islands.

3. Likewise, the border political boundaries are graphed: in the north, with the Plurinational State of Bolivia and the Republic of Paraguay, to the east with the Federative Republic of Brazil, the Oriental Republic of Uruguay and the Atlantic Ocean; to the South, with the Republic of Chile and the Atlantic Ocean; and to the west with the Republic of Chile.

4. Regarding the natural geographic composition, Argentina is made up of plains, mountains, a maritime platform to the east and south, and the Andes mountain range along its extension to the west. It is a wide territory useful for obtaining raw materials, and developing agricultural, fishing, mining and industrial activities as well as livestock and oil, among others. Without prejudice to these benefits of the

1. http://www.ign.gob.ar/ (available on Apr. 19, 2019).

territory, in recent years and because of the coming of new technologies, there has also been the generation of several technological clusters in different sectors where technological activity is promoted.

II. Cultural Composition

5. Argentina, unlike other countries in Latin America, is a country with a scarce population belonging to indigenous peoples and does not have a great African influence as a result of the national territorial expansion against the former and also by provisions sanctioned against slavery, both in the River Plate Assembly of the Year XIII and in the constitution of 1853[2] that prevented slavery from Africa.

6. After its independence from Spain in 1816, Argentina adopted by its constitution of 1853 an open policy on immigration, especially European,[3] and, as a reflection of it, the majority of its population belongs to descendants of different immigration flows that were established throughout its history, with a marked European influence, mostly Italian and Spanish, although there has also been immigration from other sectors of that continent. The most pronounced immigration occurred in the late nineteenth and early twentieth centuries.

7. In the late nineteenth and early twentieth centuries (1889–1914), immigration was characterized as being overseas in Europe and ranked second in density in America below the United States. Then, immigration was maintained to a lesser extent toward the middle of the century and, finally, at the beginning of the twenty-first century, immigration was mostly composed of people from other South American countries, that is Bolivia, Paraguay, Peru and, more recently, Venezuela together with citizens of Asian origin.

8. It is a secular State with cultural and religious diversity, although the federal government supports the Roman Catholic Apostolic cult, where the most spoken language is Spanish, notwithstanding the coexistence with small doses of languages belonging to native peoples and current immigration (German, Arabic, Armenian, Chinese, Korean, French, Yiddish, English, Italian, Japanese, Portuguese, etc.).

III. Political System

9. The constitutional political system adopted by Argentina for its government is the representative, republican and federal form.[4] As a Federal State, each province has autonomy over issues and faculties not delegated to the nation at the time of its formation or subsequent reforms, and a provincial constitution has been issued in each State that is consistent with the principles, declarations and guarantees

2. Article 15 of the National Constitution of 1853.
3. Article 25 of the National Constitution.
4. Article 1 of the National Constitution.

adopted in the NC. In coherence with the established system, it is a representative democracy as long as people do not govern or deliberate except through their representatives,[5] who are elected by all the people of the nation according to the universal compulsory voting established for their equal and secret exercise.[6]

10. The Republic stands on the three powers of the State: executive, legislative and judicial. The balance among the three powers according to their executing powers, sanctioning and controlling laws, must be kept permanently to ensure the balance provided by the constitution. It is prohibited to grant the Executive Power extraordinary prerogatives or supremacies or those that imply holding the whole public power, by which the destinies of the nation are at the mercy of a government or any person.[7]

11. Likewise, the public and judicial acts of a province have faith in the others, and equal rights as well as guarantees to the citizens of one province are certainly guaranteed in the rest. There are no internal customs offices but only one common external customs office, without prejudice to the signing of regional integration agreements with other nations.

12. What is more, a right to which we will refer to later and which is guaranteed to every Argentine citizen is to associate with useful purposes, and we must point out that it is included in Article 14 of the NC.

IV. Population and Employment Statistics

13. Argentina presented in 2010, 40,117,096 inhabitants;[8] at present, it is believed that the number ascends approximately to 44,270,000. According to statistics from the National Institute of Statistics and Census, in the last quarter of 2018, there was an unemployment rate of 9.1%.[9] Notwithstanding this, it should be noted that the country has a high percentage of informal workers not registered (32.2%) and that, on average, 50% of registered workers work in the public sector.

14. What is more, the aforementioned data contribute to a huge fiscal burden imposed on the private sector to sustain current public spending, which also prevents the possibility of self-financing for the State to carry out structural material reforms. Considering this reality of impotence to cope with costs, current public spending is financed through the issuing of currency or external debt, both of which are difficult options causing a great impact on the economy and an uncertain future.

5. Article 22 of the National Constitution.
6. Article 37 of the National Constitution.
7. Article 29 of the National Constitution.
8. Available in Apr. 2, 2019, www.indec.gob.ar.
9. La Nación newspaper, Mar. 27, 2018, based on Indec publications.

V. Enterprise, Corporations, and Partnership Statistics

15. Argentina is ranked 119 out of 190 countries that are part of the Doing Business ranking.[10] This is the result of many reasons, including bureaucratic complications to start a company in terms of registration, opening a business (at present the position in this field is 128 in the ranking), financing or access to credit, constitution of legal entities, ratings, etc.

16. In June 2017, there were 605,626 active companies in Argentina, of which more than 99% (602,079) were small and medium enterprises (less than 200 workers), 0.6% were large companies (3,547), and 72% were concentrated in four jurisdictions.[11] According to these data, the companies providing services at that date reached a total of 207,530 and manufacturing ones a total of 61,471. However, taking into account the average of annual opening and closing of companies in the country, according to the report, around 70,000 are opened while another 68,000 are closed; these fluctuations happen in relation to changes in demand, financing, sectional trends and regulatory aspects.

17. In addition to this, it is important to highlight that there is no national index of companies incorporated under the structuring of societies as it is about local registries that receive the registration of the legal persons as a consequence of the autonomy of the provinces. Without prejudice to this, in order to make a graph that is not extended to the rest of the jurisdictions, in the autonomous city of Buenos Aires that presents the record with the greatest movement, approximately 11,000 companies were set up per year, and in 2016, 60% of them were established as limited companies and the majority of the remaining were limited liability companies (SRL). At present, as a consequence of the enactment of Law 27,349 to support entrepreneurial capital (the regulatory body that introduced simplified stock companies), the latter have reached a percentage of 31% in the last twelve months, due to their advantages over the others in matters of formalities.

VI. Social and Cultural Values

18. Argentina is a country that establishes equality before the law in its constitution,[12] including foreigners,[13] individual liberties and property rights.[14] It is worth saying that no prerogatives of blood or birth, no personal privileges or titles of nobility are admitted, being every single person admissible to any employment; the only necessary requirement is competence applied to both natives and foreigners. Likewise, the property is inviolable, and no inhabitant can be deprived of it except as a sentence based on law.

10. Available in April 2019, www.doingbusiness.org.
11. GPS Argentine companies, Ministry of Production of the Nation.
12. Article 16 NC.
13. Article 20 NC.
14. Article 17 NC.

19. These referred rights and guarantees, added to others, should not be understood as a denial of other rights and guarantees not listed, but they must be interpreted as being derived from the principle of sovereignty of the people and of the republican form of government.[15]

20. The compliance of the NC must be guaranteed at all times, even when it is interrupted as a result of acts carried out against the institutional and democratic order, all of which will be of absolute nullity.[16]

VII. Privatization Efforts

21. During the 1990s, reforms were carried out in the State, so it delegated some services to private companies, allowing, in turn, the privatization of state enterprises. By Law 23,696 (1989), the privatization of a considerable number of State companies that managed the Public Services of Petroleum Supply (Yacimientos Petrolíferos Fiscales (Fiscal Oil Deposits) or YPF was acquired by the Spanish company REPSOL), air transport (Aerolineas Argentinas SRL and Austral Lineas Aéreas Cielos del Sur SRL were also acquired by the Spanish company IBERIA), as well as railroads, water, electricity, etc.

22. The law in its eighth article established the need for a State company to be declared "subject to privatization" (before its privatization) by the National Executive and approved by the law of parliament. In this way, acts of total or partial privatization or the dissolution of companies, establishments or productive farms whose property belonged totally or partially to the Argentine National State were carried out. With the passing of the law, some necessary investments by private capital to remodel the structures and improve the benefits of the different public services were allowed. Then, some years after that reform, it can be concluded that in some cases, the results have been positive and in others not so much, but the reform was totally necessary, although due to the inefficient control of the State, in some cases, the objectives pursued were not finally achieved. There are clear examples of the privatized companies YPF and Aerolíneas Argentinas, which were later renationalized in 2012 and 2008 by Laws 26,741 and 26,466, respectively. Notwithstanding the foregoing, the provision of public services has been largely transferred to private capital through concession contracts signed by the State by which the latter controls the companies in the execution.

§2. The Historical Background of Corporations and Partnerships

23. After the independence in 1816, trade in Argentina was regulated by scattered laws that continued the prevailing reality of previous years in the colonial period. This scenario lasted until the sanction of the Commercial Code (1862), Law

15. Article 33 NC.
16. Article 36 NC.

15, which established the application of the Commercial Code of Buenos Aires. The code determined trade as a profession that required publicity and could be exercised through a company, regulating the corporate contract in Articles 387–512. In Article 387 of the Commercial Code, a company is "a contract whereby two or more people join together, providing their goods or industry, or any of these things, to carry out acts of commerce, with the intention of splitting the profits that may result." Every company was commercial if its objective was to carry out acts of commerce, with the exception of the corporation that was always commercial.[17] All this was then kept and added in the subsequent Article 282 of the Commercial Code reformed and ratified in 1989.

24. Apart from this, between the 1862 code and its reform of 1889, the Civil Code (CC) ratified in 1869 (Law 340), had admitted in its Articles 32 and subsequent, the legal entities in general and also civil societies in Articles 1648 and subsequent.

25. That Code of Commerce of 1889 was in force until 2015 (however, modifications were done at different times as it was the derogation of the third title called "the companies or societies" because of the sanction of Law 19,550 of Commercial Companies), when it was totally revoked and replaced by the Civil and Commercial Code of the Nation (CCCN), sanctioned by Law 26,994. This last regulation also modified the denomination of Law 19,550 that used to be called the Law of Commercial Companies and turned into the General Companies Act (LGS).

26. We describe the evolution of national regulations on companies in four stages, namely: (a) Commercial Code of 1862; (b) Commercial Code of 1889; (c) Law 19,550 of Commercial Companies of 1972 reformed in 1983; and (d) LGS 19,550 reformed by Law 26,994. It is worth saying that, from 1869 to 2015, when it was finally sanctioned the Civil and Commercial National Code, the CC sanctioned in 1869 (Law 340 that had its more substantial reform governed in 1968 by Law 17,711) had been in force simultaneously with the Commercial Code. This will be explained below.

I. 1862 Commercial Code

27. As we have previously expressed, the code of Buenos Aires was nationalized in 1862 (Law 15) and in its Articles 387–512, it regulated companies and societies. In this normative body, it was established that the partnership agreement, except for accidental or joint ventures (Article 446), had to be formulated in writing when its value exceeded ARS 1,000 and this act could be implemented by public or private instrument (Article 393) and then registered in the Public Registry (R.P) of Commerce (Article 397). These requirements were confirmed for the existence of a

17. Code of Commerce (1862). Art. 403.

company (Article 399), providing for the silent partner (who is a member but is not included in the contract) a personal, joint and unlimited responsibility (Articles 401 and 454).

28. In addition to this, it is possible to enumerate some notes that the partnership contract presented in this first regulation, since they will be useful to show the evolution that the institution has had in the national law since there are regulations that have been kept by subsequent governments even up to the present. It is worth saying that this first regulation acknowledged the companies or societies as a mere contract, without generating a legal subject or legal entity, something that would later be reinforced by the Commercial Code of 1889 (Article 282) (except for the corporation in this last regulation) and that therefore was so much criticized. This concept is derived from the systematic location of the company in the second book devoted to contracts, after the articles following the mandate, instead of being in the first book devoted to the businessman. In this regulation, the partners were trustees of each other, and in the collective society, the social signature was equivalent to the signature of each of them who were jointly and severally bound (Articles 454 and 455), implying the bankruptcy of the company also meant one of its partners (Article 1530). What is more, the limited partnership had two categories of partners: a collective partner with joint and unlimited liability authorized to manage the company and another silent partner responsible for the funds declared in the contract, without powers to administer (otherwise, he could be punished) and would be liable as a collective partner, as it is currently established in the regulatory body (Articles 425, 430–432). However, the latter could carry out acts of inspection, advice or opinion and surveillance. By the way, the collective partners were represented and jointly and severally obliged to each other, while the silent partners were considered commission agents without representation before third parties (Article 299). In addition, the declaration of bankruptcy of a silent partnership implied the bankruptcy declaration of the collective partners, without having the same effect with respect to the silent partners, a result that still persists in the current regulations. Finally, the code in Article 435 regulated the authorizations or societies of capital and industry also with two categories of partners: one identical to the collective partner and another industrial that contributed with his own industry forcing himself to be liable up to the limit of the unacquired profits without being able to represent the society, since the latter could only be so for the first ones who responded jointly and therefore should be included in the company name. The abovementioned solutions for the collective partners in the silent partnership are also established for the capitalist partner in this society, in the event that it has a social signature (Articles 437 and 1530).

29. In addition, in the accidental or participation entities that were also admitted and not subject to the aforementioned formalities (Articles 444 and subsequent), only the partner who had participated in the direct negotiation was obliged to third parties since, although he acted on behalf of the other partner did not oblige him to third parties.

30. To conclude, the joint-stock companies (SAS) had a particular treatment in the second chapter of the third title; we should point out that the SAS are associations of capital for the development of any company and they are commercial, as it has already been expressed, regardless of their purpose (Article 403). According to the code, although the partners were not responsible for the obligations of the company (they were responsible for the social fund or accumulated benefits), the latter was not a subject of law or legal entity (Articles 409 and 410). In this sense, the managers were agents of the partners who were responsible only for the value of their assets or to the extent of their interest and the company had no business name (Articles 405, 307 and 409). To be established, if it had some privilege (some concession provided by the State), the corporation needed authorization from the National Executive Power and it had to be set up for a specific period of time (Article 405). This regulation is based on the Spanish Code of 1829 (Article 294).

II. 1889 Commercial Code

31. The Commercial Code of 1889 was ratified by Law 2,637, which devoted its third title, with ten chapters, to "the companies or societies" (Articles 282–449). Then, this title was repealed in 1973 by the enactment of Law 19,550 of Commercial Companies.

32. The code showed, in addition to a restructuring in the articles, some modifications with respect to the SAS; for example, it required State authorization for all of them (Article 318, paragraph 4). It is worth saying that, until this time, the companies were not considered legal persons, which was granted in 1968 after the reform of the CC of 1871 (Law 17,711).

33. Likewise, the Commercial Code of 1889, in its sixth chapter, included the cooperative society as a commercial company (Article 392) without meaning a special form of society, and may consequently adopt in its constitution any of the legal types provided by the code and applying the provisions of the type adopted with the modifications established in the particular chapter of the cooperatives. This particular treatment of cooperative was repealed in 1973 (Law 20,337) that determined a particular régime and also provided the application of the rules related to SAS (Article 118).

34. Next, a reform of great importance for the Commercial Code of 1889 was the one established in 1932 (Law 11,645 Articles 1–3), by which the SRL was included as a commercial company subject to all its effects on the Commercial Code and complementary laws, whatever their purpose. It was also possible for them to have a company name or to be named according to their purpose or by the name that the partners attributed to them, preceded or followed by the "limited liability" attachment, and the possibility of carrying out any civil or commercial operation with the exception of the ones carried out by banks, insurance, capitalization and savings.

III. 1871 Civil Code: Reformation in 1968 (Law 17,711)

35. Once the CC was in force (Article 32), the person of ideal existence or legal entity was recognized. Besides, it introduced the regulation of the civil society (Article 1648 and subsequent) which did not constitute a legal entity (this was modified in 1968 as amended by Law 17,711); it could not be engaged in trade; the partners were liable in equal shares unless otherwise agreed upon; and, finally, it did not punish the partner that did not appear in the contract, as he/she was not liable to third parties in accordance with the existence of a non-representative civil regulation. After the reform of the code provided by Law 17,711, under the terms of the new Article 33, civil and commercial companies were recognized as private juridical persons, and in the case of the SAS, it was recognized as a legal entity from the moment it had got the State authorization (Article 45).

IV. Law 19,550 of Commercial Companies

36. Law 19,550, notwithstanding its successive reforms, is still in force. That is why we will be analyzing it thoroughly in the following chapters and sections. In spite of this, it is worth noting that the original text of the Commercial Code (1972) that revoked Articles 41 and 282–449 already discussed above, beyond slight changes determined by Laws 19,666; 1,880; 20,337; 21,304; 21,357; 22,182; 22,686; 22,903 and 22,985, was subject to two substantial reforms in 1983 (Law 22,903) and 2015 (Law 26,994) that passed the current unified code in civil and commercial matters. This clearly arises from the number of articles replaced by reforms, in 1983, and the Articles were: 11; 12; 22; 33; 50; 54; 55; 61–68; 70; 72; 73; 75–84; 86–88; 94; 95; 98; 110; 129; 149; 150; 152–155; 157–160; 162; 183; 184; 186; 187; 194; 195; 197; 199; 200; 201; 203; 208; 214; 215; 223; 238; 241; 244; 245; 251; 256; 258–260; 263; 264; 267; 271; 274; 280; 284; 287; 297; and 366, and in 2015, the articles were: 361; 362; 364; 365; 367; 368; 370–378; and 380–383. Also, with the enactment of Law 20,337 (Special Regime of Cooperatives), Article 372 of the Law of Commercial Companies was revoked; the latter extended the application of its rules to cooperative societies on condition that those principles did not contradict the nature of the commercial companies (Article 119). What is more, notwithstanding the aforementioned reforms, Law 19,550 has two chapters: one referring to the general part of companies applicable to any company without considering its particular type except as expressly modified in the section devoted to each of these and, the other chapter, which acknowledges the different types of companies. It is worth saying in a preliminary way, something which will be analyzed later on, that the second chapter has historically admitted six corporate types, namely: Collective Society; Limited Simple Partnership; Capital and Industry Society; SRL; Public Limited Company (Sociedad Anónima Unipersonal (SAU)); and Limited Joint-Stock Partnership.

37. Let us point out that we will refer to the Informal Companies (Simple or Residual) that are in the first chapter and are the result of the 2015 reform replacing the irregular or de facto companies of the previous text, as well as simplified stock companies created in 2016 (Law 27,349) that are not introduced in the second chapter but are ruled by this special law and, likewise, allows the application of both the LGS (19,550) (in issues related to social bodies) and the CCCN.

§3. Definitions and Structure of Corporations and Partnerships

I. Different Forms of Corporations and Partnerships

38. Legal entities in the Argentine system present a general regulation established in the CCCN, Articles 141–167, a special part of the same legal body devoted only to civil associations (Articles 168–192) and to foundations (Articles 193–224), and then special laws or microsystems that rule other legal entities such as societies in general (Law 19,550), insurance companies (Law 20,091), mutual associations (Law 20,321), cooperative societies (Law 20,337), and simplified stock companies (Law 27,349 to support entrepreneurial capital). It should be noted that the Civil and Commercial Code distinguishes between public and private legal entities (Article 145, CCCN), corresponding the first ones to the national, provincial, autonomous city of Buenos Aires, municipalities, self-sufficient entities and other organizations constituted in the Republic to which the legal system attributes such character, foreign states, organizations of public international law with legal personality and any other legal entity incorporated abroad whose public nature results from its applicable law, together with the Catholic Church (Article 146, CCCN). All of them will be ruled by the laws and regulations of incorporation (Article 147, CCCN) in terms of their recognition, beginning, capacity, functioning, organization and purpose of their existence.

39. However, regarding private legal entities, the code lists the following: societies; civil associations; simple associations; foundations; churches, religious confessions, communities or religious entities; mutual cooperatives; horizontal property consortiums; and any other contemplated by provisions of the code or special laws (Article 148, CCCN). The fact that the State participates in private juridical entities does not imply any change, and let us remark that by means of special regulations, there can be a special treatment of any particular issue (Article 119, CCCN).

40. Having made the distinction between public and private juridical entities (we should remark that the formers are exempt from the code in the terms indicated above), we must focus on the treatment provided to the latter; especially, we will concentrate on most of the subject matters since they coincide with the regime imposed in the LGS. In this sense, in the first place, the Civil and Commercial Code establishes a normative priority system that defines a certain coherence of general and special principles that regulate the same subject (Article 150, CCCN). In this way, the mandatory rules of the special and general regime will be applied in an unavoidable manner, after the contracting parties have provided in the constituent instrument without contravening the aforementioned regulations and, finally, if there has not been an opinion expressed by the parties in this sense, the supplementary regulations of the special regime will be observed first and then those of the general regime of the same characteristics. This order of precedence will be the guideline of interaction between the general regime and the specialized bodies previously mentioned.

41. Once the coherence of the system was described, it should be noted that the Civil and Commercial Code defines the legal entity as "any entity to which the legal order grants the capacity to acquire rights and duties for the fulfillment of its purpose and the purposes of its creation" (Article 141). Soon we will see that this concept, which has been recently regulated, has been in force since the end of 2015, and it shows an improved version (it is a project that will become a law) and it is being reviewed at present. This is because Article 141 of the CCCN reissues the doctrine of ultra vires, inasmuch as it limits the capacity of the entity to its object and constitutive purpose, a position that had been overcome in 1973 with the ratification of Article 58 by which the representative of the society obliged the company for all acts that were not notoriously different from its purpose, a concept that still exists and that clearly does not consider the purpose as a limitation to its capacity.

42. Apart from this, the general regime establishes that the legal entity begins its existence from the moment of its constitution unless there is a special provision to the contrary (Article 142, CCCN); also, it determines that the company is established as a different subject from the members that comprise it (Article 143, CCCN) and that, unless otherwise provided, the latter are not liable to the duties of the entity. Finally, the unenforceability of the legal entity is provided when the proceeding of the latter is "aimed at the achievement of purposes unrelated to its personality, constitutes a mean to break the law, public order or good faith or to prevent rights of any person, it is attributed to those who as partners, associates, members or direct or indirect controllers, made it possible, who will be jointly and severally liable for the damages caused," but the application of this punishment will not modify the third parties' rights of good faith or release other participants of the facts that may cause any harm (Article 144). This regulation, although it has a more complete wording in the terms already exposed, presents its similar in the third paragraph of Article 54 (Law 19,550). This last concept refers to the partners or controllers, but it does not refer to the members as the general regime does, which clearly expands its capacity.

43. What is more, as it is common in the different legal systems, some attributes are granted to legal entities (such as name, address and registered office, assets, duration and object—Articles 151–156). In this regard, it is important to simply specify some concepts related to the attributes, such as the fact that the name is an identifying label of the legal entity that must meet the assumptions of truthfulness, novelty and distinctive aptitude regarding their situation (e.g., if it is in liquidation, it must be noted), and also as regards other names, trademarks, fictitious names or other forms of reference to goods or services whether they are related or not, of those included in the purpose of the legal entity. As regards the address, we must remark that it is essential for the notifications that the entity must receive, regardless of the fact that if it presents different establishments or branches, it can also be notified in each one with respect to the duties acquired by these representations. To conclude, regarding its duration and purpose, it is worth mentioning that the legal entity is of unlimited duration unless otherwise provided by a particular regime and that the purpose must be precise and determined, so as to protect third parties at the same time since the capacity is linked to the latter according to Article 141.

44. The operation of the private legal entity, unless modified by the special regime in question, has the following characteristics:

- In the first place, the statute will have provisions regarding the way in which the administrative, representative, governmental and inspection organizations will function, as the case may be.
- In the event that the statute does not establish anything, if all the participants of an assembly or meeting agree, interactive means can be used to allow simultaneous communication at a distance, in which case the minutes must be signed by the president and another administrator indicating the character adopted. Clearly, this includes the possibility of holding a teleconference meeting on the internet among members.

45. Likewise, the members who participate in the meeting can summon themselves without the need for prior citation and always on the condition that all members are present and that the agenda to be discussed is unanimously approved.

46. In addition, the administrators are required to behave with loyalty and diligence, and they are jointly and severally liable for the entity, third parties and other members with respect to those damages caused by their behavior by action or omission. Notwithstanding the foregoing, in the event that the managing organization is paralyzed due to conflicting positions held among its members that prevent its proper performance, any administrator must carry out the appropriate acts to prevent any harm to the entity and, in addition, to inform the assembly about this issue; otherwise, it will imply responsibility.

47. Finally, the general regime establishes dissuasive measures that initiate the extinction of the entity prior to its liquidation, assumptions that in some cases coincide with those provided by Law 19,550, Article 94. The causes may be removed to avoid dissolution and subsequent liquidation; besides, there can be some causes or reasons established in the statute that are not listed in the regulation (Article 163, CCCN). These are: compliance with the resolute condition; unanimous decision or by a contractual majority; attainment of the supervening purpose or impossibility of fulfilling it; expiration of the period of duration (in this case it can be extended before the expiration according to majorities arranged in the statute or renewed once expired in the same sense); declaration in bankruptcy (unless this becomes a reorganization proceeding or there is an agreement); fusion by absorption; the reduction to one of the numbers of partners; the denial or revocation of authorization to operate in the case where it is required; the exhaustion of the goods destined to support it; any other cause foreseen in the statute or special provisions.

48. As it arises from the last assumption, the enumeration regulation has a notifying character. Finally, after the causal and once the dissolution has been declared by the members, the legal entity must add the inscription "in liquidation" to the name and limit its purpose to the acts necessary to fulfill the pending duties by carrying out its assets, allocating the remainder to members or third parties according to the terms of the statute. In the event that this obligation of liquidation is ignored in the terms set forth, the administrators shall be liable jointly and severally together with those members who consented to such action instead of repressing it.

49. We will deepen our analysis of certain issues at the time of reviewing the general regime of companies provided by Law 19,550 that is more elaborate despite the restricted application to those entities.

II. Distinction Between Structures and Consequences

50. The LGS 19,550 presents different social types with their respective structures, typical notes and particular consequences.

51. It is possible to emphasize, before beginning, that the law defines in its first article society as "one in which one or more persons, in an organized manner and in accordance with one of the types provided by law, are obliged to make contributions to apply them to the exchange of goods or services, participating in the benefits and supporting the losses." The single-member society can only adopt, when it is constituted, one of the types of those provided for in the law, the single-member joint-stock corporation. Also, this type cannot, in turn, integrate another single-member society.

52. From the concept we can extract a clear idea of the essential requirements for the existence of a society that implies that one or more people must coincide in the contract depending on the case; we will deal with this concept thoroughly later on, and let us point out that they use a tool or legal institution that establishes a different legal entity to whom they provide with resources to carry out an organized economic activity and whose benefits and losses they will later participate.

53. That is to say, as already stated at the time of referring to the evolutionary analysis of corporate law, the company, on the occasion of the enactment of Law 19,550, constitutes a law subject and not a simple contract (Article 2).

54. The requirements established in the first article already referred to must be fulfilled in order to set up a company and they must be related to the context; but there are some other requirements exposed in Article 11 called non-typifying, which add non-essential content but they certainly constitute the contract of the society, as well as those stipulations that the contract must refrain from receiving (Article 13). It is worth mentioning that the essence of the regulations established in the first article allows us to demonstrate the existence of a society contract even though it is not materialized in writing, as is the case of the traditional factual society that is not written and that today is a kind of informal society corresponding to section IV.

55. Apart from this, the second chapter of the corporate law deals with social types in particular, according to the characteristics of each one. Beyond establishing requirements typifying each society of the second chapter, in order to comply with their effects, they ought to be registered with respect to the type (Articles 5–7). That is to say that the registration declares the existence of a society but attributes to it, from its entry into the registry, the effects of the type. That is why, both atypical societies, as those de facto, as those that have adopted a type provided in the second chapter but have not been registered, belong to section IV established residually as a means to rule every society in that any formal requirement or any regulation related to the type has been omitted. Finally, this section resulting from the reform of 2015 (Law 26,994, Articles 21–26) has meant the necessary modification of Article 17 of the law that declared the atypical society as null. At present, this consequence has been modified and the atypical society is established in the fourth section of the law, without implying the elimination of the type principle, a principle that is still in force according to the first article (in an organized way and "in accordance with one of the types provided by law … ") and the whole second chapter of the law that approves of the different types of companies.

III. Commercial and Civil Corporations and Partnerships

56. After the amendment of Law 19,550 by means of Law 26,994, the Law of Commercial Companies was modified in its denomination and was called "LGS," so it includes all the societies acknowledged by the Argentine Law (except the Simplified SAS that is in an independent system regulated by Law 27,349 System of Support for Entrepreneurial Capital) without distinction of a civil or commercial nature.

57. Prior to the reform, the Argentine Law receipted the Civil Companies in the CC, whereas the commercial companies were established in the 19,550 Law of Commercial Companies. As we have already stated, the companies could be commercial either by the type adopted, on condition that it was one of those included in the second chapter of the law, or by the commercial activity to be developed in the case of de facto companies. It was so that the concept of the merchant (social type adopted) or the performance of acts of commerce (activity developed by the society) determined the commercial nature of the society.

58. Furthermore, when the new CCCN was ratified in 2015, the Commercial Code was revoked together with the concepts of commercial act and merchant, and both of them have been replaced in the new code by the notions of business and organized economic activity. Likely, the change of denomination of the current LGS in that sense and the omission of the civil society as a particular type of the normative system, so that all the societies are ruled by the LGS, have brought about as a consequence that there is no longer difference between civil societies and commercial ones.

59. Then, considering what we have just mentioned, if we concentrate on the concept of society already explained in the first article of the LGS, we will notice that the commercial activity has not disappeared nor diminished; on the contrary, we would say that it has been imposed as a consequence of both the presence of this concept and the omission of regulation of the civil society.

60. That is to say that, the concept established in the first article of the law prescribes what society is the contract by which one person or more people in an organized manner and in accordance with the types prescribed by law are obliged to make contributions to apply them to production and exchange of goods or services, perceiving the profits and bearing the losses. Having said that, it is evident that the production and exchange of goods or services are a commercial activity so we can admit that, although the Companies Act has been extended to acknowledge atypical societies (as is the case of the civil society at present), the business activity included in the purpose of societies remains a characteristic feature and an ontological requirement.

61. Similarly, the treatment of commercial companies has not been modified with the reform since they continue to be regulated by the same law. Apart from this, let us remark that the treatment for existing civil societies and those that would be constituted and established after the reform of the legislation should be determined since the legal social type as such has disappeared. Thus, Article 7 of the CCCN establishes that the application of this new code will be effective with respect to the new legal relationships established once it is in force and the consequences that will occur with respect to the existing relationships. It is worth saying that there is no retroactive application of the new legal body, but it is immediate for the new relationships and the consequences with respect to those already existing.

62. In addition, we must say that the case of civil society is a particular one that deserves to be analyzed in accordance with this new reality. Currently, the treatment of civil society is the one established in section IV of the LGS, since it is an atypical society with the effects of that section to which we refer as we have previously analyzed. Likewise, the existing civil societies continue being in force and there is no ultra-activity of the old code (only for the text of the contract), notwithstanding that the latter must respect the current imperative norms of both the new Civil and Commercial Code and those of the LGS, everything according to what is set forth by Civil and Commercial Code (Article 150) that determines the normative priority.

63. Therefore, nothing prevents a new company contract from adopting the revoked provisions of the old CC (they will be regarded as an exercise of the autonomy of the will of the contracting parties), and they are applicable without any doubt as long as they do not contradict imperative norms of the general body or of special Law No. 19,550.

64. To conclude, we must point out that all companies are currently protected by the LGS without making a distinction of their activity or social type that would differentiate them in civil and commercial partnerships and, as the civil society has been omitted as a regulated type in the new Civil and Commercial Code, it is an atypical company fully regulated by the LGS (section IV).

IV. Non-profit Associations and Other Corporate Legal Persons

65. In reference to private non-profit legal entities, we must mention that civil associations, simple associations, cooperative societies and foundations are legal entities that (with the exception of cooperatives that hold a special regulatory body) are ruled and typified by the Civil and Commercial Code. Notwithstanding the fact that the cooperatives have a special regime as the companies do, as we have expressed before, this does not prevent that collaterally, and they are regulated by the new code in terms of the section focusing on private legal entities in general. Having already provided treatment to the general part of the Civil and Commercial Code devoted to private juridical entities, we will be dealing with the subjects of rights referred to in this section showing their characteristics.

A. *Civil Associations*

66. Civil associations are regulated in Articles 168–192 of the new Civil and Commercial Code. Thus, according to the regulations, it is a legal entity established to contribute to the fulfillment of a social purpose, without having a profit as their main activity as well as for the founders and subsequent associates.

67. Article 168 states that "The civil association must have a purpose that is not contrary to the general interest or the common good. The general interest is interpreted with respect to the diverse identities, beliefs and traditions, be they cultural, religious, artistic, literary, social, political or ethnic, that do not violate the constitutional values. It cannot pursue profit as its main purpose, nor can it have profit for its members or third parties."

68. The text of the precept is somehow forced since not only civil associations must include in their purpose activities that do not contradict the general interest or the common good but that it is also a duty of every juridical person. A body which does not respect racial, cult, identity, sex, gender, cultural, etc., diversity could not be established. Therefore, the characteristic note is that it cannot pursue profit for its own sake as its main objective, nor can its members or third parties profit through it.

69. In addition, the civil association is distinguished from the simple association in that the former is only going to be constituted when it has obtained the State authorization to operate, so, in the meantime, it should be considered a simple association. It is worth mentioning that the civil association must be established observing the form of a public instrument, requiring the State authorization through the controlling organization and, likewise, registering once said permission is obtained; consequently, in the future, it will be subsequently controlled in its evolution by the same State inspection body. These requirements are ontological so if any of them is present in the constituent *iter*, the entity will be treated as a simple association but not as a civil association.

70. Apart from this, as characteristic and distinctive substantial elements of the constitutive act, it must foresee: (a) the types or categories of the partners together with the duties and prerogatives of each one; (b) the regime established for admission, resignation, disciplinary sanctions, exclusion of associates and appeals against decisions; (c) the social organisms of government; administration and representation, with a board of directors, the assembly and the internal supervisory body, establishing the integration, duration, competences, functions, attributions and functioning thereof; finally (d) the purpose of the existing assets at the time of their liquidation must be established, identifying the entity of public or private common good that is not for profit and is domiciled in the Argentine Republic.

71. What is more, the board of directors (administrative body) must be composed of associates and it must have the following positions: president, members, a secretary and a treasurer, all of which are regarded by the law as the board of directors. Regarding the responsibility of the board of directors, the general criterion established in Article 160 of the Civil and Commercial Code applies, insofar as it provides that it will be unlimited and jointly and severally with the legal entity, its members and third parties, for the damages caused because of them during the time in which they hold their position or in the exercise of their duties, either by action or by omission, always analyzing the actions or inactions in accordance with the behavior established in the previous article as regards the duty of diligence and loyalty with which administrators must act. Next, in reference to the period of time in which the directors' positions are in force, it is worth mentioning that the directors cease in their positions due to death, declaration of incapacity or restricted capacity, disqualification, expiration of the term for which they were appointed, resignation, removal or any other cause that could have been provided for in the articles of incorporation, which cannot under any circumstances restrict the removal or resignation of a director. In turn, regarding the resignation of the director, it will be presented in writing to the chairman of the board of directors or to its replacement and will be accepted if it is not expressly rejected within a deadline of ten days to be counted from the moment it was announced. Notwithstanding the foregoing, the resignation so arranged by the outgoing director shall not affect the functioning of the executive committee or the carrying out of acts previously resolved by it; otherwise, the director shall remain in office until the ordinary meeting takes a decision and the resignation will be rejected.

72. Finally, regarding the directors, their responsibility is extinguished by approval of their respective management or by the board of directors as a whole, or by resignation or transactions resolved by the ordinary meeting in that regard. However, it is not extinguished if the responsibility has been the cause of an infringement or infringements of mandatory regulations, or if in the ordinary meeting, there was an express and well-founded opposition of associates representing 10% of the total. In the latter case, those who object to it may carry out the social action of liability established by the LGS (Article 276), as it is clearly stated in the Civil and Commercial Code.

73. Besides, with respect to the supervisory body, the statute may provide that it be formed by non-associated entities, who will be auditors of accounts. The account review committee is mandatory for associations that have more than a hundred associates. It is obvious that the law prohibits the inclusion in this body of those who also integrate the board of directors or certify the financial statements of the entity, extending the prohibition to spouses, cohabitants, relatives by blood and affinity (in a direct line in all grades), and collateral relatives up to the fourth grade.

74. As for the governing body, the ordinary assembly, the statute must establish and enable the participation of the associates in the acts of government, and at the same time, it can also be able to establish certain conditions such as, for example, a certain seniority and payment of social quotas (it is absolutely necessary not to register past due debt in order to participate in the act), although limitations implying a total restriction cannot be established. Likewise, the right to withdraw from the association waiving the status of associate must be unlimited, but he can be asked to pay for the due fees. However, the condition of affiliate is non-transferable and cannot be excluded from the association but for serious causes expressly provided for in the statute, and must, in any case, allow the right of defense of the challenged associate to be exercised; besides, if the decision is taken by the board of directors, it can then be reviewed by the ordinary assembly in the short term. Finally, as it has been remarked when dealing with the general regime, the associates are not liable directly or indirectly, nor collaterally for the debts of the civil association, but they are certainly responsible up to the limit of the contributions they are forced to provide when the entity is established; also, they are liable for the contributions that they have not provided yet as well as those of the quotas and contributions to which they had already agreed on.

75. It should be noted that civil associations are dissolved by the same causes as the rest of the private legal entities, adding the particular cause of reduction in the number of associates so that it does not allow for integration of all the positions of the board of directors and supervising positions; this is the case when that situation is not corrected within a period of six months. If there has been a cause and it has not been corrected, the entity will be liquidated according to the procedure established in the statute prior appointment of a liquidator so that he or she will act under the supervision of the inspection body. If nothing has been foreseen in the statute, or even if it has been foreseen and some issues have not been included, the process will be ruled by the provisions of the LGS for the liquidation of the companies, as pertinent.

B. Simple Associations

76. In reference to simple associations, we must point out that they are regulated by the rules established for civil associations when there are no regulations clearly expressed in the code; hence, we will highlight the differences of this type. It is worth saying that as regards the content of the constitutive act, functioning, organisms and associates, it is ruled by the regulations set forth for civil associations with the modifications that were particularly marked. It is, as its name indicates, a more flexible type, which can be constituted by a public or private instrument with a signature certified by a notary public and its name should be identified by adding "simple association." Unlike civil associations, they do not need State authorization; consequently, their existence operates from the moment they are established by signing the instrument authorized for this purpose. Likewise, the number for dispense of the supervisory body is to have less than twenty associates, but this does not mean that they are exempt from certifying the financial statements and also grants the members the right to be informed through reports requested to the executive committee and direct examination of books and records.

77. In addition, regarding the responsibility of the administrators, they are liable jointly and severally with the association for the duties that the latter contracts during the personal administration period that they have integrated, in case the assets of the entity were insufficient to pay the debts and what is more, let us highlight that, concerning the administrators' patrimony, the personal creditors will have a preference on it in the execution and payment. Finally, in the same case as for civil associations, members who have not participated in the administration are not liable with their personal assets for the debts of the simple association; however, they are responsible up to the concurrence of the contributions they have already agreed on as well as the contributions which have not been provided for together with the ones agreed upon or quotas unpaid to that date.

1. Foundations

78. The foundations are legal entities whose main objective is to ensure a common good purpose. It can be said that foundations are private non-profit legal entities that collaborate with the State in the achievement of altruistic purposes, hence the fiscal benefits they do have and the permanent State control they are subject to. They are now regulated in Articles 193–224 of the CCCN, after the repeal of the previous regime of foundations included in Law 19,836.

79. They can be established by other legal entities or human beings through a public instrument and even, in the latter case, they can be set forth by an act of last will. Likewise, in order to exist, they need State authorization.

80. Once it is established, the foundation must rely not only on the principles it has but also on the initial patrimony that is granted to it for the fulfillment of its purposes. In this sense, there is what is called the three-year plan, which is the financing project prepared by the foundation at the time of incorporation to accredit these extremes, and that includes contributions not only from its founders but also from third parties. All this will be subject to review by the State comptroller body set up for this purpose, which may also authorize the incorporation for other reasons in addition to those already mentioned, bearing in mind the potential fulfillment of the objectives set forth in the articles of incorporation pursuant to the guarantee which would represent the background of the founders and the characteristics of the program to be developed. The refusal of State authorization ordered by the controlling entity, as any other decision of the entity that affects the foundation, may be judicially appealed in a Court of Appeals of the jurisdiction in question, using grounds of illegitimacy and arbitrariness, a procedure to which a summary trial must be agreed on.

81. However, at the moment when the foundation is set forth, its statute is prepared to be shown to the State controlling authority, and it must have the following information: the data related to the founders; name and address of the foundation; designation of the object in a precise and determined way together with the initial equity and future resources; in this respect, contributions in cash and securities must be deposited during the authorization process, while the contributions of assets must be accounted for and valued in an inventory made by a national public accountant and future promises are irrevocable after the State authorization has been granted (unless before the date set for compliance, the statutory object has been modified and the donation has been expressly agreed on according to the previous object); what is more, the foundation is able to exercise all the actions tending to make it effective. Apart from this, it must also include the following data: the term of duration, the organization of the board of directors (including the duration of the positions, the meeting schedule and the process to appoint its members) selecting the first members, the operation and internal organization, the closing date of the annual exercise, the regulations that determine the dissolution, liquidation and destiny of the remnant assets (public entity or Argentine private juridical entity with the purpose of public utility or non-profitable common good), a three-year plan of action (it must be renewed every three years and in each case, the nature, characteristics and development of the activities necessary for compliance must be indicated precisely, as well as the economic funds that will be available to develop them), the appointment of the person empowered to carry out the constitutive process and, finally, to obtain the State authorization to operate.

82. In addition to this, the founders and administrators hold in the constitutive stage joint and unlimited liability toward third parties until the foundation is granted the State authorization to operate. During this period, those persons will be liable for their personal assets to third parties, but the individual creditors of each of them will have preference over those assets. Also, during the validity of the entity, the founders and their heirs cannot contract with the foundation without the prior authorization of the State comptroller, except in the case of donations; as a result, any other contract between these parties will be totally ineffective.

83. As for the administration and government body, it is called the board of directors and will be formed by a minimum of three unpaid persons (except reimbursement of expenses); besides, the founders are able to have the possibility of holding positions in the council (something that has to be established in the statute) as well as to hold the power to appoint those who are members of them in case of vacancy or expiration of the positions in their case (they may be permanent or temporary). We must also remark that the latter may even be delegated to public or private non-profit institutions. In the case of vacancy and due to the impossibility of appointing new members or when the entities do not accept the position and they are therefore vacant, the State controlling authority may reorganize the administration, appoint its new authorities and modify the statute in the relevant sections.

84. The faculties of the board of directors are broad and therefore include everything necessary for the fulfillment of the purpose of the foundation, but they must always be in the terms determined by the statute. With respect to the operation, the statute may establish that certain decisions must be approved by the permanent members, even including the appointment of temporary members.

85. Furthermore, with regard to the functions of the board, these can be developed by an executive committee (remunerated or not) provided for in the statute that is made up of members of the board of directors or by third parties and that must be responsible to the council for what has been done. Likewise, merely executive functions may be delegated to board members or third parties, but they must always be human beings. In addition, everything concerning ordinary and extraordinary meetings of the board of directors and the multi-personal executive committee, as the case may be, must be stipulated in the statute, and in order to hold the meetings, a constituent and functioning quorum of half plus one of the members must be held. Also, the resolutions ought to be adopted by a majority vote of the members present and, in the case of a tied vote, the chairman shall have a casting vote or double vote, except for the cases of removal of a member, modification of the statutory purpose and merger and dissolution: in these cases, it is necessary to have the favorable vote of two-thirds of the body. Regarding the purpose, it can only be modified when the statutory purpose is impossible to fulfill. The meetings must be registered in a special minute's book authorized by the State controlling entity.

86. Furthermore, the rights and duties of the board of directors are stated by the mandatory regulations and the provisions of the statute; besides, the mandate regime shall be applied to them. In case there is a breach of the legal or statutory duty, the foundation or the State controlling authority can demand action of liability against the members of the council, apart from the fact that the foundation is subject to administrative sanctions.

87. During its operation, the foundation must allocate its income to the fulfillment of its purposes and also keep its patrimony; besides, it is not able to accumulate funds except for future projects strictly defined and approved by the supervising authority.

88. Finally, as it has been pointed out, the State supervising authority has a special monitoring function in relation to the foundations during their operation. Thus, within its powers, we can highlight the following: (a) to have the possibility of judicially requesting the integration of vacant positions in the administration and government body; (b) to avoid the carrying out of resolutions taken in board meetings or the executive committee when it understands that what is provided is contrary to the law or the statute and consequently judicially request the nullity of that act; (c) to request the authorities to remove or suspend administrators who ignore the duties they certainly have and, consequently, to request the appointment of new provisional administrators; (d) to summon the council meetings when it is requested by one of the members or when serious irregularities are detected; (e) to determine a new purpose when the one established in the founding statute is or makes its compliance impossible; and finally (f) to arrange the merger or coordination of activities between two or more foundations.

2. Cooperatives

89. Cooperatives are legal entities included in Law 20,337 and are used by cooperative members as a tool to organize and provide services based on mutual effort and help, education and cooperative integration. To be established regularly and for any future statutory reform, they need authorization from the State enforcement authority (National Institute of Associativity and Social Economy (INAES)).

90. It is a private legal entity with the following features that characterize it: (a) the capital is variable and the contributions of the associates must consist of certain assets and it is susceptible to forced execution; (b) the partners are jointly and severally liable for the effective integration and correct valuation of the assets contributed; (c) they do not have a maximum limit of members, although they do have a minimum of ten in order to be constituted, and each of them has only one vote, no matter how many social quotas they may have; (d) the partners can be both human beings and legal entities, including SAS; (e) the social quotas have equal value and one or more of them must be represented in registered shares that can be transferred among associates with the agreement of the board of directors; (f) the partners may distribute surpluses resulting from the activity as a difference between the cost and the price of the service provided to the associates; (g) they do not allow the distribution of the constituted social reserves and the remaining assets once liquidated must not be given to the partners; (h) it must add limited cooperative or its abbreviations to its corporative name; (i) they can associate with people of another legal nature in order to comply with the corporate purpose; (j) they cannot be transformed into societies or civil associations; (k) they are constituted as a single act and by a public or private instrument, as a consequence of a constituent assembly that must include the following: the identification of the initiators, the draft statute, the subscription and integration of social quotas, and the appointment of counselors and trustees.

91. Next, regarding the statute, it must have the following data: (a) company name and address; (b) precise and determined reference to the corporate purpose; (c) cost of social quotas and right of entry expressed in the national currency; (d) organization of administration and oversight bodies, as well as the assembly regime; (e) provisions relating to the distribution of surpluses and contribution to losses; (f) conditions of entry and exclusion of the cooperative member; and finally (g) provisions related to rights and duties of associates and the dissolution and liquidation of the entity.

92. As for the assemblies, the law of cooperatives includes: (a) the ordinary and extraordinary kinds, with exclusive competences regarding the treatment of the financial statements; (b) reports from the receiver and the auditor; (c) distribution of surpluses; (d) merger and incorporation; (e) dissolution; (f) change of the corporate purpose; (g) election of the board of directors, etc., which must be informed to the application authority and the competent local body at the time of being appointed.

93. Furthermore, the board of directors responsible for the management of social operations and the liquidation of the entity (unless otherwise provided by the statute) shall be composed of human beings who will remain in their position for up to three fiscal years, although they may be reelected indefinitely unless otherwise provided in the statute. The board administers and the representation is held by the president, notwithstanding that the statute may provide for plural representation. In the latter case, in case of infringement of the system of plural representation, the same solution as that provided in Article 58 of the LGS applies; that is, the company is bound in the cases of securities, contracts in forms or adhesion contracts together with distance contracts, except when the third party knew the infringement at the time of contracting.

94. In addition, the board may order the creation of an executive committee composed of some of its members to ensure the continuity of ordinary management. The conformation of the committee does not exempt the council from responsibility for the acts carried out by the committee.

95. The directors are jointly and severally liable for the acts they carry out and breaching the law, the statute or the regulations, but may be exempted from liability if they had not participated in the act or if they prove by means of a record in the minutes that they have voted against it.

96. In reference to private control, the body can be integrated by one or more trustees (it must always be an odd number), which will have a duration of three fiscal years in office and are eligible for reelection under the conditions authorized by the statute. Some of its functions include: (a) summoning the assembly and the inclusion in the agenda of topics when the call is made by the council; (b) supervising the administration; (c) verifying the cash status, titles and values of any kind; and finally (d) verifying and facilitating the exercise of the rights of the associates, etc.

3. Simplified Shares Company

97. The global situation of the corporate legal systems, tends to create mechanisms that seek a compatibility of the regulatory regime of the legal entity with a changing and challenging world, open to great changes and reluctant to the administrative bureaucracy, with pragmatic qualities and desires of freedom without implying a decrease in its responsibility, has come to conspire against this new type of company emerged as an option offered to entrepreneurs, but whose scope certainly exceeds this task.

98. Our position (which definitely agrees with this new regulatory body whose incorporation into the national law we requested in previous critical publications of the Sole Proprietorship Corporation) absolutely coincides with the regulation in general, with some observations that we will point out throughout this written work. The truth is that we will devote an extensive section to deal with this particular type since it is currently one of the legal tools most used by the market and is envisioned as a type that will leave those included in the LGS as secondary resources.

99. With the inclusion of the Simplified SAS in the Argentine Corporate System, the deficient regulation of the SAU (granted by the 2015 reform of the LGS and subsequent modification in 2016 with respect to the plurality of its bodies) has been replaced. By means of these acts, it was simply possible to resort to the constitutive sole proprietorship act or due to situations that have developed over time, but which in turn imposed such rigor and control on the new type that practically isolated it from small and medium enterprises. We have previously mentioned that perhaps its residual space is destined for the interest of foreign companies that do not wish to share the social group with a local society.

100. What is more, we must remark on certain merits that exceed the mere possibility of being a sole proprietorship because it is there where this new social type marks a substantial difference with its deficient precedent, since considering the regulation in force, the Simplified SAS show advanced characteristics as regards the concept of social capital, extension of the corporate purpose, composition of its organisms, transfer of participations, participation in secondary financing markets and the relationship with the digital environment regarding its constitution and subsequent operation.

101. Thus, we are truly satisfied with the ratification of Law 27,349 which supports entrepreneurial capital as a body that, among other benefits, brings to Argentine people this flexible, versatile, agile, and comprehensive social type of the national and foreign businessman's demands. Later on, we will focus on the fact that there are still some points to review and whose effective application will support the feasible alternatives regarding a possible improvement in regulation.

§4. Sources and Hierarchy of the Law on Corporations and Partnerships

I. International and National Sources

102. As it will be expressed in the section related to companies incorporated abroad, the Argentine legal system in relation to the regime of companies and legal entities, in general, is made up of the provisions contained in our autonomous source, such as: the LGS No. 19,550; Law 20,091 of Insurance Companies; Law 20,321 of Mutual Associations; Law 20,337 of Cooperatives; Law 27,349 of Support for Entrepreneurial Capital; the CCCN of Law 26,994; and the conventional source which comprises international treaties that in some cases has a constitutional hierarchy and in another superior to laws, all by virtue of Article 75 paragraph 22 and subsequent articles of the NC; let us remark that, especially in the second case, we can refer to Treaties of Montevideo (1889 and 1940) and the Second Specialized Inter-American Conference on Private International Law (CIDIP II). In other words, in the case of an international question because of the existence of such a connection point, first it will be necessary to consider whether there is an agreement between the countries of which the parties are national or not (in this case the law has established the criterion of prevalence of the subsequent treaty over the previous one, at the time of the priority application of CIDIP II over the Treaties of Montevideo) and, in the absence of these, to the provisions of the autonomous regime of Private International Law of the country. Besides, if the matter is not of Private International Law, it will be resolved according to the regulations of the domestic regime that were previously related.

103. The legislation, according to the legal pyramid, is composed, in the first place, of the Argentine NC which establishes the legal principles determining the block of constitutionality. These principles must be interpreted in coherence with each other and, also, the legislations that are dictated regulating the constitutional dispositions must not contradict the spirit of the mandate included in the NC. Thus, the laws must not alter the purpose that the constituents had in view at the time to incorporate the constitutional norm, under sanction of unconstitutionality. It should be noted that, in Argentina, the control of constitutionality operates in a diffuse manner; consequently, every national judge can declare the unconstitutionality of a rule because it does not correspond to the provisions of the NC.

104. Following the hierarchical order, by virtue of Articles 31 and 75, paragraph 22, treaties signed with foreign powers are operational (of direct application) and hold *supra* legal hierarchy, except human rights treaties that have a constitutional hierarchy. This means that if there is a conflict of domestic norms with those provisions included in an international treaty, the latter will prevail over the former.

105. In reference to conventional regulations, we referred to them at the time of dealing with Private International Law of companies in the relevant section.

106. Finally, at the foot of the pyramid, there are the local norms of autonomous law. Among these regulations, as we pointed out, there is in turn a relationship of specialty and imperativeness between the general and special bodies. Thus, as we have already highlighted on other occasions, the system of priority of regulations on private legal entities is included in Article 150 of the Civil and Commercial Code, which establishes first the priority application of the mandatory regulations of the special law and of the general body, then what is provided by the autonomy of the will of the parties; third and subsidiary, the special regime will be applied and finally, the general one.

II. Relationship Between Bylaws or Articles and Legislation

107. In accordance with the provisions, the relationship of the bylaws with the legislation has the limit set by the mandatory rules of the special regimes (Laws 19,550; 27,349, etc.) and the general body (CCCN). Thus, in the corporate contract or statute, the parties may agree on everything that is left to the autonomy of the will that does not contravene provisions of that nature, under penalty of having the contractual clause that establishes it declared void. Likewise, in reference to the issues omitted by the statute, the special regime will rule first and second, the general regime will do so in a subsidiary manner.

III. Hierarchy of the Law on Corporations and Partnerships

108. As we have stated before, the 19,550 Company Law and regarding its hierarchy, is placed below the NC and the international treaties on the subject subscribed, a topic that we will reinforce at the time of dealing with the rules of Private International Law. As we have already pointed out, with respect to the CCCN, this special law has priority precedence for its specialty, although there must be a certain coherence and integration regarding the principles both bodies have. All this is in accordance with Article 150 (already established) of the CCCN.

§5. International Private Law (Conflicts of Laws Rules)

109. In this section, it is necessary to carry out a detailed analysis of the regulations prevailing in the Argentine Republic regarding the regime of companies established abroad and legal entities in general. Thus, the regulatory scheme is made up of the provisions contained in our autonomous source (Law 19,550 hereinafter LGS and the CCCN, etc.), which is a conventional source with international treaties that in some cases have a constitutional hierarchy and in some other cases, it is superior to the laws, all by rule of Article 75, subsection 22, subsequent and related provisions of the NC (especially, Treaties of Montevideo of 1889 and 1940 together with the CIDIP II) and, finally, the dominant jurisprudential criterion in the matter. It must be kept in mind that, beyond the adjustments made by the special regulations for each case, it must be based on the basis set forth in Article 20 of the NC by which "Foreigners do have in the territory of the Nation all civil rights of the citizen."[18]

110. Although the analysis that is carried out later is organized not by regulation but by matter to be treated (capacity and existence, isolated or habitual acts, central administration or effective headquarters, etc.), it is essential to point out that the application of the standards is made according to the legal pyramid. That is to say that, in the case of an international issue because there is a certain connection in that field, first, it will be necessary to consider the existence of an agreement or not between the countries of which the parties are national (in this case, the law has established the criterion of prevalence of the subsequent treaty over the previous one, at the time of the priority application of CIDIP II over the Treaties of Montevideo) and, in the absence of these, the provisions of the autonomous regime of International Private Law of the country.

111. However, we clarify that we will approach this topic from those cases in which the company, as an economic concept, is developed by a personified legal structure that sets it in motion.[19] That means that we will focus on the analysis of the recognition of the private foreign legal entity.

I. Argentine Law: Its Conventional Autonomous Source

112. Throughout this chapter, we will carry out a thorough analysis of the Argentine regulations in relation to the recognition of legal entities constituted abroad, a study that will be carried out considering diverse matters (capacity, existence and form, isolated acts as well as habitual ones, development of its main objective in the Republic, etc.).

113. As we have already stated before and as an initial premise our Constitution states that "foreigners have all the civil rights of citizens in the territory of the Nation" (Article 20). It is essential to keep this principle as our goal when interpreting each general or special rule applicable in the matter since it establishes the principle of non-discrimination in order to guarantee equal treatment to any foreign person, human or legal when it is established in the national territory. Above all, it is an inspiring guide to resolving doubtful suppositions or where there is no legislation at all and this can result in denying a capacity held by legal entities of the country.

18. The CSJN has repeatedly stated that existing companies abroad established here can enjoy all the rights agreed by Argentine Laws, according to Arts. 33, 34 and 35 of the CC (now repealed), analysis in: D.R. Vitolo, Manual de Sociedades, Estudio, Bs As, 2016, p. 356.
19. H.R. Ferro, Legislación de la Empresa, Astrea, Bs As, 1979, pp. 100 and 101.

114. Having mentioned this, it is worth noting that our autonomous regime had Article 34 in the revoked CC, which provided recognition to the legal individuality of societies established abroad.

115. Thus, the provisions regarding national juridical persons determined in the previous principle were also applied to foreign ones and consequently, their regulations as regards duties and rights were also accepted.

116. Later on, the CCCN was enacted, but it does not have a similar concept in its articles; consequently, it does not differentiate when referring to the private juridical individuality as regards its nationality or the place where it was established.

117. Thus, Article 148, in its first paragraph, states that societies are private legal entities and that those incorporated abroad are ruled by the provisions of Article 150, last paragraph, of the same legal source.

118. However and in general terms, the Argentine Law of conventional source is composed of the Treaties of Montevideo of 1889 and 1940; CIDIP II; the Argentine-Brazilian Bi-national Society Article, etc. When dealing with an international question as it is the case of the legal entity established abroad, the priority of sources is the following: verification of the existence or not of an agreement among the countries whose parties are national or residents and, in the case there is no agreement, the Argentine autonomous regime in matters of Private International Law. That is to say that, except for the compatibility clause, when there is the possibility of applying more than one international agreement for the specialty of the topic, the most important is the subsequent one.

119. Since this is an analysis according to the different subjects, we will focus on the regulations of all sources regarding each topic, trying to determine the way in which they complement and integrate the law as a whole, as a system. So, we will first concentrate on the reception of all sources by the Argentine Law regarding both the theory of incorporation and the place where it has been established, focusing on the diversity of isolated or habitual acts that can be performed by the legal entity established in a foreign country, its accounting, typology, participation or constitution of a juridical order, liability regime, etc., as well as the exceptional case in which our regulations take the effective headquarter theory in order to safeguard its international public order. We will be dealing with this below.

II. Theory of Incorporation or Establishment: Its Application

120. Regarding its general regime, Argentina is largely inspired by the theory of the place of incorporation or establishment, except in the case in which the company incorporated abroad has its head office in the country or its main objective is intended to be fulfilled in it.

121. In this sense, Article 118 of the LGS provides a general guiding criterion to identify the *lex societatis*, determining that "The society established abroad is ruled, as regards its existence and characteristics, by the laws of the place where it has been established … ."

122. It is an indirect rule that establishes the criterion of incorporation referring to the legislation of the place of creation of the entity as *lex societatis*. Two aspects are obtained from this set of rules: what is meant by a Constitution as well as the manners established in order to get the benefit of legal individuality. Let us point out that the place of incorporation must not necessarily coincide with the place where the contract or constitutive act has been carried out since the latter can be absolutely circumstantial and inconsequential and it could have a remote connection with the plurilateral relationship of the organization which has been established.[20]

123. Considering the conventional source, the Treaty of Montevideo of 1889 on International Civil Law, applicable as the case may be in Argentina (Article 4), reaffirms its position when it states that "The existence and capacity of private legal entities is ruled by laws of the country in which they have been recognized as such. Their characteristics fully enable them to exercise beyond the place of their establishment, all the actions and rights that correspond to them"; second, the Montevideo Treaty of Civil Law of 1940, which in the same article states that "The existence and capacity of the Legal entities of a private nature, are ruled by the laws of the country of their domicile. Their features fully authorize them to carry out the actions and rights that correspond to them beyond the place where they have been established. When referring to acts related to their own objectives, they will be subjected to the prescriptions established by the State in which they intend to perform such acts, the same rule shall apply to civil societies." Likewise, this is supported by the CIDIP II with respect to the subject "Inter-American Convention—Law Conflicts—Mercantile Societies," since it establishes in its second and third articles, that "the existence, the capacity, functioning and dissolution of mercantile societies are ruled by the law of the place of their establishment. By 'law of the place of its establishment' is meant the State where all the appropriate requirements to create such companies are met 'and that' commercial societies duly established in one State shall be legally and fully recognized in the other States. The recognition of full right does not exclude the power of the State to demand proof of the society's existence according to the law of the place of its establishment. It is worth mentioning that the capacity acknowledged to the societies established in a State by no means could be superior to the capacity granted to the societies established in the State that has recognized it."

124. While it is true that the State of destination can demand verification of the existence of the legal entity according to the law of the country of incorporation, the recognition is the full right and this is another premise to keep in mind later at

20. H. Roitman, *Ley de Sociedades Comerciales Comentada, Commentary to Article 118*, T. II, La Ley, Bs As, 2006, p. 771.

the time of resolving somehow complex assumptions since the *ipso iure* recognition of the entity guarantees the freedom of establishment.

III. Purpose and Capacity: Their Relationship

125. In the precept referred to above, the CIDIP II provides that "in no case, the capacity recognized to companies incorporated in a State may be superior to the capacity that the law of the State of recognition grants to the companies incorporated in the latter." As regards the Argentine case, the capacity of the company incorporated abroad is hardly diminished when our system is applied since not even the purpose limits the capacity of the entity. In this sense, we have evolved with respect to a classic doctrine[21] because we understand that, according to the terms of Article 58 of the LGS, the purpose not only does not limit the capacity but also the society regards any act that is not notoriously different from its purpose, a differentiated imputation center. Capacity and center of imputation are two independent issues that even allow a society to accept by its own will an act that is notoriously different from its purpose. A common sample that usually depicts this is the purchase of a lottery ticket by a company that does not enclose such an act as an activity related to the rest of the purpose and if the latter limited its capacity, then it would result in its nullity. Nothing prevents the society from benefiting from the lottery prize and the act is not null at all. Even today, with Simplified SAS and its multiple purposes we have gone even further regarding the concept of not being imputable to the greatest number of acts up to the point that a doctrine supports the considerable relativity of the social object.[22]

126. At present, there has been a debate considering Article 141 of the CCCN, while its text certainly circumscribes the capacity of the private legal entity to its purpose together with the purpose of why it has been created. Beyond its unfortunate wording, it is absolutely pointless to be involved in this debate since this rule does not apply to legal entities established abroad; let us emphasize that according to Article 150, last paragraph of the CCCN, these legal entities are ruled by the LGS. Notwithstanding the foregoing, the deficiency of Article 141 of the CCCN has been noted and, in this sense, there has been an amending text of the CCCN recently provided to the Executive Power in September, in which its replacement has been proposed in accordance with the aforementioned.[23]

---

21. A. Boggiano, *Curso de Derecho Internacional Privado*, ed. Abeledo Perrot, Bs As, 2003, *supra*, p. 517.
22. A. Ramirez, *El Objeto Social en la Sociedad por Acciones Simplificada*, La Ley, Vol. 2018-B, Bs As, publication dated Apr. 18, 2018, p. 1.
23. Proposed draft reform of the CCCN (Dated September 2018, by lawyers Julio Rivera and Daniel Pizarro). Replace Art. 141 CCYC for the following: Art. 141. Definition. Legal entities are all entities to which the legal system recognizes their ability to acquire rights and contract obligations. They have no other disabilities than those resulting from their nature or from a legal provision.

IV. Isolated Acts

127. As a premise, in our autonomous regime, the General Societies Act (LGS, Article 118) enables companies incorporated abroad to perform isolated acts and be on trial, without having to comply with any prior formality in the country.[24] That is, this capacity is granted in general terms, beyond the demands required by the particular act. This appropriate solution is a logical consequence of the *ipso jure* recognition of the foreign legal entity.[25]

128. In order to regulate this section together with the ones corresponding to the habitual acts, the legislation has taken into consideration the dual capacity of the entity, generic and specific. The generic is related to the capacity that the act holds as such, while the specific refers to those acts intended to fulfill its social purpose. Both capacities are ruled by the law of origin, although it is necessary to remark that it should not refer to that regulation discriminating against the legal entity established abroad with respect to those created in the country. Let us point out that the rule is the capacity and in accordance with the principle established by Article 20 of the NC, both capacities should not be inferior to the one granted to national domestic companies by the national regulation.

129. The distinctive criterion of both capacities is qualitative-quantitative in a cumulative way, so the rule takes into account both, whether the act corresponds to one or the other from the qualitative point of view, and their reiteration or the time they last which lets it qualify as habitual. Thus, the acquisition of real estate in the Republic does not represent an isolated act. In this sense, the subscription of repeated mortgage loans,[26] or the ownership of a real right of guarantee, determined by the society established abroad, together with the mortgage and pledge, would not

24. The CNCRIM and CORREC, in a ruling dated Feb. 10, 2010, records: "PC H. and LRC" stated that "The text of the general and special power provided by the complainant press has acquired authenticity with the Apostille (convention of The Hague 1961—Law 23,458), certifying the signature and the character with which the signatory of the document acted. From this point of view, it is not necessary to demand that in a notarial act celebrated abroad, other titles be demonstrated than those that the domestic law of the place of celebration deems sufficient to achieve its end, creating the notary's intervention the presumption 'iuris tantum' of its legality and compliance with the laws of the place, and this is sufficient to prove the status of the president, in accordance with the doctrine of the CSJN"—Faults 48:98 and 194: 232 cited in CNCP, Room II, case No. 9,046, reg: 12.068, "Web Computing s/ appeal", rta.:7/7/08-.
25. The CNA Com., Room C,—File No. 20871.06—Court No. 20—Secretariat No. 40, in records: "OCTAVE-1 FUND LTD C/ PARQUE INDUSTRIAL AGUA PROFUNDA S.A. S/ Precautionary Measure" said that "The injured party is right. Indeed, the inscription referred to places the plaintiff in the first part of Article 118 of the Company Law, insofar as it provides that its existence and form are determined by the 'laws of the place of its constitution'. Therefore, in accordance with the criteria of hospitality that such a provision holds, it is appropriate to recognize the subject of the right to the aforementioned society, with sufficient capacity to be on trial (this Chamber in cars 'Deliceland SA c/ Cadehsur SA s/ summary', from 11-4-03; *idem*, 'Salt Card SA c/ Probursa Sociedad de Bolsa SA s/ ordinary' of 24.6.05)."
26. CN Com., Room D, Judgment of Oct. 24, 2017 in proceedings Contretas, Lucas and others c/ "Contreras Hermanos SAICIFA on the Incident of Article 250 of the Procedural Code," Journal of Societies and Reorganization Proceedings, Year 19-2018-1, Bs As, p. 254.

constitute an isolated act due to the fact that the registry entry referring to its head office is destined to last a certain period of time during which it will bring about the registration effects of publicity, priority, rank, etc.

130. From this position adopted by the national system, we should refer to the right of the society that rules its existence and form. Having complied with that system of origin, the society is fully empowered to perform isolated acts and be in court.

131. What is more, regarding isolate acts, we should mention that in the autonomous city of Buenos Aires, the recognition of full right has been ignored by the enacting of Resolutions No. 7/2005 and its subsequent 7/2015, by which the General Inspection of Justice (IGJ) established a register of isolated acts. At present, we are truly satisfied with the fact that this record has been annulled by means of Resolution No. 6/2018 since we believe it was contrary to the provisions of Article 118 of the LGS. This position adopted by the national system refers to the society that rules its existence and form. Having complied with that system of origin, the society is fully empowered to perform isolated acts and be in court. Finally, we warn the reader about the IGJ resolutions that we refer here, since that organization is completely reviewing it's regulatory regime established for companies incorporated abroad at the time of this edition.

132. However, the procedural authorization to be in court is a necessary consequence of respect for the constitutional guarantee of the defense in court.[27] Thus, the IGJ returns slowly to its usual function to check and regulate without altering the features of the regulation.

V. The Purpose or Object: Its Habitual Exercise

133. In order to carry on its specific capacity habitually in the country, the company established abroad must comply with certain requirements determined by the regulation and the legal provisions according to the corresponding jurisdiction. Thus, Article 118 of the LGS establishes that the company must: prove its existence in accordance with the laws of the place of establishment, determine a domicile in the country by completing the corresponding registration and publication duties, and also justify the decision to create a permanent representation in the country and appoint a representative for that purpose. However, when it must establish a branch and in accordance with the corresponding special laws, it ought to assign the required capital.

134. To develop a habitual activity in the Republic implies that the entity must be settled in the country through any type of representation and, therefore, there are

27. CSJN, Judgment of Jul. 31, 1963 in proceedings: "Corporación El Hatillo en Potosí S.A. c. Cóccaro, Abel F."

some unavoidable requirements to be complied with that have been established considering the national activities.[28] Regarding the branch, when it comes to certain special activities (banking and insurance), the law requires the allocation of capital. As we know, it is an exception to the liabilities of the branches, since they do not have differentiated legal representation from the main company. However, in the case of a branch of a company set up abroad that is established in the country to perform certain special activities, such requirement must be fulfilled.

135. Besides, this assertion does not invalidate the fact that the branch is considered a tax subject for the purposes of taxation or that its assets may be separated from that of the main company so as to protect national creditors in case of its tender in the country where it was established first or in case of a branch in our country, all in accordance with the fourth and second articles, subsection two, of Law 24,522, respectively. In both cases, there is an absence of a differentiated legal personality, despite the complexity and risk of certain activities, capital must be provided thus fulfilling one of its functions which is to guarantee.

136. In this particular case, capital does not provide either its production functions or a scheme of social participation, but it must be observed as an element of retention and equity balance. This should be reflected in the separate accounting that the branch should have in the country as we will analyze later on.

137. It has been said that capital has lost this function of guarantee according to the new concepts proposed by a doctrine and that would even be supported by a new legislation, for example, Law 27,349, which supports the enterprising capital: a normative volume that requires a capital of two minimum wages for simplified stock companies.

138. The truth is that it may have lost its production function in the sense that societies are usually financed by external capital to fulfill their purpose and consequently, the capital-purpose relationship has also lost its validity, but the capital continues holding its guarantee function. This is supported by what we have referred to before; the guarantee function is not determined by the amount of capital, but by its function of equity balance as derived from Articles 94, paragraph 5; 96 and 99, second paragraph, of the LGS. The new Law 27,349 does not modify the guarantee function of social capital as it is intended to be understood; in fact, except for the SAS and these new companies for simplified shares, no other company has a minimum amount of legal capital assigned and this principle has been preserved by the enacting of the LGS.

28. The Federal Chamber of Appeals of La Plata, Room II—May 8, 2001, in proceedings: "Fomento de Construcciones y Contratas S.A. c. Municipality of Avellaneda," vote of Dr. Frondizi, said that "The imposition of restrictions on foreign companies that intend to participate in the bidding of public services—in the case, waste collection in the Municipality of Avellaneda—is adapted to the constitutional principle of reasonableness if it is proportionate to the purpose pursued—that is, protection of the common good and national capitals—and does not breach the principle of equality before the law and the rights of foreigners—Articles. 16 and 20, National Constitution."

139. Apart from this, considering the necessary requirements, it is of vital importance to establish a venue in the Republic to be able to carry out the permanent representation and where that foreign company will be notified of any act.[29] We also assume that, if the registration system allows it, apart from the venue, there can be an optional electronic mail where the company established abroad prefers to be notified. A feature of the optional one determines that it should not be obliged to do so as long as it prefers to be notified by material means, but nothing prevents it from setting an electronic address if it wishes to do so. The one who will be notified can certainly decide where and how he/she desires to be so. Digital media relies on the fact that there are safety measures that are much better than traditional ones and hence regulatory tendencies will be increasingly prone to their admission.

140. With regard to the registration itself, we should remark that the social contract and its amendments, together with the instruments that justify the decision to create permanent representation, and the appointment of a representative ought to be provided to the R.P. Besides, you must also register in the registry of SAS if the social type is included in that category. Next, the representative appointment as well as its discontinuance must be published in terms of Article 60 of the LGS.

141. However, due to the lack of compliance with the assumptions established, the debate arises regarding the punishment that should be applied to the company established abroad.

142. Some propose to penalize the society for irregularity in compliance, today known as informality, further the terms of Articles 21–26 of the LGS, whose framing will be used with respect to the society and its acts carried out in the Republic.[30] This position was questioned because it was different from the provisions of the regulation itself that the society, in terms of its existence and nature, is ruled by the laws of the country where such partnership was originally settled. Thus, the character of regularity or irregularity of the entity is defined further by the regulations of origin and in the same way was delegated by our precept.

143. Two other positions are focused on the impact derived from the non-registration in terms of opposability. One of them, with which we agree, states that the non-opposability is relative only to those who have not been linked to the

29. CNAT, Room II, "Acosta, Cintia Delia c/ Gemoe S.R.L. s/ Dismissal," Oct. 3, 2018, available on Oct. 11, 2018. In the judgment, the Chamber resolved the rejection of a nullity of notification filed by the defendant company, attentive to the fact that the address to which the contested notification was made was the address informed by the IGJ as registered by the company and to which the law attributes virtuality as such, without prejudice to the existence of another address that the company could have. This decision of the court is consistent with the scope of Art. 206, inc. d., of Resolution No. 7/2015 of the IGJ, that gives the registered office identical effects as those given by Art. 11, inc. 2, second paragraph, of the LGS.
30. D.R. Vitolo, *Manual de Sociedades*, ed. Study, Bs As, 2016, p. 366.

partnership[31] and another more radical position is absolute with respect to every person, regardless of whether such person has knowledge about the existence of the entity or not.[32] Our adherence is based on the understanding that the relative opposability is consistent with the effects provided by the reform of Law 26,994 in the absence of registration.

144. The inscription is constitutive and declarative further to the type and existence of the partnership, respectively. This means that in matters of publicity, the principle of knowability is established and the juridical person *erga omnes* becomes opposable.

145. Prior to the reform, the non-registration made the entity between partners and third parties unenforceable, but this has been modified by the regime established by the current section IV of the LGS. In clear consistency with the duty of diligence, the theory of proper acts and good faith should prevail in every relationship; there is no possibility of denying something that has been consented to and validated. It is also worth mentioning that the new advertising system of section IV determines that knowledge is even more important than being knowable, and may oppose the legal entity to any third party that has known about its existence by any probative means that proves this circumstance (Articles 22 and 23).[33] The same solution applies to the case of a company established abroad that has not registered and that takes the precedent of the High Court of Justice (CSJN).[34] In other words, in order to oppose the clauses of the social contract, the burden of proof relies heavily on the society and it must be strictly valued.[35]

146. Likewise, Resolution No. 6/2018 of the IGJ has fortunately come to modify Resolution No. 7/2015 in terms of inscription assumptions, modifying the detail of requirements contained in the original text of the latter in this matter, removing, for example, among others, the need to prove that the economically significant business activity and its board of management are not within the limits of the Argentine Republic. Therefore, as previously stated, there is a regulatory evolution of the natural functions of the supervisory entity and that seems to be disclosing the regime of Resolution No. 7/2005 that established the need for companies settled abroad to prove that once they are abroad, they: (a) had another permanent representation, or (b) had interests in other companies that qualify as non-current assets, or (c) were

31. R. Manovil, *La Consecuencia de la Falta de Inscripción de una Sociedad Extranjera que Actúa en el País no es su Irregularidad*, Derecho Societario Argentino e Iberoamericano, Ad-Hoc, Buenos Aires, 1995, t. II, p. 505.
32. R. Nissen, *Curso de Derecho Societario*, Hammurabi, Buenos Aires, 2015, p. 354.
33. CN Com, Room F, Judgment of Nov. 2, 2017 in proceedings: "GeoAllianz SRL S/ Bankruptcy—review incident." In the ruling, the Chamber indicates that it cannot exonerate the executed from the consequences of the execution that was directed to her, because that would violate the basic principle of Private Law relations (Art. 9 CCC), when the executed one knew perfectly the nature of his/her tenant (society incorporated abroad) from the moment the contract was entered.
34. Rolyfar S.A. c. Confecciones Poza S.A.C.I.F.I., Oct. 8, 2004, Lexis No. 4/52.701.
35. R. Belmaña, *Acerca de las Sociedades comprendidas en la Sección IV de la LGS*, in M.C. Mercado de Sala, ed., *Empresa y Sociedad*, Lerner, Córdoba, 2018, p. 100.

holders of fixed assets in their place of origin, all this under penalty of refusal to register those that did not comply with any of those requirements.

147. What is more, a brief reference should be made to section 11 of the preliminary draft of the CCCN that was suppressed in its enacting and that was devoted to the companies established abroad. In Article 66 of that revoked section the commission advocated the subject tried to gather the requirements that were scattered among the international conventions, the LGS, the Resolutions 7/2005 and complementary, as well as of the ones held by the doctrine and jurisprudence. Some sections of the standard were included in Resolution No. 7/2015 (Article 206),[36] now in force, but reformed by Resolution No. 6/2018 as indicated.

148. Without analyzing each assumption included in the precept which was never enacted, it is worth noting in the section referring to the draft regulation with respect to "offshore" companies, or that are incorporated, registered or incorporated in jurisdictions considered low or no taxation or categorized as non-collaborators in the fight against "money laundering" and "organized transnational crime," establishing the faculty of comptroller to assess with rigorous criteria compliance with the established general regulations and, also, to demand the additional information it deems necessary. In this regard, we understand that the LGS contains organizations to punish law fraud and other illegal acts that arise in the specific case, so we did not agree with this text as it appeared to place, a priori, social types in non-valuable or pathological categories, in the understanding perhaps that they were preferably predestined to the illicit in respect to others and that, therefore, the comptroller should be even harder on them. The comparative advantages, the possibility of control through lift banking secrecy in most countries, the cross-checking enabled by the internet and the agreements signed among states, etc., encourage us to think differently and not to regulate from the pathology.

149. Next, it is essential to mention that we have found in Argentine Private International Law from a conventional source a correlation with what we have been pointing out regarding the autonomous regime. Thus, the Treaties of Montevideo of Civil Law of 1889 and 1940 (also Article 8 of Montevideo Treaty of Commercial Law of 1940), in their respective fourth articles, suppose the delegation, to local legislations, of the regulation of these acts. Thus, they support in the same way determined for foreign companies that "to be able to carry out acts included in the special purpose of their establishment, will be subjected to the prescriptions determined by the State in which they intend to perform said acts." Consistent with this, CIDIP II provides in its fourth article that "for the direct or indirect exercise of the acts included in the corporate purpose of the mercantile companies, these will be subjected to the law of the State where they perform them. The same law will apply to

36. Among others, the need to prove that the economically significant business activity and its management center are outside the Argentine Republic (section deleted from Art. 206 of Res. 07/2015 by Res. 6/2018); the solution that such registration is considered sufficient in the event that the company decides to integrate or establish a company under the terms of Art. 123 of LGS (current 214 of Res. 7/2015 amended by Res. 6/2018).

the control that a mercantile society, which develops the trade in one State, obtains over a company incorporated in another State."

150. To sum up, in terms of freedom of establishment and from comparative law, we can take the well-known jurisprudence established by the Court of Justice of the European Union in the judgment "centers."[37] In this case, a company incorporated under English law, made up of a Danish married couple, carried out commercial operations in Denmark and the State of destination did not allow them to register a branch since they interpreted that the founders had avoided the Danish right by resorting to a *lex fori* to establish the entity, when, in fact, the main activity and the effective headquarters would be settled in Denmark. This was even admitted by the founders themselves. Thus, the European Union Court of Justice (TJEU) received a prejudicial consultation and it understood that under the terms of Article 48 of the current treaty included the European Community (EC)[38] (now replaced by Article 54 of the Treaty on the Functioning of the European Union (TFEU), a precept that presents the same wording), companies that have freedom of establishment within the integrated territory and may be constituted under the laws of one Member State and established in another one. In this judgment, the CJEU not only applied the aforementioned precept literally but also interpreted it considering the fundamental principles of the TFEU and its objectives of suppression of frontiers. This is so because the integration makes the free movement of both human and legal persons and it does not admit the concept of a State preventing a society from residing in its territory because it was established according to the laws of a country with which it has no relationship at all.

151. The TFEU is in a hierarchy superior to national rights and its objectives and precepts should prevail in case of contradiction with domestic regulations.

A. Participation in the Local Society

152. 1According to Article 123 of the LGS, companies established abroad that intend to set up a company in Argentina must: prove that they have been established according to the laws of the country of origin and that they have been registered in the R.P and, in the case of SAS, they ought to prove that they have introduced in the register its constituent documents, amendments and other documentation as well as its legal representatives. Although the rule refers to the establishment, this belief also extends up to the point of participating in an Argentine company that has already been set up.[39] The wording of this concept is incomplete

37. CJEU, case C-212/97.

38. Article 48 TCCE: "Companies incorporated in accordance with the legislation of a Member State and whose registered office, central administration or main activity center is within the Community shall be equated, for the purposes of applying the provisions of this chapter, to the national natural persons of the Member States … ."

39. B.K. Orchansky, *Nuevos Enfoques Respeco de la Actuación en Nuestro País de las Sociedades Constituidas en el Extranjero*, Advocatus, Córdoba, 1996, p. 276; J.O. Zunino, *Régimen de Sociedades*, Astrea, Bs As, 2016, p. 119; E. Zaldivar & A. Rovira, *El Artículo 123 de la Ley 19550. Una*

and this has been reviewed in the preliminary draft amendments of LGS and also of the CCCN that focused on this subject matter.[40] Considering this, the rule that was removed in the final version of the CCCN incorporated some extracts from the preliminary draft amendments of Article 123 of LGS and of the enacting of Private International Law, which included both the constitution and the participation. There was also a proposal in order to make a distinction between active and merely speculative participation by the company incorporated abroad, considering it not only in terms of quantity, such as the participatory percentage in capital or the political incidence in decision-making but also in terms of qualitative concepts with respect to acts of acquisition of real estate since they are fundamental principles in the national economy. Also, further to the representatives, the rule clearly stated their faculties regarding the purpose of the mandate conferred on them for the exercise of social rights, notwithstanding the fact that there could be other representations that should be expressly conferred and that do not arise from the said mandate. To end up, the precept established a sanctioning regime regarding the lack of registration, depriving the non-registered company of the exercise of the rights of the partner (with some peculiarities when the participation has been acquired in the stock market, allowing, where appropriate, the exercise of patrimonial rights) or to dispose of the owned property.

153. It has been argued, with regard to participation in an already established company, that the company established abroad must only complete these requirements if the acquisition of shares has been for the purpose of performing the role of an active shareholder and not that of a minority partner who has acquired them for mere speculative purposes. In the latter case, the acquisition should be considered a mere isolated event further to Article 118 of the LGS and should not be registered. Notwithstanding, the verification of speculative purposes or of active participation must be established in each case, taking into account that a minimum of social participation ensures the power to repeatedly exercise certain rights of such seriousness that imply internal activism in the entity involved, as to mention: the right of information included in Articles 55 and 294, subsection 6, of LGS, or the possibility of ensuring the exercise of social or individual actions of responsibility with respect to administrators and trustees in terms of Articles 275, 279 and 298, of LGS. This is not intended to hold a first minority to make the participation fit in the category of activist, but the objective is to concentrate on the role actually played by the shareholder.

Polémica Concluida en Torno de su Alcance, Jurisprudencia Anotada, comment on the ruling of the CN Com, Room D, Fallo Squibb SA; E.H. Richard & O.M. Muiño, Derecho Societario, Astrea, Bs As, p. 853.

40. CCCN preliminary draft. Art. 71 of s. 11 (Incorporation of a company and acquisition of participation): "To establish a company in the Republic or to acquire a stake in already constituted companies that reach ten percent (10%) of the share capital, or five percent (5%) of the capital or ten percent (10%) of the votes in the case of companies authorized to the public offer, as well as for the acquisition of real estate, companies incorporated abroad must previously accredit before the comptroller authority that have been constituted in accordance with the laws of their respective countries and register their social contract, reforms, modifications and other enabling documentation, as well as that relating to their legal representatives, constituting a special domicile for that purpose in the Public Registry of Commerce or in the records that apply, if applicable".

154. Even though there has been an attempt to make the position stated in the preceding paragraph more flexible by including the principle of reality that will prevail in each case, it is also true that the rule does not make any distinction in the percentage of participation either in the constitutive moment or through the subsequent acquisition of shares. It simply refers to the act of establishment. The distinction of assumptions has led to differentiate between the cases in which the majority of votes in the assembly are held by the non-registered company set up abroad[41] and also those cases whose assembly decisions are submitted to be tested where a shareholder has participated as a member of a non-registered foreign company.[42] This leads to consider the vote of the company constituted abroad as a vote of abstention and to verify if, even so, the decision-making was valid.

155. Notification to the company incorporated abroad regarding its membership is not made in the terms of Article 122 of the LGS arranged for the trial location. In other words, with reference to this, the particular notification to the partner company established abroad is not made to the agent or representative but must be made to the registered head office. Notwithstanding, we should remark that it can also be done at the address set up, especially for that purpose, whether physical or electronic, deeming the fact that this results from an express waiver from the partner company itself to be notified at its registered head office and, in the case of private relations, there is no impediment to do so. In addition, regarding collective calls by formal means provided by the LGS for the case of the SAU, as it can also be the case of SAS, they may be summoned to assemblies, thus; the way in which they are summoned does not vary from that of the foreign partners since the publicity is carried out by mass media and it has *erga omnes* effect.

156. In this respect, it has been agreed that the lack of registration in cases of active participation leads to the suspension of partner rights, both political and proprietary.[43] On the one hand, this consequence, which is still put into practice, could vary if we consider the current advertising regime adopted by the LGS. On the other hand, direct opposability has been accepted when it is derived from the relation whose parties had the specific knowledge of the existence of the legal entity and that their participation has been consented to. For this reason, it is worth questioning the

41. The CN Com., in proceedings: "SAAB Scania Argentina SA," ruling dated Jul. 20, 1978, determined that "the resolution which denies the registration of a statutory reform of a company incorporated in Argentina is set according to law, if the shareholder majority, shareholding company, has not registered its statutes in the country Register, since otherwise it would be important to breach the provisions of Article 123. Article 123 includes both the case of foundation and participation in the constituted company. The term constitute used by the aforementioned Article includes both 'being part of' and participating in an existing company in the Republic and the truth is that, analyzing the legal nature of the partnership contract in high terms so much is a company that is originally associated with another to establish a society, like that which is associated with other people, and partners in an existing society."
42. Resolution IGJ No. 433/03.
43. CN Com, Room B, Judgment dated Dec. 12, 2001 in proceedings: Rosario de Betesh, E. c/ Rosarios y cía SA and other—Sumarísimo; R. Nissen, *The Legal Situation of Foreign Companies That Are Members of Argentine Companies in Violation of the Provisions of Article 123 Law 19,550*, VI Conference of Commercial Law Institute.

inexorable observance of registration in the case of Article 123, since the registration does not work as a guarantee of any kind in defense of the Argentine economic community, but the guarantee is the application of the rules that punish abuse of rights, fraud, etc., all more effective means than mere registration.[44]

157. Also, it is worth analyzing whether a foreign company, registered or not, could be established or participate in an informal society from which it takes the fourth section of the LSG. We do not oppose this option, attentive to the principle of non-discrimination of the entity established abroad and to an interpretation consistent with the spirit of the reform produced by the enacting of Law 26,994. In such case, this situation must be confirmed by any means of proof and its impact evaluated in accordance with good practices and good faith standards (Articles 22 and 23 of LGS, and 9 of the CCCN), all in the interest of determining the primacy of reality respecting what the parties have recognized and agreed upon.

158. Regarding the IGJ, the general Resolution No. 7/2015 in its amended text (par 6/2018) has made the treatment of the case included in Article 123 of LGS flexible in relation to the previous text provided by general Resolution No. 7/2005. Thus, Articles 245–257 of Resolution No. 7/2015 focus on the regulation to register and participate in a partnership and they establish the requirements and functions of the administrators,[45] the precautions for the subsequent registrations (Articles 247–250) and the subsequent action (Articles 256 and 257). Regarding the subsequent action, it is worth mentioning that with the issuance of Resolution No. 6/2018, five precepts that regulated the information regime in Resolution No. 7/2015 have

44. Orchansky, *supra*, p. 277.

45. Resolution No. 7/2015, Art. 245. For the registration prescribed by Art. 123, Law No. 19,550, the following data must be handed over: (1) Certificate provided for in Art. 206, para. 1 of these Rules. (2) Contract or constitutive act of the company and its reforms in notarized certified copy or by registry authority, in both cases of the jurisdiction of origin. (3) Resolution of the social body to register the statute for the sole purpose of participating in society, pursuant to Art. 123, Law No. 19,550 with the following data: (a) the decision to register under the terms of Art. 123, Law No. 19,550; (b) the closing date of its fiscal year; (c) manifestation that the company is not subject to liquidation or any other legal procedure that imposes restrictions on its assets or activities; (d) manifestation that the company is not subject to liquidation or any other legal procedure that imposes restrictions on its assets or activities; (e) head office in the autonomous city of Buenos Aires, set with accuracy (Art. 66, last paragraph)—whose registration will have the effects provided by Art. 11, subs. 2, second paragraph, of Law 19,550—the representative may expressly be empowered to fix it; (f) the appointment of the legal representative who must be a human being, and comply with the provisions of Arts. 206 and 208 of these Rules. (4) Written report with the signature of the appointed representative, with notarized signature certification or if he/she were a professional lawyer or accountant with his signature and professional seal; the provisions of subs. 5 of said Art. 206 being applicable. (5) Powers of the representative: The appointment of the representative must include the granting of special power to participate in the incorporation of companies and/or acquire participation in them, exercise the rights and fulfill the obligations of the foreign company proper to its condition of partner and respond to judicial or extrajudicial legal actions carried out in the registered head office in accordance with Art. 122, subs. b), of Law No. 19,550 or where applicable, at the representative's special domicile in all related with such condition and the obligations and responsibilities derived from it (Text in accordance with substitution resolved by General Resolution IGJ No. 6/2018, BO dated Aug. 29, 2018).

been repealed (Articles 251–255), subsisting only as regards recordable acts of investee companies (Article 256) and approval of financial statements (Article 257).

B. Assumptions Included in Articles 1, 30–32 of LSG

159. Finally, it remains to review the assumptions of Articles 1, 30–32 of LGS regarding the sole proprietorship, the partner company, the participation in other companies and the constitution or increase of capital by reciprocal participation.

160. In reference to Article 30, we should remark that it does not allow SAS to become a partner of another company that is not an SAS or an SRL. In the case of a limitation on capacity, and as it is expressly delegated by our legislation to the *lex societatis*, we understand that the company established abroad is not subject to the aforementioned limitation.[46]

161. The basis of the inapplicability of Article 30 to the company set up abroad is that the legal nature of the rule is imperative of internal public order, but not of international public order.[47]

162. A similar situation occurs with Article 31 of the LGS since the limitation to participation also represents an incapacity that is not analyzed by our regulations but by the law of the place of incorporation.[48] These referred rules belong to the public internal order and they are not applicable to the company set up abroad.[49]

163. Contrary to what is stated in relation to these assumptions, Article 32 of the LGS does apply to companies incorporated abroad,[50] since it is not about the incapacity of the one who executes the act but about the fact that this act is null itself. The establishment of a company or capital increase through reciprocal participation supposes the existence of a fictitious capital, non-existent, and the regulation punishes the act with nullity regardless of whether those that participate in it are local companies or incorporated abroad.

---

46. "The incapacity of Article 30 of Law 19,550 (ADLA, XXXII-B, 1760), does not reach Limited Companies or Joint-Stock Companies governed by a foreign law. Thus, the Limited Company incorporated in Switzerland and governed by Swiss Law (Article 118, 1st paragraph, Law 19,550), is not governed in terms of its ability to take part in an Argentine Limited Liability Company by any other right than from the country of its constitution and not by Argentine law" (Inval, SR L—CAN Com., Room C—LA LAW, 1982-D, 500, with a note from Manuel E. Malbrán—ED, 98-478).
47. Orchansky, *supra*, p. 275.
48. Civil and Commercial Court No. 13 of Córdoba, Judgment dated Apr. 11, 1995 in proceedings: "Construcciones Argentinas SRL c. IRPC—Constitution"; T. Machado de Villafañe, "Inapplicability of Article 31 of LSC to Foreign Companies," note to judgment Construcciones Argentinas SRL.
49. R. Manovil, *Sociedades Multinacionales: Ley Aplicable a sus Formalidades de Constitución y Contralor de Funcionamiento*, T.2005-A, Sec. Doctrine, p. 1503.
50. E. (h) Favier Dubois, *Las Sociedades Constituidas en el Extranjero frente a la Ley 19,550*, Errepar, Bs As, p. 172.

164. To conclude, it remains to be mentioned whether the companies established abroad are subjected to the limitations included in the first article of LGS and 34 of Law 27,349, respectively, in relation to the prohibition that a sole proprietorship could be composed of another sole proprietorship. We think that, as we pointed out recently when referring to Articles 31 and 32 of LGS, these rules are not applicable to companies set up abroad whose capacity is ruled by their *lex societatis*. That is to say, in this sense, if the right of origin allows the sole proprietorship of any kind, the establishment of a sole proprietorship, here it may do so notwithstanding the provisions referred to.

165. Lastly, the IGJ, by means of Resolution Number 8/2021, has implemented, to our humble understanding, a new set of impediments to the landing of foreign investment in the autonomous city of Buenos Aires. This is why we have made these comments in other collaborative texts. The following are the salient points: (a) The status of a vehicle company must be declared at the time of its registration in Argentina. The status of a surviving vehicle company is not admissible; (b) The registration of more than one SPV per group shall not be admitted; (c) The registration of SPVs shall not be admitted if their direct or indirect controlling company is registered in the Argentine Republic in terms of section 118 or 123 of Law 19,550; (d) The registration of vehicle companies resulting from a chain of control between successive sole proprietorships shall not be permitted; (e) The registration of sole proprietorships whose shareholder is only a company incorporated abroad as a sole proprietorship, whether it is a vehicle or not, shall not be admitted.

166. Referring to the points of the first article of the Resolution, it is worth noting that neither Article 118 nor Article 123 of the LGS provides the endpoints set out therein. The non-admission of cases whose prohibition does not arise from the LGS is peculiar as if the IGJ could prohibit what the LGS does not prohibit in a clear inversion of the principle of constitutional reserve. Such regulation refers that, by means of a series of prior documentary statements to be observed by the controlling foreign company, the aim is to prevent the conduit company from "implying a transfer of the business risks of the external controlling company to third parties linked to the 'conduit company,' whose legal personality is strongly weakened by the characteristics of this operation itself; and, this same purpose, at the same time, definitely highlights the precariousness of the legal personality of the 'vehicle' companies, given that they are companies lacking their own aims, of a strictly corporate nature and articulated in the interests of the companies themselves, since the latter certainly 'leads' ('drives') the aims of their controlling companies—hence the use of the term 'vehicle'—, normally aimed at isolating or limiting risks and the consequent preservation of limited liability … ." In this respect, the following question arises: Is it unlawful to limit the risk by means of a special-purpose vehicle? Is the limitation of liability limited to the subscribed capital also unlawful? Why this unconstitutional differential treatment with regard to the equality of foreigners in comparison with Argentine citizens? Apart from this, the Resolution states in other recitals that: "Articles 118, third paragraph, and Article

123, of Law 19,550, are only applicable once it has been determined that the foreign company, which intends to register in the R.P to act in a certain national jurisdiction with any of the above-mentioned scopes, does not have an effective place of administration of its business in the Argentine Republic, nor is its main object intended to be carried out there, points which lead directly to the application of Argentine Law (Arg. Article 124, Law 19,550)." In this respect, it is worth pointing out that the burden of proof is reversed, with foreign companies having to prove, *ab initio*, a negative fact (not having their real headquarters in Argentina, which constitutes a manifestation of a diabolical assumption of proof). This is based on pathology and neglects the fact that good faith and lawfulness of acts are presumed. Another question that must be considered is the following: is the prejudice a priori that the subsidiary company of a foreign holding company is constituted for spurious purposes unless it proves otherwise? Clearly not. To establish that "it is not serious to proceed with the registration of a foreign company, in a foreign jurisdiction, with the costs and formalities involved, if there are no concrete and real interests that justify such a course of action ... " will certainly imply a clear excess related with the inspection's regulatory powers, since the concrete and real interests are the exclusive property of the controlling foreign partner and should not be accredited to the inspector as a business analyst, but the foreigner should simply limit himself to complying with the law in terms of incorporating or participating in a lawful company in accordance with the LGS and registering in accordance with Article 123 for this purpose, without further ado.

167. In addition, the Resolution also errs in considering it necessary to register the holding company in all the public registers where the subsidiary has a branch, in this case, the CABA (Article 2), thus dealing with this situation in a similar way to the branches of local companies. Truly speaking, the subsidiary must be registered in the provincial registers when opening the branch, but imposing the same procedure on the holding company makes no sense either in law or in practice. The local requirement is thus exorbitant for a company which, we reiterate, must simply comply with Article 23 of the General Societies Act.

168. Furthermore, the aforementioned decision argues that although the capacity of the company is governed by the law of the place of incorporation, this does not prevent the application of supposedly inhibiting public policy rules, such as Article 1 of the General Societies Act, which establishes the impossibility of a single-member company to participate in another company with the same characteristics. In the following section, we will be explaining why this position, which is contrary to the provisions of Article 118 of the General Corporations Act, is not justified and must therefore be rejected.

169. To conclude, with respect to the third and fourth articles of the Resolution, which refer to the duty to accompany the investment plan indicating the list of the company or companies in which it intends to participate or incorporate in the Argentine Republic, the effective activity carried out by the company incorporated abroad and the effective activity of the company or companies developed that it intends to participate or incorporate, the identification of the remaining partners; the number of shares it intends to acquire; and the statement on the existence or non-existence of a final beneficiary in the sworn statement required by section 510, subsection 6°, of General Resolution (IGJ) No. 7/2015 (in the latter case, it must be documented that the leading company of the group has all of its shares admitted to the public offering or that the ownership of the shares is so dispersed among the individuals in which the share capital is finally held that none of them reaches the ownership of the minimum percentage contemplated by subsection 6°, of Article 510 of the General Resolution (IGJ) No. 7/2015), all of which leads to a position that reiterates past errors in which the inspection presumes itself to be competent to understand and rule on investment plans, management and business models, etc.; these are mistakes we have already seen in previous years with the establishment of now revived provisions on minimum capital, object and capital ratios, sole purpose, etc., all qualifications which the IGJ is incapable of analyzing and issuing rulings on. It is the very nature of the organization set up to control formal compliance and always, but always, to watch over the autonomy of will and freedom as long as this does not contravene an unavailable rule. It is clear that controlling constitutive formalities and providing opposition to their registry entries does not imply a considerable dictation of regulatory resolutions that are in no way coherent with the special corporate system and legal precepts, such as respect for the will autonomy and minimum State interference in private acts, presumption of good faith and lawfulness of conduct, among others. This unfounded inspection advocacy will not only prevent investment but also damage the market, causing all the negative collateral effects that derive from it and that we are all aware of.

C. Company of Unknown Type

170. The company of unknown type does not present major objections, since its recognition is *ipso iure* in the terms of Article 118 of LGS, notwithstanding the act of entrusting the registry judge the requirement of formalities to be completed by the foreign company subjected to the criterion of maximum strictness. Argentine Law coincides with this criterion when referring to SAU.

171. The company set up abroad is subjected to the *lex societatis* in the constitutive act and this determines both the formalities to be fulfilled and finally the recognition of its existence. Thus, in relation to the company of unknown type, it is necessary to conclude as it has been done by Article 119 of the LGS, without changing the general criterion, beyond the formalities to be fulfilled because it is an atypical entity.

172. This solution adopted by the precept could change if section 11 of the CCCN was enacted which included, in its Article 67, a reiteration of Article 54 of the preliminary draft Code of Private International Law. In this sense, a somewhat evolutionary text was proposed that exceeded the defensive vision currently held by our system with respect to society of an unknown type. It proposed a contemplative view of its own characteristics to allow the comptroller authority to place it, in terms of formalities for the compliance of the registration, in a position of reasonable analogy with respect to those similar types included in Chapter II of the LGS.[51] This would have been another step in a trend that moves toward the non-discrimination of the company set up abroad, an initiative that ultimately was not enacted but we consider it remarkable.

173. It is worth saying that, even with the validity of the previous text of Article 17 of the LGS that claims the atypical society as null, this precept did not apply to companies established abroad because of the prevalence of the rule referred to here and that deals with this particular case. Consistent with this situation, we understand that at present Article 17 does not apply in its current version, despite being different from the previous sanctioning regime and, therefore, the foreign company of unknown type does not enter for qualification in section IV of the LGS, but it is ruled to that effect by the legislation of the place where it is established.

174. Regarding the regulations provided by the IGJ, General Resolution No. 7/2015 (it replaced Resolution No. 7/2005), which was later amended by No. 6/2018, provided as a requirement to consider the register that companies must accompany the certificate issued by the corresponding registry authority that does not exceed six months, etc., in addition to the duty to explain the scope of the liability of the partners for social obligations and to publish that it is a company of an unknown type with such a nature of responsibility.

D. Separate Accounting

175. In the case of a permanent representation in a country that does not contain independent legal status, it is necessary for the company established abroad to have a separate accounting from the head company in order to regulate and monitor the operation of the assets affected by the transfer.

176. This is an argument both economic and legal as this will allow, among other possibilities, to assess its solvency and also the tax duties; what is more, it will determine the repatriation of permitted capital on behalf of the main company, to compete. As previously indicated herein, a branch of a company incorporated abroad is treated as a tax subject although it does not represent a differentiated legal personality.

177. The established forms, accounts, items and entries to keep the separate accounts arise from section IX of the LGS. Notwithstanding, it should be emphasized that the application of accounting methods and compliance with specific obligations do not necessarily impose the extension of certain prohibitions that apply to

51. Article 67 (Societies of unknown type) of s. 11 (Companies established abroad): The preceding article will apply to companies constituted in another State under an unknown type by the laws of the Republic. The registration authority shall determine the formalities to be completed in each case, subject to reasonable analogous criterion.

local companies, such as the early distribution of dividends in terms of Article 68 of LGS, since the company incorporated abroad is ruled, for that purpose, by its *lex societatis.*[52]

178. Regarding the rules imposed by the IGJ in this respect, Resolution No. 7/2015 IGJ in Article 231 determines the obligation of branches or permanent representations to present the financial statements within 120 calendar days after the date of closure, which must be made according to technical regulations, be signed by the representative and accompanied by an audit report.

179. Likewise, the IGJ will guard the maintenance, in positive terms, of the net worth of that economic unit and the preservation of capital, as the case may be (Article 232), as well as, in the event that the accounting yields negative results in this sense, the company must recompose the net assets and accredit them according to the accounting certification or request the cancelation of the registration prior to liquidation, under penalty of judicial requirement (Article 233).

E. Representatives: Their Liabilities

180. Article 121 of the LGS refers to the general criteria of liability of administrators according to the typology provided, and in the case of companies of unknown type, it will be that provided for SAU. Without prejudice to the provisions of the regulation, we must point out that the representative of the company established abroad may have been appointed through a mandate contract, in which case the consequences and effects thereof will be ruled in accordance with the provision stated in such agreement in the CCCN.

181. Moreover, should this situation never happen and in the case of the non-existence of a relation of the bodies, it is difficult to imagine the application of the behavior pattern described in Article 59 of the LGS, deeming that it is established in that way with respect to the commitment the administrator has got toward the entity and this will be the subject matter of the *lex societatis.*

182. Notwithstanding the foregoing, we understand that—in practice, and only in cases in which the executives are also administrators of the entity—what will usually occur, according to the action of responsibility in question, is that the contractual relationships between partnerships in which the responsibility of the administrators is reviewed at the request of a social action proposed by the entity before the courts of the country where the said contractual partnership was constituted (supposition of Article 276 LGS) will be ruled by the *lex societatis.*[53]

---

52. Decision of the CSJN dated Oct. 8, 2013 in proceedings "White Martins Cilindros Ltda. Suc. Argentina (TF 29.993-I) c/ DGI, Folio No. 31,776/2009," quote: IJ-LXXI-830.
53. CSJN del Oct. 8, 2013 en autos *White Martins Cilindros Ltda. Suc. Argentina (TF 29.993-I) c/ DGI*, Expte. No. 31.776/2009, cita: IJ-LXXI-830.

183. However, the responsibility of the administrators for damages to local third parties—partners or not—caused in the exercise of their functions that is valued at the request of an individual action of responsibility proposed by them before our courts (principle of Article 279 LSG) will be according to the national law and that even coincides with the place of execution of representation.[54]

184. To conclude, regarding the representatives, the IGJ, Resolution No. 7/2015 modified by Resolution No. 6/2018, Article 223, states that the registration of a new representative must comply with the formal requirements provided by Article 206 3rd, 4th and 5th subsections of the same resolution, notwithstanding the publication and registration of the cessation of the functions of the former representative. What is more, Article 224, point I of this resolution, states the documentation that should be attached,[55] and point II describes aspects related to the content of the resignation.[56]

F. The Trial: Its Summon

185. The trial summon included in Article 122 of the LGS makes a distinction according to whether it originated as an isolated act of the foreign company or if it has a head office of permanent representation in the country.

54. R. Arenas García, *Constitución de Sociedades*, in J.C. Fernandez Rozas & R. Arenas García, of Miguel Asensio, *supra*, p. 196.
55. General Resolution No. 7/2015, Art. 224, point I—(1) Instrument emanating from the company which accepts the resignation presented whether it is registered or not that it was accepted. (2) Otherwise, public deed in which: (a) the instrument for the notification of the resignation addressed to the company to the domicile that it indicated to receive communications from the representative in accordance with para. 4 of Art. 208 of these Rules and the proof of receipt of said notification must be recorded; (b) if the notification was not received, the declaration must be recorded under the responsibility of the waiver that after the registration of his/her appointment, for his/her relationship with the company, the latter did not subsequently communicate another address nor did he know; (c) details of the books signed and/or, where appropriate, of the means authorized under Art. 326 and following of these Rules, indicating date and content of the last registration made on the date of resignation and, for handbooks, last page used; (d) indication of the domicile—within the limits of the autonomous city of Buenos Aires—in which the books and supporting documentation will be retained to make them available to the newly appointed representative or the competent court if it is necessary. (3) The financial statements pending presentation—whose term is expired—as of the date of application for registration. (4) The publication of the corresponding notice in the Official Record.
56. Resolution No. 7/2015, Art. 224 point II—formalities as regards the resignation. The waiver must: (1) be formulated in express and unequivocal terms, they must not be subjected to any kind of conditions; (2) indicate a period during which the waiver will continue in office, not less than ninety days from the date of acceptance of its notification, whether positively or negatively, and for the purposes that within that period, the company shall appoint a new representative and request its registration; (3) have precise reference to the provisions of Arts. 226 and 273 subs. 2, regarding the deadline to request the registration of a new representative and the consequences of non-compliance; (4) inform the company, based on the financial statements and/or accounting certification required for this purpose, if on the date of the resignation the existing assets and funds are prima facie sufficient to comply with the obligations arising from the branch's performance, seat or representation, expired and due payable in the Argentine Republic, estimating, if it is negative, the existing deficit.

186. In the first case, the notification must be made to the person who had taken part in the act or contract from which the judicial conflict arose. By the statement referring to the proxy himself, it must be understood that is his own domicile or that established by him/her in the act in question.

187. With reference to the second case, regarding the notification to the representative, in the event that there is a permanent representation, this statement refers to the representative registered in terms of Article 118, third paragraph of LGS.

188. However, if the company established abroad is not registered, the principle of Article 152 of the CCCN shall be applied.[57]

189. The preliminary draft of CCCN, in section 11, Article 65, presented a solution to this matter. Thus, the standard transcribes in its first section the current first paragraph of Article 122 of LGS, but in the second section, it extends the alternatives of notification to the registered address beyond the person of the representative. Moreover, it has also been established that it must be applied even when there was no act of registration of the domicile. Thus, the notification can be made to both the representative who intervened in the act or contract with respect to the dispute in question and the location of the administration the constituent has in the country.[58]

190. Thus, this approach of the regulation certainly provided a greater range of possibilities; yet it was not enacted.

191. Finally, regarding the regulations set forth by the IGJ, Article 244 of Resolution No. 7/2015 of the IGJ, let us remark that it provides that any summon in court to be made to the partnership at the headquarters registered by them because of any action that these promote or in which they intervene will be entailed and will be enforced by Article 11, subsection 2, second paragraph, of the LGS. It is clear that the case refers to habitual acts and the act of registration of the company according to Article 118 of LGS, but it does not refer to the provisions of Article 123 of the same legal regulations, since the regulatory article is established in the fourth section of the first chapter corresponding to the third title of the resolution, a section dealing with the performance of the representative, but it is not applicable in case

57. Article 152 of the CCCN states: "The legal entity that owns many establishments or branches has its special domicile in the place of said establishments only for the execution of the obligations therein contracted … ."

58. Article 65 (Companies established Abroad) of s. 11 (Summons to process): The placement of a company constituted abroad can be fulfilled in the Republic: (a) originating in an isolated act, in the person of the advocate that intervened in the act or contract that causes the dispute; (b) originating in acts carried out in the Republic with intervention of a branch, seat or any other form of representation registered in the country at the registered domicile in terms of Art. 66, third paragraph, or in the person of the registered representative. When the company had to register its establishment and failed to do it, it will be validly to summon in the location of its administration in the country or in the person of the representative who intervened in the act or contract causing the litigation.

of participating or setting up a company in the country, which is regulated in the second chapter of that section and heading.

VI. Effective Headquarters in Argentina

192. The general criterion on Articles 118–123 of LGS is based on the quality or nature of the acts that the foreign company intends to carry out, varying the assumptions to be observed, it is appropriate to deal with the case in which the *lex societatis* of the place of establishment does not apply any longer and the social entity is ruled by the law of its commercial domicile, effective headquarters or place where its head office is located.

193. According to this, this assumption has its regulation in the different normative volumes of autonomous and conventional sources included in the Argentine Law; however, there are no substantial differences. Thus, as already mentioned at first, Article 124 of LGS prescribes that "The company incorporated abroad that has its headquarters in the Republic or its main purpose is intended to be fulfilled in it, will be *considered as a local society* for the purposes of compliance with the formalities of its setting up or its reform and supervisory functioning." The text of this standard is clearly inclined to the theory of the effective headquarters against these assumptions, in as much as the foreign company has its head offices in the Republic, or if its main purpose is intended to be fulfilled in it, it will be considered a local company for the purposes of compliance with the formalities of establishment, reform and functioning control.

194. Moreover, the IGJ has provided that when the submitted documentation derives in the application of this rule, the company established abroad will be required to adapt itself to the 19,550 Law,[59] under warning of requesting cancelation of its registration and the liquidation of assets that could correspond.[60] We do not agree with this license to request the liquidation of assets since, in the absence of fraud leading to nullity and the consequent duty of liquidation, the company will fall in the premises of section IV of the LGS and it will necessarily keep its assets.

195. In another sense, despite this error of the IGJ, we must highlight the acceptance by this office regarding the possibility of accrediting the incorporation of the company and the activity abroad by technological means.[61]

196. In reference to Article 124, the nature of that precept has been defined as international public order or police,[62] or as a rule that prevents fraud.[63] Then, it is

59. General Resolution IGJ 6/2018, Art. 266.
60. *Ibid.*, Art. 267.
61. I. Molinari, *La Nueva Resolución de la IGJ: Un Paso Acertado en Relación a las Off Shore*, elDial.com-CC384.
62. Vitolo, *supra*, p. 379.
63. "… Article 118 LS should be read and interpreted as a set integrated with Article 124 LS, which contemplates the problem of companies constituted 'in fraudem legis'. This is so because that first

certain that, beyond the position adopted, the subjective assumption that must be presented in the case of fraud will not always take place and the application of the rule will be activated simply by the fact that any of the objective factual situations that it involves can be proved, such as: that the company established abroad has its head office in the Republic or that its main purpose is destined to be fulfilled in it. Should this take place, Article 124 leaves the general criterion of setting up or place of incorporation and it will be applied exclusively in defense of Argentine international public order. It can happen that, the company set up abroad does not carry out any activity in any other third State or in its place of establishment, but simply in Argentina, beyond the specific activity to be developed in the country as it could be, for example, the mere holding of company shares, the company can be included in this precept as has been stated.[64] To this last respect, we must remark that the company will not be included because of the mere possession of shares but when it constitutes its sole activity.[65]

197. Likewise, the Treaty of Montevideo on Commerce Law (1940) in its seventh and eighth articles states that "the content of the social contract; the juridical relationships among partners; the relationship between the latter and the company and between the company and the third parties, are ruled by the law of the State where the company has legal domicile"; and that "mercantile companies will be ruled by the laws of the State of its commercial domicile and will be acknowledged as holding full right in the other contracting States and will be able to carry out commercial acts and to be in court." It is possible to notice that, beyond their diverse wording, such regulations clarify that the regulation ruling the company *(lex societatis)* is, in this case, the one where the company has its commercial domicile. Thus, the effective headquarter theory is put into practice if we take into account the concept of commercial domicile established by the Treaty which states, in its third article, that "commercial domicile is the place where the business or the commercial law has its main head office. However, if they establish settlements or branches, they are estimated to be settled in the place where they function and subjected to the local authorities' jurisdiction regarding all the acts that they carry on there." Besides, identical criterion is established in the Commercial Treaty of Law (1889) which in its fourth article states that "the social contract is ruled by the law

part of Article 118 LS recognizes the existence of the foreign company, as long as Article 124 LS, it just does not do it—it strictly ignores it as a foreign company—with respect to the assumption that it legislates." The resolution also supports that "that in the cases contemplated in Article 124 LS, the Argentine Republic does not recognize the existence of the entity as a foreign company; it considers it a local company and the law of the place of incorporation becomes irrelevant" (Boskoop SA s/ bankrupt s/ incident of appeal—CNCOM—SALA A—Apr. 18, 2006).

64. "In the event that the only activity denounced by the foreign society is to own a set of actions that allow it to control an Argentine company, it does not seem doubtful that the situation is truly great in the event of 124, and the regulation provided for national entities should be applied to the affected company, much more when the offshore in question has no other activity in the country where it was established or in third countries, but acts exclusively in Argentina, which can be verified through a simple examination of its financial statements" (*Juz. Com. 1st Inst. No.* 16 in proceedings: Great Brands Inc s/ reorganization proceedings, dated Oct. 3, 2002).

65. CN Com., Room C, Judgment dated Dec. 27, 2002 in proceedings: "Great Brands inc. s/ reorganization proceeding."

of the country where it has its commercial domicile regarding both, its manner and its juridical relationships among partners and even among the company and third parties."

198. In order to understand all the precepts already mentioned, the CSJN has determined that, in these cases, the commercial domicile can be granted jurisdiction in a fallible process that shows a certain insolvency due to the fact that it believes the company established abroad to be a native one. With reference to this, the Highest Court has stated that … "the required one had its head office and main activity in the Argentine Republic, Article 124, Law 19,550 should be applied since it determines that, in case of fraud, the foreign company must be considered as a local one."[66]

199. Apart from this, let us point out that CIDIP II in its fifth article accepts the possibility of states selecting the headquarter theory by providing that "companies incorporated in a State that intend to establish the effective head office of their central administration in another State, may be obliged to comply with the requirements established in the legislation of the latter."

200. Let us also remark that when there is no adequacy to the regulations of a local company, except in the case of fraud to the law, it does not directly cause the nullity of the entity and consequent liquidation of the assets of the company. We believe that it must be opposed relatively and, in turn, as it is a local society, be considered in section IV, Article 17 of the LGS.

VII. Freedom of Establishment According to Mercosur

201. The Treaty of Asunción, in its first Article, establishes: "The free circulation of goods, services and productive factors among countries … ," thus clarifying that the recognition and freedom of establishment of societies must be ensured.[67] This statement is also applied to legal individualities and this makes the first article incompatible with any denial of individuality. Then, if there has been a breach of formalities, we must be subjected to the aforementioned relative unenforceability,

66. CSJN in proceedings, case *Mihanovich, Ricardo L.* Upon Request of Bankruptcy General Business Company, Feb. 24, 2009. In its text, the ruling also states that "Article 118 of Law 19,550 regulates the recognition of the foreign company, as long as it complies with the laws of the place of its constitution, and Article 124 of the same regulation—whose application the petitioners request—individualizes the assumption in which the company incorporated abroad is not recognized as such, but as a local company. This issue arises when the headquarters or main corporate purpose are located in the national territory, a hypothesis which imposes by the application of the national legal system with the scope established in the regulation itself. Therefore, the decision about the legal treatment that, in domestic law, corresponds to the company whose bankruptcy is petitioned, is absolutely linked to the conclusion reached about the place in which it developed its main activity"; Nissen, *supra*, p. 361.
67. Alegria,H. in N.A. Gomez, *Libertad de Establecimiento de las Sociedades en el Marco de la Integración*, VIII Congreso Argentino de Derecho Societario, IV Congreso Iberoamericano de Derecho Societario y de la Empresa, Rosario, 2001, p. 101.

but we could never deny its personality type. It is possible to emphasize that the conventional precept is of direct application and can be opposed to the Member States by the operators.[68]

202. Our regional integration agreement has not reached the prevalence of the European Union (EU), despite all the efforts made. Thus, a case such as that of the CJEU center's sentence would hardly have a solution like the one that the High European Court established in a process presented before the national judges. It is worth noticing that the elimination of limitations is nothing more than a desire. Nonetheless, if we concentrate on the article previously mentioned and we agree that it encloses the legal entity among the factors of production, free circulation must be guaranteed and the LGS police regulation must not be overused. We ought to remember that a nullity act related to a society under the terms of Article 124 does not keep coherence with the first article of this treaty, except in cases of fraud to the law.

203. Apart from this, a similar position to that of the European Limited Company (Sociedad Anonima Europea (SAE)) has been adopted here by the bilateral treaty for the establishment of the statute of Bi-National Argentine-Brazilian Companies.

VIII. Bi-National Argentine-Brazilian Companies: Their Statute

204. It is a bilateral treaty signed between Argentina and Brazil, which establishes the statute of a supranational company or that of a company formed by many nationalities. The purpose has been to provide entrepreneurs from both markets with a legal tool which allows the exercising of economic activity organized in both countries.

205. It is understood that it constitutes an instrument for investors according to its first Article, which reads as follows: "the physical persons domiciled in either of the two countries; public legal entities of either of the two countries; and private legal entities of either of the two countries, in which the majority of the share capital and votes as well as the effective administrative and technological control are held, directly or indirectly, by the first two investors … ."

206. Within the characteristics of this binational type, it can be observed that in the last part of the referred regulation, the control theory is established. This means that social will is not only controlled by necessary capital and vote but also kept in Argentine and Brazilian national investors (Article 1, paragraph 2). Note that compliance must be presented simultaneously, that is to say that: (a) at least 80% of the share capital and votes must belong to national investors of the Argentine Republic and the Federative Republic of Brazil, assuring them effective control of the binational company; (b) the participation of all the national investors of each of the two

68. Boggiano, *supra*, p. 978.

countries is at least 30% of the company's capital stock; and (c) all the national investors of each of the two countries have the right to elect, at least, one member from each of the administrative organisms together with one member of the internal supervising organization.

207. Besides, the treaty has two fundamental principles for freedom of establishment, such as national treatment and non-discrimination (Article 5). This regulation guarantees the participation of the binational society within a market as a local society everywhere. Likewise, the regulatory volume provides the necessary regulation for the repatriation of capital, allowing investors to transfer profits once the obligations in the market of origin have been canceled (Article 6). Finally, the treaty encourages the transfer of workers from one country to the other without requiring greater formalism from the company (Article 7).

208. In relation to its aim, the activities included may be all those permitted in the country where the company will have its head office (Article 2); such regulation will also determine the legal form that the entity must adopt when it is established. Once the constitutive requirements have been fulfilled, the national comptroller authority will issue a certificate of compliance and registration in the Bi-National Societies Registry.

209. In terms of its social type, the company can be established under any of the provisions provided by the country where its head office is located, adding the EBAB (Bi-National Argentine-Brazilian Enterprise or EBBA) (Bi-National Brazilian-Argentine Enterprise) abbreviations to its name. If we choose an SAS, they will be nominative non-endorsable. Finally, in reference to subsidiaries, branches and agencies, we must remark that the regulations of the country of destination will be the ruling regime for such head offices of permanent representation, and therefore, the companies should be established always particularly focusing on issues related to the purpose, form and registry.

A. Synthesis

210. Following the analysis criteria expressed at the beginning and according to all the above, it is possible to express that the Argentine Republic, like the Italian Law 66, adheres to the theory of the constitution according to its regulations and, as an exception, acknowledges the theory of the effective headquarters in its Article 124 of the LGS also supported in the international conventions cited as well as in the statute of bi-national societies.

211. It is worth mentioning that all the analysis carried out is based on the relationship between Articles 118 and ss., and Article 124, of the LSC, in order to determine the situation of the company incorporated abroad, since the second rule is applicable, the possibility of applying the first and the following ones is automatically excluded. This does not necessarily imply that, in practice, in order to avoid the perpetration of "fraud to the national law" or by applying the precept as a police regulation in the protection of public order, Article 124 of LGS is not frequently admitted.

212. Likewise, it should be taken into account that, being the exception to the general criterion, the interpretation for the application of this last rule must necessarily be restrictive. Having said this, it is easy to detect the theory on which the corporate system is based: in all the cases, the theory of incorporation or place of incorporation is applied (Articles 118–123 LGS). What is more, we must mention that the *ipso jure* recognition of the foreign legal individual derives from the latter, with a single exception for the case when the effective headquarters is in our country.

213. Added to this, it should be noted that the acceptance of the theory of the constitution as a general rule is further admitted if we take into account the case of the foreign society of unknown type (Article 119) which is not denied recognition, but it is allowed to act and the capacity granted from its origin is certainly recognized although it determines applicable requirements for legal security reasons and in defense of local interests. As a direct consequence, this statement determines the inapplicability of the limitations contained in Articles 1, second paragraph, 30 and 31, of LGS, as well as of Article 34 of Law 27,349, for the cases in which, in accordance with the law of incorporation, the foreign company does not have these restrictions.[69]

214. Moreover, it should be emphasized, as we have already stated, that under the regime of relative enforceability at present reinforced by the reform of Law 26,994 that included section IV and its Article 22, the society not yet registered cannot be unknown by those who were linked to it or to its bodies.[70] Also, for the case where there is no fraud, but Article 124 of the LGS applies and the company does not conform to the forms, it will not be null but will be considered a local company under the terms of section IV as Article 17 of the LGS and allowing the continuation of the company in accordance with Article 100 of the same volume. It can happen that an entity has not been constituted in order to deceive the national regulation and has had both the headquarters in another country and also exercised its activity in many places, but when carrying out the activity has then settled its main center of exploitation and headquarters in the country, searching for comparative advantages of any kind. It would be considered a local company according to Article 124 of LGS and the Argentine corporate regulations will be applied, but there would be no fraud to the law and consequent nullity of the entity, but simply by not following the terms of Chapter II of our law, it would be placed in the fourth section of that legal volume. We should also point out that it is not possible to presume fraud, but that the latter must be accredited as well as the proof of the subjective element.[71]

69. Article 25, Italian Law 218/1995 on the reform of the Italian system of Private International Law.
70. H. Roitman, H. Aguirre & E. Chiavassa, chap. cap. *Las Sociedades—Proyecto de CCC*—Revista de Derecho Privado y Comunitario, Ed. Rubinzal Culzoni, 2013, p. 445.
71. A.V. Verón, *Sociedades Comerciales*, Ed. Astrea, Bs As, 2007, T.I., p. 1207.

215. To conclude, we must provide a last conceptualization of Article 124 as an exception to the rule; it is such a clear regulation that the explanatory statement of the LGS states that there is no need for explanation. Thus, the legislator has concluded that, in this particular case, the reason why the regulation of conflict of Article 118 is displaced, in order to add some regulated formalities to the constitution of the foreign company, must be observed in a compulsory way and it must also control its operation, considering it as a local society for such purposes. All this is evident due to the local interests that the headquarters has in the Republic as well as the question that its main objective is destined to be fulfilled.

216. For all the foregoing, we can conclude by saying that for the Argentine legislation, it is indifferent that a company constituted according to the law of a State has its real headquarters or central administration in another country than the one of the constitution, but in reference to its existence and capacity, it will be ruled by the law of the latter. With the exception of the only case in which this main establishment is in the Argentine Republic (as noted, it is not necessarily fraud to the law, but can act as a police regulation protecting the public order), in which case, the theory of the effective headquarters or of the real nature contained in Article 124 of LGS will apply.

217. To summarize, it is worth mentioning that the flexibilization of the system in the case of companies incorporated abroad does not restrict the application of the general principles of law related to good faith, abuse of rights, etc., nor does it inhibit the application of the law at all cost and its duty of avoiding any damage and extend civil liability to everyone who fits that attribution according to the general theory of responsibility for an unlawful act. All these current tools are still available to severely punish negative assumptions and thus avoid the categorization of certain foreign companies as dangerous per se or to believe that registration will guarantee the reduction of damage. The lack of registration makes the entity unenforceable except when there is knowledge, so that the personality cannot be invoked to involuntary creditors and they will stand all the implications in matters of liability actions to go to the ultimate consequences and against all those responsible for the damage.

218. In this sense, it is fundamental to emphasize that the registration of goods in the corresponding registers does not replace the registration stage of the R.P of companies and besides, it has no advertising effect on the entity (real estate, automotive, tax, etc.) since the records are established in the statutes with another objective and their effects are only adjusted to the fulfillment of such goal.

§6. The Labor Law Connection: Codetermination and Corporate Structure

219. In the Argentine corporate scheme, the workers do not participate in the decision-making of the company, unless it is established in its statutes (in the SAS incorporation act, for example). There is no legal imposition that determines the necessity of worker participation in management or profit sharing, despite the fact that these models can be adopted in statutes as incentives for them. In this way, the private character of the invested capital and its management by administrators chosen by investors who become shareholders will be safeguarded.

220. This does not mean that an administrator cannot have a dual status in his relationship with the company. He can also be an official in the exercise of the administration forming part of the body as well as a worker in the provision of a technical service or a job task in the company.

221. However, it is common for workers who achieve certain objectives to be offered prizes that consist of opportunities to be shareholders acquiring shares for lower prices (stock options). However, in terms of labor agreements, workers according to their activity are grouped by union of workers that negotiates with business chambers the agreements for the development of the tasks of the activity and requests approval from the Ministry of Labor. By the way, the worker who within the company is a representative or union delegate cannot be dismissed without cause from the company because of the union protection; otherwise, the dismissal is understood to be discriminatory and activates the right of reinstatement of the badly fired worker.

Part I. Corporations/Companies

Chapter 1. Big Corporation: Public Corporation—Share Company

§1. CHARACTERISTICS

222. For the large company, the planned structure is that of the Limited Company (SL). It is a capital company in which the partners are called shareholders and are considered investors, especially in the case of the open corporation where there is no *affectio societatis* as a characteristic element. It is worth saying that the partner himself is not a prominent element in the conception of the type, but rather the relevance falls on his contribution, beyond its distortion in reality to which we are referring. As a consequence, it is not possible to assign a company name to the corporation, but it is given a company name followed or preceded by the identification of the type or acronym thereof. This type of company does not limit the group of partners to a specific number, it can be extended indefinitely and its bodies are called: the administration, the board of directors, the government body, the assembly; and, those related to supervising: the supervisory council and a receivership. The SAU that is not included in Article 299 (Law 19,550), that is to say, the one that does not have a capital superior to ARS 50,000,000, can do without receivership. Likewise, with respect to the constituent capital, it cannot be less than ARS 100,000 and the contributions in cash must be integrated at 25% at the time of incorporation, except in the case of the sole proprietorship which must be fully integrated in that act.

223. Closed Stock Corporations (SAs) are not those that are simply not listed on the stock exchange, but in this category are all those that, in their bylaws, do not allow the free transferability of the shares, but establish a series of limitations. That is to say, however, that open companies are those that do not limit the transfer of shares, whether they are listed or not on the stock market.

224. In turn, this society accepts a subtype which is the sole proprietorship. It is the only corporate type of the 19,550 Company Law that allows the sole shareholder society, but it does have a limitation: the impossibility for that company to constitute another sole proprietorship. With the enactment of Law 27,349 to support entrepreneurial capital, another corporate type was added: the Simplified SAS that allows the constitution of a sole proprietorship and that cannot, in turn, in the case of being a sole proprietorship, constitute another sole proprietorship whether it is a Simplified SAS or a sole proprietorship.

225. In reference to SAS, there is a permanent State control if they are included in the cases of Article 299 of the LGS, that is to say: if they make a public offering of their shares or debentures; if they have a capital higher than ARS 50,000,000; if they are of mixed economy or if they are included in section VI (SAU with majority State participation); if they carry out capitalization, savings or in any other way require money or securities from the public with a promise of services or future benefits; exploit concessions or public services; if it is a controlling company of or controlled by another subject to permanent State control in accordance with the assumptions set forth herein; and, finally, as we have mentioned, if it is a one-person corporation. It is worth mentioning that, in Argentina, there is a distortion on the part of the market regarding the purpose pursued by Law 19,550 when creating the different types of companies, since the SAS has been the society chosen by the national market to operate (at least prior to the incorporation of the company by simplified shares that currently has a large number of constitutions). Thus, the number of SAS, even in the case of family companies, greatly exceeds SRL and the rest. We should point out that the doctrine is not peaceful in the debate on whether the closed corporation deserves a normative interpretation that assimilates it to the SRL and takes it away from the large company. Besides, the SAU, whether open or closed, is a SL and the market cannot vary the characteristics of the type and even claim the non-application of the natural precepts by the mere indiscriminate use of SAS for assumptions in which the type of capital is not the one that best fits personal relationships.

§2. Formation

I. Formal Requirements and Minimum Content of Articles

226. The SAS is incorporated in Articles 163–314 of the LGS and is constituted by public instrument and in sole act or by public subscription. Note that, in a law that has 390 articles, 151 articles refer to the SAS in its various manifestations. This truly shows the importance of this type of company that is regulated by more rules than the rest of the social types considered a whole.

227. Regarding the constitutive process, first, we will refer to the assumption of the constitution by public instrument and in a single act.

228. Thus, a public instrument refers to the instrumental genre that includes any of its species, for example, a Public Deed or an administrative resolution. It is worth mentioning that, as it is a federal country, the constitution by public instrument does not find a single treatment at the national level. Thus, in the autonomous city of Buenos Aires, SAS can only be constituted by Public Deed authorized by the Notarial Registry of that capital. On the contrary, in the province of Córdoba, these companies can be established either in that way or by resolution of the comptroller administrative entity which authorizes the setting up of the SAS that has been presented by the founders in a private instrument with certified signatures.

229. Furthermore, as it has been permanently pointed out, in order to be able to enjoy the effects of the chosen type, the society must previously register in the R.P. The inscription is declarative of the existence of society, an entity that exists only by complying with the assumptions established in the first article of the LGS but at the same time, it is constitutive of the social type, bearing in mind the fact that once it is registered it produces the effects of an SAS.

230. It is worth emphasizing that the SL must always surpass the control established by the provincial State organism for this purpose. That is to say, either in the case of the autonomous city of Buenos Aires, where the constitutive public instrument takes part as a Public Deed for its control from the beginning or in the case of those provinces where a private instrument takes part with certified signatures; in both cases, the State supervisory body will submit the constitutive instrument to the control of legal and fiscal requirements prior to its approval. That is to say that the instruments require State approval to be registered, regardless of their initial nature as public or private instruments with certified signatures, with the difference that in the latter case, the approval resolution will grant the private instrument the character of a public instrument.

231. When dealing with the study of the constitutive instrument, regardless of the manifestation that it has at the beginning (public or private instrument with certified signatures), it should be noted that the non-typifying legal requirements established in Article 11 of the LGS must be observed (partners' data, possible precise and determined social purpose, organization and functioning of the corporate bodies, corporate name, term of duration, partners' rights and duties, dissolution and liquidation of the company), as well as those of the corporate type adopted (board of directors, assembly, supervisory board or syndicate (where applicable), representation of capital in shares, minimum capital, etc.). They must also publish edicts as provided in Article 10, as well as apply for admission in the tax status to the Federal Administration of Public Revenues (AFIP).

232. The SAS does not have a social contract but it has a statute and a constitutive act. The constitutive act supposes the documented external manifestation of the founders of constituting a SL characterizing it in its denomination, composition and integration of the corporate capital as well as the composition of the administrative body, and it also approves the bylaws of the company. The statute has an objective regulatory nature of the structure and operation of the company in matters related, for instance, to its name, address, term, capital, shares, purpose, assembly, inspection, distribution of profits, dissolution and liquidation. Likewise, the statute can approve a regulation (it can also be done later by the assembly) that must be registered to be opposable to third parties and in which, for example, different functions are established for the administrators; let us point out that such functions will be significant at the time to attribute responsibilities to the administrators when analyzing the individual exercise of the personal attributions and duties there disposed.

233. Apart from this, the procedure by public subscription has an absolutely different process from the single act where there is a call to the general public to integrate a future society according to a proposed program, but we must remark that in order to be established, it ought to have collected previously the necessary initial capital already determined in the call.

234. In this pattern regarding its constitution (included in Articles 168–182 of the LGS), the figures of the promoters are imposed; they write the program in a public or private instrument that is subject to the approval of the audit organism and subsequent registration in the public record. The program must contain the promoters' data; the preliminary bases of the statute of the future society; the shares, the number of scheduled issues, the conditions of the subscription contract and the advance payments to which they are obliged; identification of the bank that will represent the future subscribers and advantages and eventual benefits that the promoters wish to receive. Once this has happened, the bank signs subscription contracts with the interested third parties, identifying their data, subscribed shares, integrated advances, etc., and the bank is forced to reimburse what is integrated by the third parties in the event that the public subscription finally fails. However, it could happen that the contributions given by those who are interested may exceed what is established in the call, in which case when the company is established, a decision will be taken so as to determine if the capital is increased according to what has been provided or kept and the excess contributions are prorated. To end up, the constituent assembly is held with the presence of the bank intervening in the subscriptions and chaired by the State comptroller authority; thus, it is formally established with a quorum of half of the subscribed shares plus one other subscribed share. Once the assembly is set up, the decisions will be adopted by a majority of the present subscribers that represent not less than one-third of the subscribed capital with voting rights, calculating also the votes of each subscriber that will be equivalent to the shares that have been previously subscribed and integrated.

235. It remains to be mentioned that, in the constituent assembly, the following issues must be resolved: (a) topics pertaining to the management of the promoters; (b) approval of the social statute; (c) provisional valuation of the non-cash integrated contributions; (d) appointment of directors and trustees or supervisory advisors; (e) term of duration of the company; (f) appointment of subscribers who will sign the minutes of the assembly once concluded. Once the act is concluded, the company must be registered as in any case and as we will be dealing with in the following section.

A. *Deed of Incorporation: Its Characteristics after Law 26,994*

236. As stated before, it has been expressed that the company contract is a plurilateral organization contract in which, unlike an exchange contract in which the rights and duties of the parties are established in a reciprocal and direct manner, in a society contract, we refer to juxtaposed rights and duties. That is to say that the partners are not liable to each other but to the society and the result of signing the social contract brings about a subject to rights different from the members that comprise it.

237. Following this reasoning, we should point out that with the last reform of Law 19,550 carried out by Law 26,994 in 2015 and, also, after the enactment of 27,349 Law of Support for Entrepreneurial Capital, one-member companies were introduced; it is worth mentioning that one-member corporations can adopt the features of one-member SAS or simplified stock companies. The question arises as to whether one can continue to characterize the nature of the corporate constitutional act as a plurilateral organizational contract, given the aforementioned reform and the introduction of a sole proprietorship where there would be no contract. This is because contract is any legal act at least bilateral, and then its bilateralism will depend on whether it generates duties for one or both or the other parties, hence the clear differentiation proposed as a graph of this concept in the case of donation and purchase-sale agreements.

238. We intend to differentiate the constitutive act of the resulting contract, in order to support the concept that the company contract continues to be a plurilateral contract of organization regardless of whether a single person participates in the act of its subscription. That is to say that, although in the case of the sole proprietorship, it can be said that it arises from a unilateral declaration of will issued by the constituent subject and sole partner, the truth is that from that declaration, a subject to rights emerges and it is different from the constituent law subject. We must remark that it is plurilateral since nothing prevents the constituent law subject from transferring shares to third parties without the need for any transformation or modification of the statute. The sole proprietorship can then continue as an ordinary corporation without the need for transformation as it has been incorrectly held by a doctrine since it is a subtype of a SL that from the plurilateralism in its social group, is subject to the general regime of full right. The transformation is a formal act which includes a transforming process imposed by law that in no way applies in these cases. There is no type of transformation or change; the only consequence which takes place is the one corresponding to the social group.

239. In reference to the debate on the nature of the constitutive act, we must say that regarding its origin, it can arise from the declaration of several partners or the unilateral manifestation of a single person, but it will always be a plurilateral contract of organization that brings about a different legal entity as a result.

II. Notification, Registration, Incorporation and Publicity

240. Once the partnership agreement has been issued by a public instrument, either in a single act or by public subscription, it must be submitted to the provincial State control authority to be supervised and for its subsequent registration. The process is regulated in Articles 5–10 of the LGS.

241. The supervisory authority must submit it to the law, once the instrument is registered either in digital support uploaded on the website provided for that purpose or in a physical format. This examination proposed by the supervisory authority is called legality control and qualification of the instrument.

242. Thus, a rigorous examination of the instrument is carried out in order to determine whether all legal and tax requirements have been complied with (Article 11, LGS and typifying requirements plus the tax rates) and, also if the publications of laws (Article 10, LGS) have been carried out. Regarding this topic, it is worth mentioning that advertising in a newspaper of legal publications does not fulfill the permanent objective of advertising, but it does fulfill a circumstantial goal of a society which is in a developing process as well as in a process of regularization. Finally, once the legal and fiscal requirements have been achieved, the company is definitively registered.

243. Regarding the duties, the law determines deadlines for the beginning of the referred procedure of definitive registration of the entity, something that must be carried out by the founders. Besides, corporate bylaws and their modifications must be registered in the R.P of the domicile of the company and in the branches it holds. Thus, within twenty days of signing the instrument establishing the company, it must be submitted to the State monitoring body for supervision and subsequent registration. In the event that there is a delay in the presentation and it is done after twenty days, the deed of incorporation will be registered in case there is no opposition from the interested party.

244. The legitimacy to request the registration may fall on the person appointed in the deed of incorporation (lawyer, notary public, agent, etc.) or, if nobody has been appointed, the directors must do it and, in case they do not do it, even the shareholders may urge it.

245. Once the procedure has been submitted, it must be checked so as to be registered within a period of no more than thirty days, unless the delay is attributable to the registry or supervisory authority and, in that case, the terms will be extended for as many days as those public offices would have been delayed.

246. What is more, once the society is registered, there are two effects: advertising and definitive establishment with the effects of the type:

(1) Advertising: registration advertising implies a declaration of certainty that produces the registration to the community where it shows its registration records. That is to say, as it has been said before, that the advertising effect of the inscription is the fact that it is knowable. It means that there is a possibility to know and, if somebody is interested, he or she can access the registration records. This is in opposition to the knowledge that implies a specific subjective fact of knowing the particular legal act and that can be accredited, for example, when there is a personal notification. It is often believed that it is the same to know, but it is not the same not to know something that you must

know, and that the registration records are acknowledged by everyone. That is the effect of registration: the society can oppose any person.

(2) Definitive establishment with the effects of the type: although the society as such is set up since the observance of the assumptions established in the first article of the LGS, it does not produce the effects of the type since the moment it is established but it does so from the moment in which it is effectively registered. That is why we express that the inscription is declarative of the existence of society and constitutive of the type since from the moment it is set up until its registration it is a company in the process of being set up and only after its consolidation in the registry, it produces the effects of an SAS. Once the twenty days available to start the registration process have elapsed without registering the constituent instrument to the supervisory organism or registration, the company will not be a company in the process of being set up, but a society of the fourth section of the law, regardless of whether a late registration is carried out. It is worth saying that it will remain as a company in the process of being set up from the moment it is established as long as it complies with the registration deadlines; to do so it must be registered within twenty days to the supervisory entity whereas the registration must take place in the following thirty days.

247. At the time of registering the company, there is the opening of a registry file where the registration specialty principle is complied with, and all the instruments related to the company, both at the initial moment and those that subsequently enter the registry will be recorded and attached. Likewise, in said file, there must be a chronology related to the instruments to be registered in order to provide faithful compliance to the successive preemptive rights, a registration principle that does not allow the registration of a subsequent instrument if its previous similar instrument is not registered.

248. Furthermore, in the case of a SL, the local registry must send a copy of the documents arising from the registration entry to the National Registry of Share Corporations: a single registry that has a national character. Corporations do not allow homonymous names, so the name enjoys the protection granted by its originality and consequent registration. First come, first served, that is the registration effect when registering the name of the SAS observing the registration principle of priority.

III. Contracts Made on Behalf of a Corporation/Company in Formation

A. New Section IV of Law 19,550: Its Effects—Registration Process—Its Importance

249. Articles 183 and 184 of the LGS are part of the traditional regime of the SL in training and, according to part of the doctrine, of any society that is in that formative state. In this section, the fundamental question is to distinguish the corporation from the rest of the social types, as well as to determine the incidence of the reform by Law 26,994 in relation to the registration process and to section IV as substantial reforms.

250. Prior to the reform of the LGS by means of Law 26,994, part of the doctrine supported the idea that the scheme of the company in training provided in Articles 183 and 184 of the LGS could be applied to all societies in training. There were different doctrine positions on the subject because it is about two precepts that are included within the fifth section of the second chapter, devoted to the joint-stock corporation. The systematic location of these rules made them applicable without discussion to SAS and, according to part of the doctrine, by analogy, to the rest of the companies. At present, it is worth revising these positions.

251. In the first place, we should point out that the corporation must comply in its constitutive *iter* with the legal regulations established timely and in due form to be able to fit within the regime foreseen for the companies of this type that are in training. That is to say, as already stated, that the constituent instrument ought to be entered into the supervisory body within twenty days of its subscription and, then, the legal and fiscal regulations must be complied with in order to be registered within a period of thirty subsequent days (except when there is an extension due to delay of the public office that exceeds the established deadlines), in which case, during all that time it will be regarded as a company in training. Our position is that, if the process is not initiated within twenty days of the deed of incorporation, or even if it has been started appropriately, then exceeds thirty days for reasons attributable to the petitioner, then the company will be framed in the fourth section of the law, regardless of the responsibilities for deeds performed either in the training period or those after expired deadlines. While the company was in training, the regime will be that of Articles 183 and 184. Then, if the registration process fails, the duties from the day after such failure will have the effects prescribed by the fourth section:

(a) SAS in Training: During this period, directors are able to oblige the society for those deeds necessary to be established together with those included in the legal purpose which have been explicitly authorized. Besides, the directors, the founders and the company are joint and severally liable for the consequences of such deeds when the society is not registered. Furthermore, in reference to other deeds which have not been expressly mentioned, all those who may have carried them out together with those directors and founders that may have known and consented to them will be joint and severally liable.
    Once the deed of incorporation is registered, those deeds that are necessary and explicitly authorized will be regarded by the company as if they had originally been executed by it as a registered company; thus the directors and founders will not be liable for the effects arising from such deeds. However, with respect to the rest of the deeds, the company may deal with them by resolution of the ordinary meeting at the proposal of the directors, but that option neither releases them from their liabilities nor all those who intervened in those deeds nor the

directors and founders who consented to them; consequently, they will all be liable jointly and severally to society and third parties.

Let us remark that there are those who think that what is established in the abovementioned paragraph should be extended to the rest of the societies by analogy. However, we must distinguish the case in which the registration deadlines have expired; in consequence, societies should be included in the fourth section of the act and then they rectify the assumption where the corporation restarts a new registration process through late registration.

We believe that, for all companies, except the SAS, a rectification ought to be carried out, but in the case of the latter, it will be considered a training company given the specific instrument established for the corporate type and the accentuated liability that involves all the participants, unlike what is established in the fourth section. In this case, in reference to the SAS, we could differentiate three moments: (1) an initial one where it is in training and every deed executed in this period of time brings about the particular responsibility established for the constitutive *iter*; (2) a second one when if the registration process fails, the society is included in the fourth section but it is liable for the deeds executed during the registration process and it modifies it with reference to new deeds executed when it is framed in the fourth section (in this second period it will simply be joint); and (3) a final moment when, through the beginning of the process of late registration, the State in training is renewed.

The point is the protected interest, whether it is that of the company and the partners or that of the third parties that were linked to it. This is because, if one foresees the possibility of rectification in the case of the company that was frustrated in a previous registration process, beyond the particular procedure imposed on the correction, it would be granting the dissatisfied partners the possibility of exercising the right to withdrawal and leave the society, while if the second registration is qualified as a process of late registration, the rules of the company in training should be applied so there is no right to withdrawal and liability of founders is accentuated from the presentation of the late registration request up to the definitive registration. It is worth mentioning that the case of a SL which never started the registration procedures (not even through the late registration process) is not the same as the one that did and the process failed but then it restarted the process. We believe that, in the first case, there is no doubt about the partners' willingness to frame the company in the fourth section and, in the second case, it is just the opposite, so it would be contradictory and even nonsense to authorize that second company the process of rectification and the consequent exercise of the right of withdrawal to its dissatisfied partners that have manifested their will to register before. A different solution would be contradictory to the theory of the deed itself that should prevail in these cases with respect to the partners.

(b) Companies Included in section IV: For the sake of brevity and following the aforementioned reasoning, any company, except the joint-stock society, once the registration process has failed or when the late registration process has not been carried out, will be placed in the fourth section of the LGS. In addition, regarding the SAS, if it never initiated the registry process, then from its beginning it will be in the fourth section. Ergo, if the administrative process was initiated, it will be in training while the process is pending resolution and it does not fail, while once it has failed, it will be modified and it will refer to the provisions of the fourth section. To conclude, if the registration process is initiated again by requesting the registration of the company, we understand that it would have the status of the company in training and the rectification process would not be applicable as it would apply for the rest of the corporate types. Then, in the case of the SAS, any director or shareholder may request the late registration, notwithstanding that any opposition by an interested party must be considered. Once the process has begun, the registry cannot determine whether or not a correction should be carried out; this matter is an exclusive prerogative of the competent judge.

IV. Number of Subscribers

252. Unlike the SRL that can have up to a maximum of fifty members, the SL does not find any limitation for the number of shareholders and may be constituted by one or more human beings or legal entities. Apart from this, the group of initial shareholders or founders will be formed from the very beginning, whether the establishing process is carried out in a single act or by public subscription.

V. Initial Share Capital and Contribution in Kind

253. The SAS social capital is represented in shares that can hold a value of ARS 1 or more each, and all must have the same value, although they can be differentiated by classes (A or B) and according to their political or economic rights in preferred or ordinary shares. As for the minimum amount of the initial social capital, the Executive Power has set it in the amount of ARS 30,000,000 (Decree No. 209/2024). It must be differentiated, in terms of its provision, if it is an ordinary SAS or a sole proprietorship SAS since the requirements vary in one case or another.

254. The SL, by limiting the liability of its partners to the subscribed capital, does not allow the contribution of obligations to do but as accessory benefits. You can only provide duties by means of money or ownership of assets and, in the latter case, assets that are susceptible to enforced execution. In the case of the sole proprietorship, the total capital must be provided for at the time of incorporation whatever the contribution may be. On the contrary, in the case of an ordinary joint-stock corporation, contributions in cash must be provided for, at least twenty-five per account (25%), and the residue within two years, while the contributions of owned assets ought to be provided for at the moment of incorporation in all cases.

255. As we have previously indicated, the issued shares may belong to different classes (A or B) that will determine the respective participation in assemblies according to the classes (ordinary assembly class A or ordinary assembly class B);

besides, they can grant their owners various rights. It is worth mentioning that privileged shares give their holders benefits in terms of political rights (more than one vote per share and up to five votes), and preferred shares have benefits in terms of property rights such as, for example, priority to the dividends collection. Those that do not grant great political rights (one vote per share) or patrimonial benefits are called ordinary shares. Unlike the Societies for Simplified Shares, there can be no differences in the same category of shares.

256. As we have already stated, capital is an intangible and invariable account except for the cases established in the LGS. This implies that the capital can only vary by legal provision or by the partners' will. Finally, in terms of functions attributed to social capital (production, guarantee and participation of partners), we refer to what has already been explained when dealing with the matter with a general criterion applicable to all social types.

§3. Essential Elements of the Legal Person: Seat, Name, Objects Clause and Character

257. In relation to this section, it is possible to list briefly the attributes of the legal *entity* according to special Law 19,500 and to the LGS and the CCCN, relating the different systems and referencing the particularities where the regimes are different from each other.

258. Consequently, we can enumerate the following elements: name, domicile and registered office, assets, term and purpose.

259. The name, according to Article 151 of the CCCN, is an identifying attribute of the legal entity and must necessarily be accompanied by the specification of the social type adopted so that third parties know the effects that this entails (similar to Article 11, paragraph 2) of Law 19,550). Also, if the person is in the liquidation stage, it must also be expressed together with the name (similar to Article 105, third paragraph, Law 19,550).

260. Furthermore, the name must meet the following assumptions: truthfulness, novelty and distinctive ability, not only to differentiate the legal entity from other ideal entities but also to differentiate from other distinctive companies' features and products such as brands, names of fantasy, commercial name, etc. At present, the names of internet domains can also be added to these distinctive categories. Likewise, it is worth pointing out that names contrary to the law, public order, ethics or good practices cannot be used, as well as those names which mislead the class or the purpose of the legal entity.

261. Besides, the name of the legal entity or company name, if applicable, does not necessarily coincide with the company's commercial name. It is worth mentioning that the commercial name is the name of the person in relation to the kind of activity that is acquired with the use, but it is not his/her personal name. The legal entity can transfer the commercial name of its property that is an asset of the goodwill, while the proper name of the legal entity is an attribute of the personality that accompanies it until the extinction except for modification of the constituent instrument and consequent substitution of the name or company name. What is more, the corporate name, as already indicated before, takes place when the name of the legal entity or company is identified with the name of one or more partners; this assumption is present in personal companies. On the contrary, a company name implies the identification of the company with a name different from that of the partners and that is compulsory in the cases of SRL, SL and SAS. Finally, as it has been stated, there is a national registry of corporations that dilutes the possibility of homonyms in that social type.

262. Regarding the domicile and the registered office, the domicile established by the jurisdiction must be differentiated from the registered office that identifies the precise place of the main establishment or operation center of the legal entity and in which it will be notified of any act. Article 152 clarifies that in the case that there are branches, they will have their special domicile in the place of the situation for the execution of the obligations that these representations have contracted. The headquarters can be set by a separate document from the statute, which will imply that, in case it is modified, the constitutive instrument should not be modified. On the contrary, in the case of a change of domicile, the constitutive instrument must necessarily be modified. The duty to establish the domicile in the constitutive instrument, in the case of companies, arises from the eleventh article, second paragraph.

263. The aforementioned has been modified in the particular case of Law 27,349, with respect to simplified stock companies, which have the novelty of enabling partners to endow it with multiple purposes and, also, of an insignificant capital established in a minimum of two adjustable minimum living wages. The flexibility of this individual system is related to the fact that this social type is intended for entrepreneurs and, in those cases, the entrepreneur needs freedom to develop ventures of all types not limited by the purpose, as well as the investment partner when contributing to the society does so primarily by trusting the person of the entrepreneur, not by a particular activity established in the purpose. It is worth saying that, in this way, there are two objectives of the Law of Support for Entrepreneurial Capital that coincide: (1) to allow freedom of entrepreneurship; and (2) to make it possible to be financed without the fact that the funds have an application determined by the corporate constituent instrument.

264. We have already dealt with these attributes extensively not only to develop the introductory part but also in the assumptions of each particular social type, so we will not reiterate the concepts to which we refer in the interest of brevity.

§4. CAPITAL AND SHARES

I. Functions of Capital Stock in Current Businesses

265. The subsistence of capital stock as a budgetary element in a company has been the target of much criticism recently and even a certain amount of consensus can be seen in an important sector of the doctrine with respect to the termination of some of its classical functions.

266. The production and guarantee functions of capital stock have been questioned by part of the doctrine due to how little this account would be considered by third parties when contracting with the company. Notwithstanding, this paper will attempt to assign to capital its real importance in business, taking into account both the above and the legal effects caused by its total or partial loss.

267. (a) Its guarantee function. In particular, it must be acknowledged that when third parties enter into a contract with the company, they take its equity into account, not the amount of capital. This is because the common pledge of receivables comes first and it is logical for the statement of financial condition to be valued first to mitigate risks. However, the fact that equity is the primary guarantee of collection does not mean that capital does not fulfill this function.

268. With regard to this, it should be noted that the amount of capital does not provide the third party with any security. With simply one peso (we dare to illustrate it this exaggeratedly for the sake of clarity), its task is complete. That is why we oppose the notion that an administrative control agency or a judicial headquarters should justify the guarantee function with the amount of capital.

269. The guarantee function is statutory, not quantitative. The capital stock, insofar as it is a retention figure, operates as a guarantee of equity balance ensuring the superiority of assets over liabilities, in that amount at least. In the same way, the legal guarantee lies in the sanctions established for the loss of unrepaid capital stock, whereby the third party is entitled to make claims against the company's equity and that of others. Once there are grounds for dissolution due to loss of capital stock, the alarm is activated to stipulate either its removal or the installing the entity's liquidation and dissolution, under penalty of adjudicating liability on the administrators and those partners who sidestep these obligations by consenting to the continuation of hazardous vehicle. This is the legal guarantee of the capital stock, which bears no relation to the amount of the figure, but which addresses the sanctions provided for by its losses in the interests of third-party creditors. The loss of capital broadens the range of collection expectations held by the third party (Articles 94, subsection 5; and 99 of the General Law of Corporations).

270. The aforementioned serves to state clearly and safely that the amount of the capital stock that is arbitrarily demanded by control authorities from companies being incorporated is of no importance because no guarantee or surety of traffic lies in the amount. It is the regulatory system, in its budgetary and sanctioning coherence, that achieves these goals.

271. (b) The production function. On another note, if we agree that, in practice, what has disappeared in most cases is the production function of capital stock, then companies' financing mechanisms are usually from external sources. This may be obvious, but it needs to be established. By the way, the financing of a company by its partners is extremely costly, as the profitability they expect in applying resources is vastly higher than the market interest rates as they would otherwise choose this option which carries no risks. Also, the amount of external resources, at least in Argentina where 95% of the companies are SMEs, is much higher than the amount the partners are able to inject. Following on from this, what also emerges from the analysis is how abstract and unfounded it is to pose a necessary relationship between the capital and the purpose since the entirety of contributions, whatever the figure may be, in no way guarantees the fulfillment of the corporate purpose. Nor can the control authority of the incorporation process make an admissibility examination based on the amount of capital and the feasibility of fulfilling the purpose. The legal minimums of capital stock, though only founded on the regulation in accordance with the foregoing, are the only enforceable budget. So no one is likely to know how to carry out the organized economic activity nurtured by sufficient resources than the founding members. The control authority, whether it is administrative or judicial, lacks the tools provided by the administration sciences that make it possible to judge the propriety or not of the assignment of capital to a particular business, especially if the company's financing mechanisms are, as we have pointed out, mostly external.

272. (c) Organizational function. Although the capital determines the partners' degree of participation in the company and their relationship with the profits and in supporting the losses is a subsidiary parameter in the absence of a statutory or contractual provision (Article 11, subsection 7 of the General Law of Corporations), the truth is that, in common law systems, this can be achieved with a simple percentage detail of each one's participation with no need to equate it to any particular figure. That is to say, in these systems, the members' participation can simply be determined by percentages, with no need to express any figure at all.

Final Considerations

273. In short, it becomes clear from the relationships made, that nowadays capital stock presents its utility both in its classical organizational function (irrespective of how it is expressed) and in the legal guarantee it offers third parties, regardless of its amount. It is the production function which, in most cases, has disappeared, which is the reason for the arbitrariness of any figure demanded by either the regulatory rules or by the discretion of the controlling authority.

II. Different Concepts of Capital: Nominal, Issued, Disbursed, Minimum and Authorized Capital

274. As previously stated, the minimum nominal capital at the time of incorporation of the corporation is ARS 100,000, which must be totally paid if it is a one-member SAS or 25% of the monetary contributions if it is an ordinary SAS. Payment in kind must be fully provided when it is established. As regards the rest, we refer to the analysis already carried out (*see* section "Initial Social Capital and Contributions").

275. As for the shares, they are securities representing the shareholding in the share capital and have the particularity of being nominative and not endorsable. This implies that the natural condition of the security has been limited as an instrument of circulation to the bearer. Thus, the action must necessarily include in its text the name of its owner and be transferred as a right, but it is not possible to simply endorse the document and thereby transfer the status of shareholder to the new acquirer.

A. Alteration of the Capital Requirements

276. Capital, as we have said, is intangible and invariable, unless the law provides for its necessary modification or it is produced by the shareholders' will.

277. In the first case, the exercise of the right to withdrawal the shareholders have, in the cases acknowledged by the law, implies the reduction of the share capital unless the shares of the retiring partners are paid with extraordinary reserves or unallocated results, or through external financing, and the redeemed shares by the company are reallocated between the shareholders (maintaining those their proportions) in the term of a year. In another case, the capital will be reduced by the cancelation of the redeemed shares.

278. The invariability and intangibility of social capital is a characteristic that distinguishes it from heritage (essentially fluctuating during the activity) and it is clearly guarded by Articles 94, subsection 5, and 96 (Law 19,550). It is worth saying that the loss of social capital brings about its dissolution. What is more, the loss may also be partial, and in any case, whether it is total or partial, the cause for dissolution is removed if, at the request of the shareholders, it is fully or partially reimbursed. If the loss was partial, higher than both the legal reserves and half of the capital, and the shortfall is not repaid, it must necessarily either reduce the capital (Article 206, Law 19,550), or it is also possible, by the shareholders' will, to resolve the reduction of capital in case of losses in order to reestablish the balance between capital and equity.

279. However, the capital increase is the competence of the extraordinary meeting, unless it is established in the bylaws that it can be carried out, just once, by means of an ordinary assembly and up to a maximum quintuple. That is to say that the clause is exhausted in its first use and then any capital increase up to any amount will be dealt with in an extraordinary assembly. The explanation of such a provision will be found when analyzing the exclusive competences of each assembly, ordinary and extraordinary, since there are different constitutive assumptions in each case that correspond to the seriousness of the matters dealt with. The indiscriminate increase of capital determined by an ordinary assembly could provoke abuses in which controlling shareholders or those with a certain financial status arbitrarily increase their position in the social capital with respect to others that are not in such a situation and in this way, the rights of the latter would be reduced.

280. In reference to those cases in which a capital increase is determined by an extraordinary meeting (greater than five times) and this requires disbursement by shareholders, those who refuse to subscribe to new shares will have the right to withdrawal, that is to say, to leave the company and demand the reimbursement of the value of their shares, payment that must be refund within one year after the assembly that gave rise to the partial resolution was closed (Article 245, Law 19,550). Similarly, in cases where reserves, dividends, or other funds are capitalized, it must be carried out in such a way that the shareholders shall keep the previous proportion in the capital.

281. Finally, we must mention that in the cases of capital increase, unless expressly established exceptions, the rights of preferential subscription of the shareholders must be respected; in consequence, the latter can accordingly subscribe to all the necessary actions to keep the proportion they hold in the share capital.

B. Preferential Right of Subscription

282. The right of preferential subscription is in the public interest, that is to say, a legal issue that cannot be denied in the statute nor ignored or limited at the time of capital increases (Article 194, in fine, Law 19,550) unless the limitation is expressly stated in the agenda and the new shares are paid with contributions in kind or the capital increase would correspond to a capitalization in payment of preexisting obligations (Article 197 Law 19,550).

283. The preferential subscription is the right that the shareholders are granted so that they can keep, in case of an increase in capital, the proportions they hold in the social capital. However, failure to exercise that right or if it is partially exercised by some shareholders, the other shareholders will have the right to subscribe to the shares they leave unsubscribed and thus materialize the right to increase which they certainly have.

284. To ensure the proper exercise of the right of preferential subscription, the company must offer the shareholders by means of notices for three days in the newspaper of legal publications and, also, when it is an SAS included in Article 299 (Law 19,550) so that they exercise the subscription option within thirty days following the last publication unless the statute establishes a longer term. The option term may be reduced to ten days by an extraordinary meeting if the company makes a public offering of its shares.

C. Issuing Shares at a Premium and Below Par

285. As it is known, the shares hold a nominal value and a real value. The first one corresponds to what is established in a constituent instrument and quantifies the invariable and immutable social capital, whereas the second one has a direct relationship with the patrimony. While the real value of the shares is constantly changing as it is directly linked to the equity, the nominal value is not modified and is directly linked to the capital.

286. The issuance of shares below par or below their nominal value is null. This is clearly the result of the minimum relationship that must exist among shares, capital and equity. It is worth mentioning that, according to its function to guarantee, the capital must remain unchanged, and its monetary expression results in the minimum positive net worth that society must keep. That is why, an issue of shares below the nominal value would break that relationship by entering fewer values than those expressed in the capital and therefore would disrupt the minimum balance between capital and equity.

287. What is more, the share with premium refers to the difference between the nominal value of a share and its real value, and the subscriber must pay for the real value of the share to be able to acquire it, regardless of the nominal value that arises from the title and for the sole purpose of reflecting in the share capital. The latter takes place when it has been agreed on by an extraordinary meeting (except for companies that make a Public Offer (OPA), where it is the responsibility of the ordinary meeting, considering that it is an act of the business itself and, in these cases, the premium can be established by the board of directors, determining certain limiting parameters) and as long as equality is maintained in each issue.

288. There have been some debates and even regulatory precepts regarding the obligation to issue shares with a premium have been carried out by the State supervisory authorities, taking into account the strict justice that the issue premium seeks to establish. The law does not establish any duty and it provides the possibility simply to choose in that sense (Article 202, Law 19,550). Let us remark that we believe that the law can be imposed in cases where the subscribers are third parties that do not belong to the social group of the company, who must necessarily pay the difference between real and nominal values so that the shares of the preexisting partners are preserved. In this way, there is equity in the different moments of acquisition or subscription of the shares.

289. The difference between the nominal and real issue value, that is to say, the premium, will be a particular reserve account that can be later distributed.

1. Public Issue Requirements and Promoters

290. The legal structure of the capital market is made up of the 27,440 Productive Financing Law, which modifies the 26,831 Capital Market Law (Ley de Mercado de Capitales (LMC)); the Regulatory Decree No. 1023/13; the General Resolution No. 622/13; Law No. 17,811 (1969); and the Decree No. 667/01. Law 26,831 in its explanatory statement establishes the need to promote participation of small investors, trade unions, business associations, and professional organizations in the capital market, favoring mechanisms that encourage public savings as well as their productive development. It also seeks to strengthen mechanisms to protect and prevent abuses against small investors, and to promote market access for small and medium enterprises and it also seeks for the creation of an integrated market through mechanisms for the interconnection of computer systems. The principles on which the public offering regime is absolutely sustained are those of advertising, information and transparency. In turn, the legislation referred to in the previous paragraph imposes the National Securities Commission as enforcement authority, an autarchic entity dependent on the Ministry of Economy of the Nation and with a board of directors appointed by the National Executive Power. This authority is financed through national budget items, fines imposed on those who participate in the stock market activity, as well as other resources available to them.

291. The National Securities Exchange Commission is the controlling entity of the stock markets and the open contributing companies that participate in that market so their resolutions are the regulatory provisions of the activity.

292. The National Securities Exchange Commission is in charge of the following: (a) to authorize the OPA of negotiable securities; (b) to regulate, supervise, punish and inspect people who develop activities related to the OPA; (c) to declare the irregularity and ineffectiveness for administrative purposes of the acts subject to its control; (d) to determine minimum requirements to be observed by the firms that audit those who participate in the stock market activity; (e) to fix the patrimonial budgets to be filled in order to operate in the stock market; and (f) to dictate complementary norms.

293. Likewise, it may: (a) request reports and instruct summaries to the entities that participate in the securities market; (b) search places in order to instruct summaries; (c) initiate legal actions, even criminal, in which it may act as plaintiff.

294. The 26,831 LMC has been substantially modified by the 27,440 Law of Productive Financing as follows: the powers that enabled the National Securities Exchange Commission to appoint observers with veto power and even to intervene in a society are removed (the previous text allowed the appointment and suspension of administrators of the contributing companies in the event that rights of securities holders are breached); in addition, it is important to clarify that the denial of the authorization of OPA cannot be based on reasons of opportunity, merit or convenience; besides, the power of intervention of the Central Bank to limit in general and for as long as it deems necessary the OPA of new issues of negotiable securities established by the current LMC is eliminated. In this way, the National Securities Exchange Commission is restored a power which is the possibility to enact that kind of proceedings according to its nature of application authority.

a. Stock Exchange Introduction Requirements

295. In order to finance themselves in the capital market by issuing any of the securities (stocks, bonds, etc.), issuing companies must obtain a double authorization: on the one hand that of the National Securities Exchange Commission to legalize the public offering of the securities in the market and, on the other hand, the authorization of the particular stock market that must give its permission so that said securities can effectively be listed there.

296. The stock exchanges are the establishments where the stock markets work. While the stock exchanges are non-profit civil associations, made up of different sectors of the economy, the market values are established SAS and are composed of a limited number of shareholders, brokers and finance companies. Both legal entities are supervised by the National Securities Exchange Commission. Thus, on the one hand, the stock exchange authorizes contributing companies to use the financial tools available for investment, and it distributes the pertinent information in this regard, on the other hand, the security market enrolled in the stock exchange is the one that negotiates, liquidates and guarantees the operations that take place within it.

b. Issuance

297. In order to issue a public stock offering, a prospectus must be prepared including the subjective, objective and formal elements, as well as other relevant information and guarantees against the offer made. Among the first ones, we find the following: (a) name and registered office of the affected company; (b) social denomination; (c) social headquarters; (d) registered office; (e) social purpose; (f) identification of the corporate group the offeror belongs to; (g) people responsible for the prospect; (h) detail of the negotiable securities of the affected company owned by the offeror, its controlled and controlling companies; (i) agreements between the offeror and the board members of the affected company; (j) information on the nature of the activity, business, economic and financial situation of the offering company.

298. Second, regarding the objectives, the following information must be detailed: (a) the negotiable securities to which the OPA extends, indicating percentages or maximum and minimum number intended to be acquired and the number to which the offer is restricted; (b) offered consideration; (c) established guarantees; (d) statements regarding a possible future indebtedness of the offering company or of the affected company in order to finance the offer; and (e) a description of the financing offer and the origin of said financing.

299. Finally, in reference to the formal principles, the following should be established: (a) dates of issue and terms of acceptance of the takeover bid (OPA); (b) steps to be taken to show acceptance of the offer and the term in which they will receive the consideration; (c) appointment of authorized intermediaries to act for the offeror; and (d) expenses borne by the recipients of the offer.

300. Other information that must be provided is related to the purpose pursued with the financing (continuity of the business, investments, restructuring, increasing the workforce, etc.) and the guarantees, etc.

301. Furthermore, Law 27,740 of Productive Financing allows the National Exchange Commission (CNV) to regulate the private offer in the case of those issues that do not qualify as a public offering. This allows the development of secondary financing markets in digital platforms that work with security systems or safe harbors (*safe* harbors) and allow to carry out private placements for qualified investors that do not require the same amount of information as those who participate in the public offering. The CNV will be able to delimit this area with precision and regulate this type of placements.

c. Information and Transparency: Abuse of Privileged Position

302. Let us remark that Law 26,831 establishes the behavior that contravenes transparency in the public offering; by these misbehaviors, we understand all that constitutes an abuse of privileged information and therefore it prohibits any sort of manipulation or deceitfulness and it intervenes or offers in an unauthorized manner. It is worth mentioning that abuse of privileged information means all that information which, if it had been published, could have influenced substantially under the conditions, the placement price or the negotiation course of the negotiable securities offered.

d. Directory

303. The commission, in accordance with its faculties, has issued Resolution No. 730/2018 which establishes the need for these companies to adapt the structure of the administrative bodies after December 31, 2018, in the first assembly prepared for this purpose, so that directors can be regarded as independent. To fulfill this, it is necessary to observe the following characteristics: in order to appoint the directors, it is essential to concentrate on their professional standards; the directors must not exceed ten years exercising the position; they must not have kinship up to the third degree of consanguinity among them and at least two of the members of the board must be independent.

304. According to Law 26,831, directors must act with loyalty and avoid the following issues: (a) to make use of social assets and any confidential information for private purposes; (b) to take advantage of business opportunities of society; (c) to overreach in the exercise of their powers as provided by the statute, law, assembly or regulation; (d) to act with interest contrary to society; (e) to disclose any information to which they have direct or indirect access because of their position.

e. Audit Committee

305. As for the audit committee, this is an obligation for the companies that make an OPA and must be formed by at least three members that are independent directors according to the criteria indicated before. In reference to the audit committee's duties, we should mention the following: to issue an opinion regarding external auditors; to supervise the internal control and administrative accounting systems related to the accuracy of public information; to supervise the information regarding the risk management policy applied to society; to identify conflicts of interests and give its opinions about them; to check that there have been reasonable expenses when issuing negotiable securities; to verify adherence to the rules of corporate behavior; to express an opinion on transactions with related parties (operations that represent a relevant amount need the approval of the committee); and to review the internal or external audit plans and evaluate their performance, expressing an opinion on the matter.

f. Takeover Bid for Shares with Voting Rights: Shareholders' Protection

306. The OPA to acquire shares with the right to vote may be mandatory or voluntary. In the first case, it is necessary when dealing with the transfer of shares to obtain control of the social will either directly or indirectly, individually or in an arranged manner, and even in one or more successive deeds. This is also compulsory when a voluntary withdrawal is activated by shareholders or when it involves the acquisition of residual holdings.

307. In the case of voluntary retirement, the offer must be extended to all shareholders who did not vote in favor of the withdrawal and to all the duties which could be changed into shares and other securities that give the right to their subscription or acquisition. Likewise, those who voted in favor must immobilize their shares until the period of acceptance of the takeover bid (OPA) has elapsed. Regarding the price, it must be the equitable value of the shares considering the special balance for the purpose of voluntary retirement, value of the company according to discounted flow of funding, liquidation value, average price of the last six months prior to the meeting that voted for the withdrawal (whatever the number of sessions in which the securities were traded) and finally last price of takeover bid or exchange throughout the last year, although it should never be lower than the average price of the share in the last semester. In this regard, the price must be supported by the board of directors, the supervisory body and the audit committee, and the dissenting shareholders may challenge the right in courts or arbitration within three months of the last publication.

308. In the event of a public offering of residual shares, the event is described as the situation of almost total control held by a person who directly or indirectly holds 95% or more of the subscribed capital. In this case, the controlling or controlled company is obliged to inform both the National Securities Exchange Commission and the stock market about the situation of almost total control, within the ten days in which this situation arose. The effects of this situation can be summarized in the following manner: the minority shareholder will force the parent to purchase shares from all minority shareholders, and the controlling shareholder may issue a unilateral declaration of will to acquire the entire share capital within six months after the situation of almost total control. The aforementioned unilateral statement must be resolved by the board of directors of the controlling company; thus, because of the acquisition of the total share capital, the ultimate consequence can lead to the withdrawal of OPA and contribution of the shares.

2. Classes of Shares

309. The shares are nominative, not endorsable, issued in titles or in writing, and may include greater political or economic rights, depending on the type of share. Thus, the preferred shares include economic advantages without political rights (they do not grant voting rights, except for the extraordinary cases included in the final part of Article 244 of Law 19,550, such as the change of the object or purpose; change of the address abroad; concentration operations). However, privileged shares grant advantages in terms of political rights, and shares of this type may be issued that grant up to five votes. Finally, ordinary shares do not grant advantages of any kind, neither political nor economic, but they cover both economic and political rights alike. That is, they do not grant an advantage in the collection of dividends and they grant one vote per share.

310. In turn, the shares can be of different classes, A or B, and accordingly, the proprietary shareholders will participate in the special meetings held for each class.

3. Transfer of Shares

311. The transfer of the shares is free unless a right of preference has been agreed. In that case, the statute must establish the particular procedure of its exercise whose observance is inexorable prior to any transfer. If the right of preference is not exercised by the shareholders, the seller assigns the share to the buyer and the assignment is noted in the shareholders' register, a record that is in a book kept by the company itself. However, in the event that there is a right of first refusal, the selling shareholder must offer the share to the rest of the shareholders and notify the price offered by a third party, so that they can exercise the preferential option. However, once the price has been notified, the disagreeing shareholders can challenge it and initiate a judicial appraisal process to establish the real value of the share. The costs of this procedure will be borne by the party that established the value more distant in relation to the price determined by the appraiser. Once the value of the appraisal has been established, neither the shareholders who challenged are obliged to buy the shares for that value nor the selling shareholder to sell them for that amount.

4. (Mortgage Bonds) Debentures and Other Securities That Do Not (Yet) Represent Capital

a. Debentures

312. Debentures can be issued either by SAS of all kinds or by limited partnerships for shares, in order to get external financing, either publicly or privately. The company that is financed in this way enters into Article 299 (first paragraph) of the Law, so it must comply with the precepts derived from it (plurality of directors and trustees, among others.) This issue is regulated in Articles 225–260 of the LGS.

313. The debenture titles may be registered or bearer bonds, endorsable or non-endorsable, and must be of equal value and may even imply more than one obligation. They must have the following information: data of the society that offers them; the serial number and order of each one; its nominal value; the security guarantees of the title; trustee data; date of the act establishing the issuance of the titles and data of its registration in the R.P; the predisposed interest; data of the time and place of payment; and the amortization period, etc.

314. In order to carry out the placement of the securities, a trust agreement must be entered into with a financial institution. The trust agreement is in charge of managing the subscription portfolio, supervising payments and deposits, and representing the future debenture holders for the defense of their rights and interests during the entire term of the loan until their full refund on the terms agreed upon in a term of office and which will be ruled by the provisions of Article 375 (paragraphs H and I) of the CCCN and finally, it is in charge of presiding the debenture holders' assembly. Notwithstanding the foregoing, it is worth mentioning that the requirement that it must be a banking institution only affects the periods of issuing and subscription, and then the trustee bank can be replaced as provided by the debentures' meeting; besides, we must point out that such a meeting can also remove any fiduciary at any time and without specifying the cause. If there is no removal agreement, any debenture holder may request the judge to carry out that dismissal with a righteous cause.

315. In order to comply with the task, the trustee may do the following: to review the documentation and accounts of the debtor company; to attend with voice and without a vote the meetings of the board of directors and assemblies; to ask the judge of the corporate domicile to revoke the board of directors when interests or amortizations of the loan are owed, or when the debtor company has reduced its assets by more than a quarter, or when the dissolution or bankruptcy of the company occurs, and the fiduciary can continue with the business of the company in all cases and to assist the bankruptcy trustee in that particular case.

316. In the event that the offer for financing is public, this must be done through the preparation of a prospectus which must have the following information: the same specifications that are required of the debentures; a record book detailing the activity of the society and its evolution; names of the authorities and members of the union; the result of the last two years in office and the transcription of the special balance prepared for this deed. Besides, fiduciaries, directors and trustees are jointly and severally liable for the faithfulness of the data included in the prospectus. What is more, the directors are liable with respect to the damages derived from any infringement of the duties that have been imposed on them, but such responsibility ceases regarding the trustee in the case of any other assumption that is not related to the contents of the prospectus; in addition, let us remark that the trustee is responsible in case of his intentional performance or serious negligence in the observance of his duties. Against debentures, the company will provide special common and floating guarantees. So, in the first scenario, the common guarantee assures debenture holders the possibility to collect their credits as unsecured creditors. Second, those secured by special guarantee will have an asset affected to credit security. Thus, in the event of the collateral on real estate, they will have to comply with all the precepts established for a mortgage not only instrumental but also registry, with the benefit that in this case, the real guarantee may last up to forty years.

317. Third, the floating guarantee extends over the entire patrimony of the company, granting the privileges recognized by the pledge, mortgage and antichresis guarantees in each case, without having to complete the formalities that each of those guarantees require in isolation, but simply the mere manifestation of granting floating guarantee plus the corresponding inscriptions.

318. Through the guarantee we have referred to, the debtor company has the full administration and disposition of its assets, but with the applicable limit of what is necessary to carry out the commercial turn; this may be carried out even when the assumptions related to the pledge become enforceable. In this sense, this guarantee enjoys protection as it is enforceable with respect to all the assets or part thereof (in this second case, the non-enforceable assets must be identified and that particularity must be recorded in the respective registers) if the company does not comply with the payment of interests or amortization in the agreed terms, or if during the commercial turn it loses a quarter of its equity with respect to the one it held at the time of subscription of the guarantee, or if it dissolves or goes bankrupt, as well as if its transfer comes to an end.

319. The placement of the debentures gives rise to the bondholders' assembly who will have the right to authorize or oppose certain acts of the debtor company. Thus, for instance, bondholders may oppose any division or merger that the debtor company intends to carry out; also, those bondholders guaranteed by a floating pledge may not authorize the issuance of new debentures that have priority or equal rights to collect them.

320. Furthermore, when there is an option for the debentures to be changed into shares, the shareholders have the right of preferential subscription over those and even the right to accrue. Besides, this possibility of being changed determines that the capital cannot be amortized or reduced (all this while this option is being analyzed). What is more, the capital cannot be increased by incorporation of stocks or profits. Also, it cannot distribute stocks or modify the statute regarding the distribution of profits. Finally, if it were a debenture issued below par, the conversion cannot be carried out if it affects the social capital.

321. It is worth mentioning that the offering company is strictly forbidden both to reduce the social capital in a greater proportion than that which determines the reimbursement of the debentures (except for a case of forced reduction) and to receive its own debentures as a guarantee.

5. Valuation of Intellectual Capital

322. Argentina has faced a circular social and economic challenge for the last four decades (with some economic springs), which has been presented as a matter of interest for this analysis in the first chapter, but the country's great human capital in this environment constitutes the comparative advantage that allows for the production of quality intangible assets at a low cost and their ulterior commercialization at international prices, giving the process superlative profit margins in any segment.

323. The valuation of intangible assets is of vital importance for the appraisal of a company. In annual balance sheets, this valuation is not usually formalized but usually takes place when the company is sold or a partner leaves, among other assumptions. It is only when the intangible assets are added that we learn the real value of a company. Establishing a conceptual framework, three essential characteristics can be identified in the definition of assets: that the asset has the ability to generate future economic benefits, that is, to contribute, by itself or in combination with other assets, to future cash flows, either directly or indirectly; that the entity has control over those benefits, which implies both the ability to obtain future economic benefits and to prevent others from obtaining them; that there is a fact that has already occurred, a transaction or an event, which gives rise to control over future economic benefits by the entity.

Preliminary Considerations

324. The valuation of intangible assets admits a variety of mechanisms based on the factors to be considered, whereby the price conforms to the objective value of the good. Thus not only initial values stemming from the actual price paid to acquire the good, where applicable, or the compared price with respect to a similar good on the market should be taken into consideration, but also other factors such as adjustment for inflation (in Argentina) and the amortization resulting from the passage of time with regard to the depreciation of the good. In the case of intangible assets, their depreciation does not arise from their wear and tear resulting from use over a period of time, as they are not individual tangible goods, but rather from an intellectual property right which, in some cases like patents or designs, lose value as their expiration date as exclusive right approaches and, in the case of others such as software, their obsolescence unless new versions are created (2.0, 3.0, etc.) It may be true to say it is the other way around for trademarks and designations, as a trademark that remains in business and maintains its registration in force over time is one that increases its prestige and subsequent value every year.

325. Below is an enumeration and brief explanation of the factors related to the valuations of related intangible assets, irrespective of the particular circumstances that will be the subject of a subsequent analysis.

326. Acquired intangible assets: In the case of intangible assets acquired by the company, such as IP assets (the acquisition of software or patents, or the right to use or trade IP assets), the value will be determined by the price of the transaction. The method of evaluation is appropriate because it consists of the price the market has assigned to a particular good thereby submitting to the laws of supply and demand. Unlike other mechanisms based on comparing similar products, no objection whatsoever corresponds to this modality as it is the price established individually with respect to the good in question.

327. Self-generated assets: The situation changes if the assets are self-generated, since there is no transaction value as a reference and the development costs do not reflect the real value, whenever the real or market value comprises the manufacturing cost but must necessarily be made up of other elements. In this case, we must take into account other factors, including the reference price of a similar IP asset in the market.

328. Adjustment: Time affects an asset's value due to amortization and inflation factors experienced by a country. Since Argentina has experienced a high inflationary index for years, an asset's value must be adjusted in real terms to have a stable quantification base. It should be noted that the adjustment for inflation is necessary because it addresses the particularity of its market of origin, besides the fact that a stable reference currency may be established. That is to say, inflation or the local valuation of prices does not always maintain a direct relationship with the devaluation of the currency (in Argentina the currency is the Argentine peso) whereby a stable currency can be established as a reference but accounting adjustments must be based on inflation. Especially when, in Argentina, accounting regulations establish that goods must be valued in legal tender and this country recognizes the Argentine peso and the Argentine gold, there is no bimonetary system that makes it possible to establish book values in dollars or any other currency.

329. Amortization: Amortization is the decrease of an asset's value due to wear and tear. In IP assets, it is somewhat inappropriate to speak of wear and tear. The obsolescence of a good can be taken into account, as well as the owner's remaining years of monopoly or exclusive property. This applies to definite intangible assets, such as patents, industrial designs, copyright, tech-transfer contracts, etc. However, we have indefinite intangible assets or assets with uncertain expiration, such as brands, commercial and industry secrets, know-how, market share, goodwill, etc.

330. Having referred to the previous general concepts that are necessary as a prologue to the particular treatment of each asset, it is now necessary to analyze each case in particular:

(a) Valuing brands: Regarding brands, whether they are trademarks or trade names, we must distinguish the cases in which the brand is acquired (purchase cost) or developed by the company. For the latter, the historical cost of creation must be taken into account, quantifying the amount spent on the brand since its creation, a comparative market value of a similar brand that has been subjected to a transaction, or the rent—or income-based royalties.

(b) Valuing patents: Again, their value depends on self-generation or acquisition. For the latter, the accounting expression is simple. It must reflect the transaction price. For the former, both the direct and indirect development costs must be considered, as well as the expected royalties based on projected units for sale before the patent's expiration date. While it is true that losing the patent due to its expiration leads us to consider the amortization that must be applied (the closer we are to the expiration, the lower the value of the patent), a patent associated with a brand will make the product remain competitive in the market, with a leading edge after the patent expires, since the market associates the quality of a product with the manufacturer's brand, regardless of whether competitors later manufacture the same product that is already in public domain.

(c) Valuing copyright assets: We must distinguish the cases of acquired works or self-generated works. In the first case, the transaction cost is the value to be considered. In the second case, we must also differentiate the nature of the work. In the case of contemplative works of an artistic, scientific and literary nature, the generation costs (including registration costs) must be considered, as well as the projected royalties of copies sold according to programmed editions. In this case, the right is long-lived (at least fifty years, except for photography). Finally, in the case of software and databases, the assumptions are similar to patents: although they are protected for long periods of time, obsolescence is short-term. They need permanent investments in technological updates, which should be quantified at all times to revalue the assets.

(d) Valuing goodwill: Different proposals have been developed, such as the current value of super-profits or the American system for buying profit years. In the first case, the average net profit of the company's last accounting periods or years is considered compared to the competition and, in this analysis, the super-profit or excess profit is indicated. This system is usually used in countries with unstable economies, thus the drawing up of an average. It must be expressed in real terms (adjusted for inflation). In the second case, ordinary profit is simply taken into account and multiplied by a certain number of accounting periods or years, which is frequent in stable economies. When the company is quantified according to its net or ordinary profit, intangible assets are included in the calculation, but they are not itemized; they are taken into account regarding their impact during the year. If we use net worth during the quantification process, problems will arise, since it does not consider the self-generated intangible assets that are not expressed in most financial statements.

§5. Shareholders, Management and Control

I. Shareholder Control Mechanisms: Right to Information, Calls, Social Action of Responsibility and Judicial Intervention

331. As we have already expressed before, the governing body of the SAS is the shareholders' meeting. The assembly, unlike the board of directors, is not a permanent body and meets at least once a year to discuss the company's financial statements.

332. In SAS where a receivership has been dispensed with, shareholders may examine the corporate books and collect from the directors the reports they deem pertinent, all in accordance with Articles 55 and 284, last paragraph, of the LGS. Notwithstanding this right the shareholders have, their exercise cannot be abusive in a way that obstructs the normal performance of the administrative body.

333. Later on, we will have to differentiate the position each shareholder has in accordance with his/her share in the share capital. It is worth mentioning that, in order to request the board of directors to call assemblies, including points on its agendas, the shareholder(s) making such request must represent at least 5% of the share capital. The same percentage must hold the shareholders who oppose the approval of the administrators' management so that the consequent social action of responsibility is expedited. Besides, we will be dealing with this topic thereafter.

334. Likewise, in regards to the right to information of the shareholders and their exercise in those companies that hold receivership, in order to request reports from the trustee, the shareholders must represent at least 2% of the share capital, all in accordance with the provisions of Article 294, paragraph 6, of the LGS.

335. Furthermore, in terms of management, the shareholder is not involved in it (unless it is in turn administrator or belongs to the supervisory board empowered to decide on certain administrative acts) and can only control this matter at the time of dealing with the administrators' management. However, in the event that the management body performs irregularly endangering the company, the shareholders may file a precautionary measure of intervention where they request the competent judge to appoint an observer, co-administrator or administrator, as the case may be, to mitigate and redirect the situation. To this end, the shareholder, with no limit on participation in the share capital, must certify the following: the status of shareholder; that he has already made use of all the internal mechanisms of society through claims without positive results; the authenticity of the right and the danger in the delay; to lend against cautiousness in the court to guarantee the remedy of any unnecessary damage due to the measure requested; and have initiated action to remove the administrator(s) of the measure.

II. Shareholders Meeting (Kinds, Convening, Proxies, Powers)

336. As we have already stated before, the shareholders' meeting is an organism that meets at least once a year to deal with issues related to corporate turnaround; among these matters is the analysis of financial statements. It must be carried out at the headquarters or in a place specially selected for the purpose in the call corresponding to the jurisdiction of the registered office and the summary of the act with the specific expression of the decisions must be recorded in the minutes. The regime is established in Articles 233–254 of the LGS.

A. Assemblies: Their Competences

337. Assemblies are distinguished, according to their competences, as ordinary and extraordinary. Thus, issues related to social turn are subject to the ordinary assemblies according to the following detail: capital increase up to a quintuple and only once when it has been foreseen in the statute; responsibility of directors, trustees and members of the supervisory board; appointment and removal of directors, trustees and members of the supervisory board, as well as the fixing of all remuneration for the exercise of those positions; approval or disapproval of the balance sheet, statement of income, distribution of profits, a report and an annual report of the receiver, and any other measure related to the corporate turn, the board of directors, the syndicate and the supervisory board, which has not been delegated to the extraordinary assembly.

338. However, regarding the extraordinary assemblies, the competence resides in those matters that have a certain seriousness and importance so, besides the questions that have been expressly submitted to it, it also has competence over everything that has not been delegated to the ordinary assembly and that therefore places the extraordinary assembly as a remaining one.

339. That is to say, in this sense, that the issues submitted to the extraordinary meeting are the following: increase of the capital in all cases when its increase has not been foreseen by ordinary assembly up to the quintuple; reduction and reimbursement of capital; redemption, reimbursement and depreciation of shares; fusion, transformation and dissolution; appointment, removal and compensation of the liquidators; consideration of the accounts and management of the social liquidation; limitation or cancelation of the right of preference in the subscription of new shares; issuance of debentures and their transformation into shares; and bond issuance. We point out once again that any matter whose treatment has not been expressly delegated to the ordinary assembly will be the competence of the extraordinary assembly.

B. Competencies and Call

340. Assemblies, whether ordinary or extraordinary, must be summoned by the board of directors or the trustee in the cases in which the law provides, or when said bodies consider it necessary, or when the call has been requested by shareholders representing at least 5% of the social capital. In case it is requested by shareholders, the statutes may aggravate the necessary percentage of social capital to legitimize the request, but the request must always specifically indicate the topics, and the assembly must be convened and held within a maximum term of forty days once the request has been carried out by the board of directors or the receivership. If these bodies do not do so, the assembly, at the request of the shareholders, may be convened by the supervising authority of the corresponding jurisdiction or by the domicile judge.

341. Once the call has been resolved by the board of directors, the chairman must summon. If he refuses to do so, any director may summon or even the trustee.

342. In the SAS, the call is made by publications in the newspaper of legal publications for a period of ten days, and it must be done at least ten days in advance and no more than thirty days before the date on which the meeting will take place. In the case of companies included in Article 299, publications must also be made in a newspaper of greater national circulation. The publication must provide the following information: type of assembly (ordinary or extraordinary); date, time and place of meeting, agenda, and the special collections required by the statute for the shareholders' attendance.

343. In the event that the meeting has been convened in due form but has not been carried out, a second call may be carried out for the assembly to be held within the next thirty days; this call must comply with the same requirements but there will be a difference: the publications will last three days in the newspaper of legal publications and they must be carried out at eight days in advance. The first and second calls can even be held simultaneously so that the assembly, in either the first or second call, is held on the same day, provided that the statute authorizes it. Regarding the schedules, we should point out that there must be an interval of at least an hour in each call for the assembly to take place. Companies that make a public offering of their shares are not authorized for simultaneous calls.

344. Finally, the call may be omitted through publications in the journal of legal publications in the case of a unanimous assembly. This takes place when shareholders representing the totality of the share capital meet and the decisions in said assemblies are taken by unanimity of the shares with the right to vote.

345. The persistence of the call for publication in a newspaper has been criticized in recent times since the shares are nominative and non-endorsable, so, according to its share register, the company knows exactly who the shareholders are. Thus, nothing would prevent each one from being notified at the domicile, and in this way, the shareholders will not have the responsibility of checking permanently the newspaper of legal publications to be notified of any call.

346. Furthermore, to attend the assemblies the shareholders must deposit the shares in the company or a certificate of the same issued by an authorized entity, all this should be carried out three days before the date of the meeting; in return for this deposit, the company will issue a receipt. In the case of deed or registered shares held by the company itself, the shareholders will simply have to notify the willingness to attend in order to ensure registration in the attendance record for the meeting in the same way, that is to say, three days before the meeting. Once this has been done, and until the closing of the meeting, the affected participation will not be available, except in cases of cancelation of the deposit. This prohibition is of total interest since the assembly may be canceled when it is taking place and there can be an interim until it is resumed within a maximum term of thirty days, during which the participation of the attending shareholders cannot be assigned.

347. Shareholders may attend the meetings by a third party, as proxy; in order to do so, a private instrument with certified signatures stating the procurement will be necessary. In addition, directors, trustees, members of the supervisory board, managers, and other employees of the company are forbidden to exercise any representation.

348. Finally, once the assembly is established, the agenda set in the call is not subject to revision or modification, except when it is unanimous and the decisions regarding topics not included in the agenda were adopted unanimously.

C. Quorum, Majorities and Minorities Rights

349. In order to be established, the assemblies need the presence of shareholders representing a certain number of shares with voting right. Thus, in the case of the ordinary assembly, the quorum regarding the first call is that of the shareholders representing the majority of the shares with voting right, and in the second call, it is established with the shareholders who attend it.

350. In addition to this, in the extraordinary assembly, the constituent quorum required in the first call is for the shareholders representing 60% of the shares with voting rights and, on the second call, the shareholders representing 30% of those shares. That is to say that the quorum is not only constituent but also operational since it must be preserved all along the assembly so that it can operate with legitimacy.

351. In both assemblies, regardless of their nature, the majorities necessary for decision-making are those that bring together the present shares representing the majority of votes that can be issued with respect to each decision, except when the statute requires a greater number. The majority only computes votes that can be issued, since those shareholders that have an interest contrary to any issue on the agenda should abstain from voting. Examples of these assumptions would be those in which the shareholder is, in turn, a director or trustee or member of the supervisory board, and its management, appointment or removal is voted. The decisions that have been reached computing the votes thus expressed contrary to the provisions herein shall be null and void and, as a result, the shareholders who voted favorably will be jointly and severally liable regardless of the responsibilities that may be assigned to the directors, trustees and members of the board.

352. In reference to the calculation of the majority, this one presents a particularity in the special cases of Article 244 (last part), where the shares with plurality of votes will not be held as such but with a singular vote. The assumptions are as follows: transformation, extension or renewal (except for companies that make OPA or quote their shares); early dissolution; transfer of the company's domicile abroad; fundamental change of the purpose; total or partial reimbursement of capital and finally, fusion and split.

353. In these cases, except for those of early dissolution, or in the case of the partners of the acquiring company and in the division, those non-conforming shareholders who were present may exercise the right to withdrawal within the following five days and, the absent non-conforming, within the following fifteen days, counting from the assembly's closure.

D. Types of Assemblies

354. In cases where there is a diversity of shares, special assemblies can be held when the decisions to be taken affect the rights of a particular class. The special assembly is ruled by the regulations of the ordinary assembly.

355. In case the appointment of authorities of the society has been fragmented into different types, then, after removing these authorities, the right corresponds to the same class that appointed them, except judicial removal.

E. Contest of Decisions

356. The decisions taken in the assembly can be challenged by the shareholders who were present and who voted against, by those who were absent, or by those who were present and voted favorably but with unintentional behavior with no freedom. This can be carried out by a contest against the company. They can also be challenged by directors, trustees, members of the supervisory board and the supervisory authority. The challenge period is three months after the meeting has been closed.

357. Once the objection has been imposed, the objectors may request the judge to cancel the execution and the effects of the contested decision, on condition that they need to provide a countermeasure, there are serious reasons and this does not cause any damage to third parties.

358. What is more, if during the challenge process an assembly is held to revoke the contested decisions, then said procedure must be filed, regardless of the responsibilities incurred by the effects produced by those who voted in favor of the null decision, as well as the responsibility which corresponds to the directors, trustees and members of the supervisory board, in each case.

III. Annual Account Report: Profits and Dividends

359. The company must have corporate and commercial books. Among the first ones, we can list: (a) the minute's books corresponding to the administration body (directory record book); (b) the governing body (assembly minute's book); and (c) the plural supervisory body (Article 73, Law 19,550), as well as the books for the registration of shares and the registration of attendance at the meetings and the deposit of shares. When referring to commercial books, in this category we should include all the books that are mandatory for anyone who develops an organized economic activity arising from Article 323 and following regulations of the CCCN. Thus, entrepreneurs must have a daily book where all the transactions of the course of business are detailed and, also, an inventory book and balance sheets. The basic financial statements must be registered in this last book.

360. The books can be either in an analog manner or by mechanical or digital means duly authorized prior technical opinion; in the latter case, they must be kept in a private server of the society or an external server on a State platform, as required by the enforcement authority in the jurisdiction to which the company corresponds. Although the daily book could have been replaced by mechanical or electronic means, the truth is that with the enactment of Law 27,349, it has been imposed that societies for simplified shares should use the digital methodology to have their books, this includes the inventory book and balance sheets and this situation has been extended in practice to the rest of the corporate types because of local regulations.

361. It is worth mentioning that the preparation of the financial statements by the board of directors is annual in accordance with the end of the fiscal year established in the bylaws or constituent instrument (except for certain circumstances that demand a special balance such as the withdrawal of a member, the sale of the company, etc.) and complies with the accounting technical regulations that may, depending on the case, be of international or national nature. Those companies listed on the stock exchange must adapt their balance sheets to international accounting standards, while closed local companies must do so in accordance with the technical regulations issued by professional Economic Science boards.

362. When dealing with the analysis of the financial statements, these are included in Articles 61–73 of the LGS and can be summarized as follows: statement of financial position or balance sheet; state of development of net worth; income statement or profit and loss account; and cash flow statement. In addition, the companies that make up a group must carry out the consolidated financial statements that unify the graph of the patrimonial position of those that are related by reason of a common control. In other words, the duty to present a single statement of financial position is imposed as if the group were a single company.

363. Now, we go on to detail the content required in each of the basic financial statements:

(1) As regards the balance sheet, it is conceived as a photograph of the state of the assets of the company at a given time. Thus, it must include all the rights and duties of the legal entity at the financial year-end or the special situation that needs a circumstantial balance. As mentioned before, in this state we can appreciate the role of guaranteeing the social capital insofar as it serves as a reference as a retention figure that guarantees the equity balance and the consequent capacity to face the obligations contracted by the society with respect to either shareholders or third parties. Simply mentioned, the asset consists of a current asset (assets and investments realizable and applicable credits within the year) and non-current asset (tangible and intangible assets and investments and credits realizable and payable after twelve months); the liabilities of a current liability (obligations due within one year) and non-current liabilities (obligations which will be due after twelve months), and in the liability column but as a separate account there is the net equity, which results from subtracting the asset from the liability and it consists of the following: social capital; unallocated results; irrevocable contributions; reserves of all kinds; etc. We ought to point out that everything that has financed the asset is placed in the liability column whether it comes from external financing of third parties (liabilities) or internal coming from the shareholders (equity).
What is more, the operating capital that the company has (also called funds) to support the current course of business results from the difference between current assets and non-current liabilities, a situation that will demonstrate the capacity of the legal entity to face its duties, since given a state of cessation of payments, it does not necessarily mean financial insolvency. It may happen that a legal entity has sufficient assets to meet the total liabilities, but it can have insufficient liquidity to do so with respect to the current liabilities in the terms imposed by these obligations.
(2) Income Statement: the income statement is also known as profit fiscal year. Unlike the static status statement, this account is dynamic. Then, the income statement can be subdivided according to whether certain obligations or circumstances are considered or not, for example, taxes, inflation, reserves, etc., then we will have the result before and after taxes, before or after the reserves have been retained and set, as well as the unadjusted or adjusted result because of inflation. The cost of money and its loss of value due to inflation should not be computed within the profit. That is to say that whether the company has had

profits or not in the fiscal year arises from this account. It is worth mentioning that we ought to concentrate on the term utilities, as it is not synonymous with dividends. However, the profits are limited to the year in question and the evolution of the previous periods must be reviewed to determine if those profits can be converted into dividends or not. Once the losses of previous years have been covered, the remaining profits must guarantee both the legal reserves and those facultative ones that correspond to a reasonable criterion and cautious administration. Only after that, the balance can be proposed as dividends to be distributed to the shareholders. However, if there are profits that have not been assigned to any of these concepts, they will be called unallocated results, and they present the risk of being questioned by the shareholders since if there is money left over in the company, they should be liquidated as dividends.

(3) State of Evolution of Net Equity: The statement of changes in net equity determines the change in net worth in the different fiscal years. In this way, we can observe the patrimonial growth that society has experienced over the passing of time, although growth is sometimes unrealistic if adjustment for inflation is not allowed. Such is the Argentine case, where only in 2019 this has begun to be admitted for tax purposes since it cannot be thought of to pay taxes that are not real. Besides, from Article 62 (last section) of the LGS, it is inferred, with respect to this matter, that the financial statements related to fiscal years or interim periods of a fiscal year must be prepared in constant currency.
This State complements the statement of income and must establish the causes of the variations in each item of net worth.

(4) Statement of Cash Flow: The cash flow statement is a dynamic account showing the cash variation that the company has suffered during a given fiscal year and hence its capacity to generate liquid funds. This is not a minor fact, since a fundamental element for the valuation of a company is its ability to generate funds and its projection over time.
In addition to this, in the case of the companies that are included in Article 299, the enforcement authority (National Securities Commission) may require additional documentation to the balance sheet and a statement of origin and application of funds for the fiscal year that has ended. This refers to the duty of aggravated information imposed on all those companies that obtain savings from the public or quote their shares.
Notwithstanding the duty to prepare the aforementioned basic financial statements, complementary notes and explanatory annexed charts must also be prepared, detailing the content of the global accounts, providing the corresponding details of their components, as well as establishing in those notes, what criteria were used for the preparation of each State.
Another instrument that should accompany the financial statements is a record. Through this document, the board of directors carries out a thorough analysis of the company's financial situation, the causes of that state and its future projection. Among some other concepts, this means that the record will establish the reasons why the assets and liabilities have varied, the explanation of extraordinary expenses and profits; the reasons for the constituent reserves (this should be done in accordance with a reasonable and cautious criterion);

reasons why the distribution of dividends is determined; relationship of the company with controlling and controlled companies; etc.

A. *Financial Statements: Its Procedure*

364. The financial statements, such as their instruments and supplementary reports, must be at the registered office fifteen days in advance before being dealt with by the assembly. The supervisory authority will be sent copies of the financial statements and, if it is applicable, of the consolidated balance sheet. To deal with the financial statements in order to approve or challenge them is an indisputable right of the shareholders that forces the assembly to be held at least once a year after the fiscal year has ended. We ought to remark that the approval of the financial statements does not imply the approval of the management of the board of directors or the receivership or the supervisory board.

B. *Dividends*

365. In order to distribute dividends, it is necessary to deal with this issue in advance and they must be sustained on realized and liquidated profits on the balance duly prepared and approved. Consistent with this, anticipated dividends cannot be distributed, except in the cases of companies that are included in Article 299 (19,550 Law). If profits are distributed contrary to what we have mentioned above, the directors, trustees, and members of the supervisory board are jointly and unlimitedly liable for such payments, and the dividends thus distributed are repeatable, except those that have been obtained in good faith.

366. Apart from this, dividends cannot be distributed when there have been losses in previous fiscal years, without previously being paid. Let us mention that this turns out to be an obvious prohibition since fiscal years are not considered in isolation but as members of the developing society, so those positive fiscal years must support others that have had negative results.

C. *Legal and Discretionary Reserves*

367. It is worth highlighting that to have legal reserves that include realized and liquid profits determining the income statement is mandatory. They shall be quantified in 5% of said profits until reaching 20% of the social capital. Failure to do so will prevent the distribution of dividends until the shortfall is paid.

368. Besides, as already stated, extraordinary reserves turn out to be discretionary and involve the withholding of possible dividends; this is the reason why the law imposes the need to have a reasonable and cautious criterion. Thus, when these exceed the total amount equivalent to both the capital and legal reserves, a majority of shares with a voting right is required for the SAS without regarding the plural vote.

IV. Workers Participation

369. See §6. "The Labor Law Connection: Codetermination and Corporate Structure," under the General Introduction, paragraphs 219 to 221.

V. Administrative or Management Body

A. *Directors and Administrative Board (Appointment, Requirements, Remuneration, Dismissal)*

370. The management body of the SAS as already expressed is called a directory and constitutes one of the typifying assumptions of the social type regulated in Articles 255–279 of the LGS. It is a permanent body that must meet at least every three months unless the statute requires a greater number of meetings. In this section, we will deepen the analysis of this body that has already been briefly referred to in previous paragraphs.

1. Composition

371. The board of directors may be unipersonal or plural, except in the companies included in Article 299, where a plural board composed of at least three directors must necessarily be established. The members may be appointed by the shareholders' meeting or by the supervisory board, as the case may be, against the provision of a guarantee that the statute stated and that must be maintained throughout the period when he is in office emphasizing that the duration of the mandate in the first case cannot exceed three fiscal years and in the second one, it must not exceed five years, although the positions are always renewable indefinitely. Notwithstanding this, the appointment is always revocable only by the assembly and the director, even with the expired mandate, and will remain in office until being replaced.

372. Among the requirements the board must hold, it is established that the majority of the directors must be Argentine residents, also, all the members must establish a special domicile in the country where all notifications related to the position will be valid; in this way, they will be able to carry on with their position.

373. Similarly, when the societies have to do without an authorized receivership (SAU that are not included in Article 299 and decide not to adopt the internal supervisory body), substitute directors must be appointed to be in office temporarily in the cases in which the senior directors are unable to exercise the position. The companies that hold receivership are not subject to this imperative, although there is nothing to prevent them from appointing alternate directors because the trustee is the one who seeks to reestablish the functioning of the vacant administration body, unable or temporarily absent.

2. Appointment of Authorities

374. The appointment of directors is made by the assembly, as we have indicated before, but may also be carried out by category of assembly, as appropriate, in the case that there are various types of shares that belong to various categories and the statute provides that the appointment of one or more directors corresponds to each of them. In this case, only the category that appointed the director has the power to remove him, except in cases where there are incompatibilities or judicial removal as a result of the social action of responsibility.

375. In reference to the election of the board of directors, its members can be elected by the cumulative voting system. This system consists of guaranteeing minorities the possibility of trying to appoint an administrator within the directory. Thus, the system consists of multiplying the number of vacancies to be filled, by the votes that the minority shareholder has, applying the result to the election of a third of the available vacancies. That is to say that if there are three vacancies to fill and one shareholder holds ten votes, the latter can compete in the election of a single position with thirty votes, whereas he will not be able to compete in the appointment of directors for the other two vacancies.

376. The procedure must be guaranteed to the shareholders, and it will not be possible to reconstitute the board in a partial manner or in different stages if in this way the right of the minority to exercise the cumulative vote is curtailed.

377. Thus, when appointing directors, shareholders wishing to make use of this tool must notify the company at least three working days in advance and identify the procedures through which the right will be exercised. The option by a single shareholder of this system benefits the rest of the share capital, who must be notified of such option by the society in case of requesting it and, likewise, the company president when chairing the assembly, must inform the rest of the shareholders who have that right. Then, once the option has been exercised, just before voting, when the assembly is being held, each shareholder ought to be informed about the votes they hold when making use of this system. It is worth mentioning that, even before the vote is cast, all shareholders may vary the procedure or voting system.

3. Director: Prohibitions, Incompatibilities and Dismissal

378. To be part of the board of directors, directors must not be affected by certain incompatibilities and prohibitions set forth in the corporate law. Referring to those who are unable to hold the position of director are those who cannot exercise the trade; are under the condition of failed and have not been rehabilitated; have been sentenced with accessory penalty prohibition to hold a public office or have been convicted for the crimes of theft, fraud, bribery, issuing of checks without funds and crimes against the public faith, etc., until ten years after the sentence has been served; and officials of the public administration up to two years after they left their public office, provided that the position exercised is related to the corporate purpose.

379. If any director or trustee is found in any of the cases indicated in the preceding paragraph, any director or trustee must call a meeting at his own initiative or at the request of any shareholder to deal with the removal of the affected director or trustee and must do so within forty days counting from the moment the assembly is requested in the event that a shareholder demands it. In addition, once the removal is dealt with but fails to proceed, any director, shareholder or receiver may request it judicially.

380. Furthermore, there is a prohibition when coming into office: the director is not allowed to contract with the company unless those are activities in which the company participates and the contracting conditions are those of the market. In all other cases, under penalty of nullity, the prior approval of the union or board of directors shall be required and the assembly shall be informed. In case the assembly does not approve what is authorized by the board of directors and receivership, they shall be jointly and unrestrictedly liable to the company for the damages and losses caused.

4. Powers of Management and Representation (Managers, Executive Committee, Representation and Remuneration)

381. The position of director is personal and non-delegable, notwithstanding that the board may appoint managers as hierarchical employees with certain executive powers and under the full responsibility of the board of directors. This implies that managers hold the same responsibility as directors with respect to society and third parties, but they do not release those who are guilty of choosing them for that function (directors).

382. Similarly, in the event that the bylaws provide for the creation of an executive committee composed of some directors and for the management of ordinary businesses, the board of directors shall be responsible for the supervision thereof and under its responsibility.

383. Moreover, the representation of the company corresponds to the chairman of the board of directors, and if the bylaws establish it more than one director may act. The scope of Article 58 of the LGS is applicable to the representation, a topic that we have already developed in the general part of this monograph so, in the interest of brevity, we refer to it.

384. To conclude, with regard to remuneration, we have already referred to Article 261; consequently, we will briefly mention that it will be provided for in the bylaws; failure to do so, the assembly shall have to decide. The law establishes a maximum limit for the remuneration that the director may receive for tasks of all kinds (including those technical-administrative ones), which may not exceed 25% of the company's profits and will be limited to 5% when dividends are not distributed; moreover, the remuneration may be proportionally increased for the case there are distributions of dividends that do not constitute a total distribution of the profits. Similarly, the technical-administrative tasks of the directors may be remunerated in cases in which there are no profits gained, provided that this was arranged by the assembly and this concept has been established as an issue to be dealt with in the agenda.

385. It is worth mentioning that the constitutionality of Article 261 is questioned since it establishes the possibility of not remunerating or remunerating with a limit certain tasks unrelated to the role of director, such as those technical-administrative ones, which could be considered even within a working relationship. We know that the rights of the worker are inalienable, so we believe that Article 261 does not reach the concept of a working relationship, which will be dealt with independently, and the director, in turn, a worker, will get the corresponding remuneration for the job according to that particular regime.

5. Board Meetings and Call

386. The board of directors, as we have already referred to, must meet at least quarterly, unless the statute provides for a greater number of meetings. This has led some doctrines to support the idea that it is not a permanent body, but semipermanent and that it is the management which carries out permanent activities. We understand that this is not the case, since management acts under the orbit of the board of directors and by delegation of certain powers or executive functions granted by managers.

387. To carry out the meetings, they must be convened by the chairman of the board of directors indicating the topics to be discussed and to meet within five days subsequent to the call. The trustee may participate in the meetings. Also, in the event that the president does not summon a meeting, any other director may do so.

6. Liability of Directors

388. Beyond the responsibilities that fit the incompatibilities and prohibitions already mentioned, the directors cannot compete with the company either in their own name or through a third party; to do so they need the written authorization of the assembly consenting to it and provided that the director follows the pattern of conduct established in Article 59 (to be diligent and a good businessman).

389. In relation to the guideline of conduct of Article 59, in an SAS, this regulation must be associated with Article 274, which provides for the unlimited and joint liability of directors against the company, shareholders and third parties, for poor performance in their positions in terms of the first rule referred to, as well as for any infringement to the statute, regulation or law and for any damage caused with dishonesty or serious negligence.

390. As stated in the previous paragraph, it is worth concluding that the responsibility, in general terms, is collective. However, it ceases to be so in some cases and consequently, the director who has been assigned special functions (in a registered social regulation) and who has not participated in the deed that did not fall within his/her competence, as well as the one who, although competent in such deed, has voted against its execution in the board meeting, will be released from responsibility. It is necessary to state said opposition in the minutes and give notice to the assembly before it is denounced.

391. However, unlike the assumptions analyzed in the previous section where the responsibility never arises, in some other cases, where the responsibility has been caused is extinguished by management's approval of the directors, or by explicit refusal of the assembly to start legal proceedings or by the transaction agreed upon between the latter and the directors.

392. It is worth mentioning that the approval of the directors' management by the assembly, or the refusal that the latter expressly made in order to claim compensation for the damages, or, finally, the transactional agreement by which directors and the assembly make reciprocal concessions in order to achieve a reasonable balance of interests and compensation for damages, extinguishes the directors' liabilities. To achieve this, there must be no opposition of 5% of the share capital, since if this is the case, the corporate liability remains unimpeded, nor should the entity be in a case of insolvency or coercive liquidation.

393. Apart from this, it is possible to emphasize that when voting the managements in cases where there is no assignment of special functions by registered regulation and consequently the board of directors has a collective responsibility, the shareholders, who also make up the board of directors, should refrain from voting; otherwise, they will be jointly and unlimitedly liable in the terms of Articles 241, 248 and 254, of the LGS.

394. Finally, once the responsibility of the administrators has occurred and the management has been disapproved or approved by the assembly with opposition of 5% of the share capital, the social action of responsibility is unimpeded. It is a deed of a corporate nature since it is exercised on behalf of the company and in defense of its assets (Article 276). However, if the management of one or more directors is disapproved by the assembly, they will be automatically removed from their position, while if approved with opposition of 5% of the share capital, they will retain their position during the processing of the liability action, except for a judicial procedure that may be filed in parallel by the non-conforming shareholders (e.g., a preventative measure of judicial intervention of the administrative body).

395. Once the initiation of liability action has been resolved, the directory must start it. If, within three months of the action being unimpeded the board of directors does not initiate it, any shareholder may promote it on behalf of the company. Besides, if the company is insolvent or declared bankrupt, the action may also be exercised on behalf of the company by the trustee or the creditors.

396. As regards the responsibility of the administrators in reference to the society, we must point out that it is a contractual responsibility and its liability has a triennial prescription which is suspended as long as the administrator continues holding the position.

397. In order to conclude, with respect to shareholders and third parties, the liability is extra-contractual and therefore they hold the individual action of responsibility as unimpeded in defense of their own assets and in the terms established in Article 279. This is an ordinary act of liability that can be exercised directly by those affected against the director or directors and that has not previously been dealt with. It also prescribes three years later, but the prescription begins when the harmful event occurred and is not suspended even if the administrator is still holding his/her position.

VI. Supervisory Board

398. The supervisory board (Articles 280–283) may be provided for by the statute as an internal supervisory body that coexists with the syndicate or it does not. It is composed of three to fifteen shareholders, appointed and removed by the assembly in the same terms as the directors; in consequence, we refer to the sections in which we have already explained the appointment procedure. The members of the board are reelected indefinitely and are responsible to the society to the same extent as the directors, other shareholders and third parties are; also, the remuneration is subject to the same parameters as the board, all issues that we have already discussed and to which we refer.

399. Among the functions we can enumerate the following: to supervise the management of the board of directors and its custody of the corporate assets; to point out that the board of directors ought to submit a report on its management on a quarterly basis; to call a meeting by its own criteria or at the request of shareholders representing 5% of the share capital; to comment on certain deeds carried out by the board of directors that are submitted for approval and monitor the execution of their decisions in this regard to submit a report on the management of the board to the assembly; to investigate itself or by means of commissions deeds that have been carried out and which are denounced by the shareholders; and finally any power that is attributed to the receivership.

400. Moreover, if there is dissidence in the councilors' meetings, the dissenters who reach at least a third may call an assembly to report on the dissidence and the assembly must decide in this regard.

401. Lastly, in the event that there is a supervisory board and receivership is dispensed with, the board must contract an annual audit to replace it for the purposes of preparing reports on annual financial statements that must then be reviewed by the assembly.

VII. Auditor

402. The receivership is a private supervisory body regulated in Articles 284–298 of the LGS which is inexorable for the case of the companies included in Article 299. In the latter case and except for the second and seventh clauses of this regulation (companies with capital greater than 50,000,000 and single-member SAS), those societies must also have a plural receivership.

A. Terms: Prohibitions and Incompatibilities

403. Those wishing to become trustees must have real domicile in the country and be lawyers or accountants authorized to practice, or those companies with joint and several liability established and formed exclusively by such professionals. Those who are directors, managers or employees of the company or who hold such a position in a controlling or controlled company are unable to be trustees. Besides, those who are relatives of the impeded up to the fourth degree of consanguinity and second of affinity cannot become trustees.

404. In addition, the same prohibitions and incompatibilities applied to directors are also applicable to trustees, a subject matter we have already referred to.

B. Appointment and Dismissal: Composition and Remuneration

405. The trustees will be appointed by the shareholders' meeting and the manner to do so corresponds to the options available to the law for the directors' appointment (cumulative vote, election according to types, etc.). Regarding the duration of the position, it will be for three fiscal years at most, although they may be reelected indefinitely, and may be removed at the assembly's will at any time without the need for an expression of any cause, except for opposition of 5% of social capital. Once the term of the position expires, they will hold their position until they are replaced.

406. In addition, if the position cannot be performed by the trustee temporarily or there is a vacancy, the substitute appointed will hold it. If there is no appointed substitute or if the latter is unable to hold the position, the board of directors shall call an assembly to elect a definitive trustee until the three fiscal years are completed.

407. Furthermore, for those cases in which it is a collegiate or plural corporate organ, it will be called audit committee and must keep a book of minutes as provided in Article 73. Its operation and setup will be determined by the statute. The role of a trustee is personal and non-delegable.

408. With regard to remuneration, the role of a trustee must be remunerated in accordance with the provisions of the statute; failure to do so will be determined by the assembly.

C. Powers and Duties: Liability

409. The roles of the trustee are not limited to the financial years in which he holds the position, but it is extended to the past for any anomaly that he could detect. The law confers on the syndics a list of powers and duties, which the statute may later enlarge. These are as follows: to supervise the administration of the society at least through the quarterly revision of books and other documents (we believe that this power is depleted in the legitimacy of the manners of the deeds, but does not meet the criteria of convenience that motivate the directory to act); to verify the availability of the securities and their registration in the accounting documentation; to attend board meetings as non-voting members; to ensure the constitution and conservation of the guarantees provided by the directors in order to hold the position; to inform the assembly in writing of its opinion regarding the financial statements; to notify requesting shareholders representing at least 2% of the share capital about any matter submitted to their jurisdiction; to convene the assembly at its discretion or in the case of the omission of the board of directors; to ask the board of directors to include some subject matters on the agenda; to ensure the legality of the manners of any of the company's deed and the faithful compliance with the statute and regulations; to oversee the liquidation of the company; and to investigate any claim carried out by shareholders representing at least 2% of the share capital.

410. In addition, trustees are liable in the same way as the directors (Articles 271–279) to the company, shareholders and third parties; this is in a several and unlimited liability for the faithful performance of the duties under their charge; besides, said responsibility is submitted to the decision of the assembly.

411. In reference to this, they are jointly and severally liable to directors for the damages caused by their deeds to the company in those cases in which said acts had not taken place or the extent of the damage had been minimized if trustees had adjusted their conduct to their duties.

VIII. Taxation of Corporations and Shareholders

412. Taxes in Argentina are distributed into federal or national taxes and provincial or local taxes. In Argentina, there are taxes that have already been discarded by other countries, such as the tax on gross income (local tax for commercial activity). Regardless of the origin of the tax, we can point out that companies must pay income tax at the end of the year, which can reach up to 35% of incomes and, in the case of partners, must pay personal property tax for their holdings at December 31 of each year (these assets include shares). The partners do not pay profits for the distribution of dividends, since it is understood that they have already been previously paid by the company as an income tax. Finally, due to the COVID-19 pandemic, an exceptional tax on wealth or large fortunes was created, which those people with considerable wealth had to face and their shareholdings were included in the calculation basis for the tax.

413. In another order, companies must retain and enter into the treasury the social security contributions of workers.

§6. Liquidation of the Corporation/Company

I. Grounds of Winding Up (Court Decision, Shareholder's Meeting, Contractual Cause, Etc.)

414. To begin with, it is worth saying that the causes for partial resolution, dissolution and liquidation arise from the law, but they can also be extended by the partners' will to other cases (LGS, Article 89). Both the causes of resolution and dissolution, once produced, can be eliminated and removed by the governing bodies of the companies, taking into account the principle of continuity of the company (LGS, Article 100). However, regarding the partial resolution or a shareholder's withdrawal, we will briefly analyze this issue, since we have already dealt with it in previous sections to which we refer.

415. In this sense, beyond the grounds that may have been foreseen in the constitutive instrument, there is a partial resolution in partnerships due to the partner's death or exclusion. In the first case, as has previously been mentioned, a partner's death in the collective society, of capital and industry as well as in a simple partnership, results in the partial termination of the contract, unless the substitution of the deceased by his/her heirs is consented, or unless there is a replacement agreement for heirs in both collective societies and a simple limited partnership. In the case of the latter, heirs may require their participation to be limited. However, as already expressed, there are different positions regarding the partial resolution that could occur in an SRL for a shareholder's death, provided that the contract is silent in relation to it. The debate arises because the regulation that establishes the partial resolution by death (LGS, Article 90) does not include in its enumeration the SRL. Notwithstanding the foregoing, Article 155 of the LGS establishes that "if the contract provides for the incorporation of heirs, the agreement will be binding on them and the partners." Said wording does not imply the automatic incorporation of the heirs, but in the case in which it results from the social contract. Thus, before the omission referred to previously with respect to the SRL and the wording of the latter provision, the debate about the solution to be provided is raised. In this regard, we have already indicated that we adhere to the position that separates the SRL from the companies of Article 90 and, therefore, there is no partial resolution due to a member's death.

416. Apart from this, as regards the exclusion of the partner because of righteous cause, it is a cause of partial resolution in all partnerships, in the SRL, and in the case of the general partners in the SAS (Article 91). The cause of "righteous cause" implies a serious breach of his/her duties by the partner, but the rule does not wisely establish special assumptions, but must be analyzed in each specific case, except in cases of disqualification, disability, or bankruptcy in partnerships.

417. Finally, once the cause has been carried out, even when it has not been removed or eliminated, the exclusion of the partner can be initiated by both the company and the rest of the partners. Once the partner has been already excluded by judicial decision, he/she shall leave the company and his quantified participation must be paid on that date according to a special balance or according to the last balance if it is relatively recent. Without prejudice to this, the partner participates in the benefits and bears the losses of the operations that are still pending until then, and the company may retain its participation until they are ended. At the time that the part is returned to the partner, in respect to the assets that he/she would have contributed for use and enjoyment, if these are essential for the progress of the company, they will still remain in the company and an amount of money will be paid to the partner in replacement of the good that has yet to be returned.

A. *Legal Grounds*

418. The legal grounds for the dissolution of any company are established in Article 94 (LGS). These are the following: by the partners' decision; by expiration of the term for which the company was established; by compliance with the condition to which the company was subordinated; by achievement of the company's purpose or due to the impossibility of achieving it; by loss of share capital; by filing for bankruptcy of the company, unless there is agreement or conversion of bankruptcy into insolvency proceedings; by its absorption by another company according to a merger procedure; by firm resolution establishing the withdrawal of authorization for the company to operate; and by firm sanction of cancelation of the company's OPA or quotation of its shares.

419. The previous Article 94 established as a cause for dissolution the reduction of the number of partners to just one, a cause that was eliminated with the reform carried out by Law 26,994 of 2015 that included the sole proprietorship. Notwithstanding the foregoing, in the following Article 94*bis*, it establishes that the reduction of the number of partners to only one is not a cause for dissolution and it provides a solution in the case of capital and industry companies and those limited by shares. Interestingly, the rule has left out collective and SRL.

420. Thus, in the case of capital and industry companies and those with a limited partnership, in the event of a reduction in the number of partners to only one member, the company must reestablish the plurality of the group of partners and their categories within a three-month peremptory period; otherwise, it shall become a sole proprietorship. In addition to the full transformation established by the regulation, this imposes the need to make certain adjustments in the corporate instruments, organisms, and eventually in the social capital, etc.

421. That is to say, that, as has already been mentioned, collective and SRL are not included, so there is a problem regarding them because the reduction of the number of partners to just one is not a cause for dissolution. We understand that the correct solution is that, if plurality is not restored, these societies will be framed in section IV of the LGS. Finally, in the case of the SAU, it does not deserve any special treatment, since in that case, it will remain as a sole proprietorship, which shall simply have to add, if it is not contemplated, the union since the sole proprietorship is included in Article 299 of the LGS.

422. Besides, when the cause of dissolution is focused on the expiration of the stipulated term for the company, the governing body may arrange its extension (prior to its expiration) or, once expired, it shall be redirected thus ensuring the continuation of the company (Article 95, LGS). In other words, with respect to the first assumption that such agreement must be unanimously entered into in the companies constituted by a person, except for the existence of an agreement to the contrary, and by the relevant majorities in the cases of SRL, Simplified SAS and an SAU, and an extension must always be resolved and requested before the deadline. These concepts are equally valid in the case of redirecting once the term has expired before the appointment of the liquidator. If the liquidator has already been appointed, the restructuring agreement must be established unanimously without distinction of the type in question.

423. In reference to the cause of loss of the share capital, it can be provoked by total or partial loss, and the cause is left without effect in the event that the loss is reinstated recovering the original amount or even increasing with respect to the latter. In this regard, we reiterate what is referred to in relation to the guarantee function of social capital as a balance that must mediate between assets and liabilities, since its loss in all or in part activates a cause for dissolution and holds managers and complicit partners responsible for their failure to observe and neglect the pertinent measures to reverse the cause or liquidate the company (Article 99, LGS).

424. Once the cause of dissolution has been carried out and declared judicially, where appropriate, the sentence will have a retrospective declarative effect at the time the cause was audited and, also, with respect to third parties, will have effects only after registering the dissolution.

425. Finally, as already stated, the principle of continuity of the company is the pattern of interpretation established in the event that there is doubt about the verification or not of a cause, for it shall always approve the continuation of a company to be socially and economically viable. Likewise, it is worth saying that once a cause of partial resolution or dissolution has been carried out, it can be removed through its elimination and consequent decision of the governing body of the corporate type in question, provided that it is before the registration of society and while there is economic and social viability for the continuation of the company, all without prejudice to the liabilities that its members had incurred (Article 100, LGS).

II. The Effect of Winding Up: Liquidation

426. Once the cause of dissolution has been audited but not removed, the administrators must exclusively concentrate on the urgent acts and direct the company toward liquidation according to the special process provided by Articles 101 and the following provisions of the LGS.

427. Thus, the liquidation of the company will be in charge of the administrative body, and the administrators will be either ratified as liquidators for this purpose or substituted, by the required majorities according to the type; what is more, they must be registered in the registry whatever the resolution is. Likewise, they may also be removed by the majority appointing or by judicial resolution at the request of the partners or the trustee if there is a righteous cause.

428. In reference to the liquidation status, it does not affect the personality of the entity although it does limit its purpose, modify its name and alter the powers of the administrative body since with respect to the purpose, its restriction comprises the acts necessary to carry out the liquidation; as regards the company name, the words “in liquidation” ought to be added for the knowledge of third parties; and, with respect to the administrators, their powers are restricted to what is necessary for the realization of the asset and the cancelation of the liability in the same terms of the purpose now limited to that end; in addition, in case of insufficient assets, the partners shall be required due contributions pursuant to social type and constituent contract.

429. Regarding the process, it is worth pointing out that the liquidators, once in office and within thirty days, must prepare an inventory and balance of the social assets making them available to the partners, under written warning of removal for non-compliance and of being liable for the damages that the same may lead to (Article 103, LGS). Similarly, during the course of the liquidation, the liquidators must report to the partners and/or the union quarterly, as the case may be, as well as prepare annual balances if the liquidation is prolonged over time.

430. Apart from this, the distribution of the remaining occurs at the end of the settlement of the liability and prior approval by the governing body of a final balance and distribution project that is then registered in the R.P, although early partial distributions may also exist during the liquidation course if social duties are duly guaranteed and requested by one-tenth of the capital in the cases of the SAU or any partner in the other types. Concerning what each partner shall receive, it will be their correlative percentage according to their share of the earnings, unless otherwise agreed on. To conclude, if the beneficiaries of these distributions do not come forward to claim what is due to them within ninety days of approval of the balance sheet and distribution project, the amounts will be deposited in their name in a bank account and there they will remain for three years to be withdrawn. Once this last period of time has elapsed, the funds shall be allocated to the school authority of the jurisdiction in question.

431. Finally, once the asset has been carried out, the liability has been canceled and the surplus has been distributed, the cancelation of the inscription in the R.P is ordered and the partner is appointed either by the partners or by the jurisdictional authority; we must point out that the appointed partner is the one who must keep the books and other social documents for ten years according to Article 328 of the CCCN. At present, since there are digital books placed on State platforms or on network servers, it is most likely that the judge simply determines that a partner shall keep a backup copy, the password and an account where the documentation is available.

§7. Mergers and Takeovers

432. The restructuring or concentration processes of the corporation are dealt with in Law 19,550, General Part. We shall refer to each one below.

I. Transformation

433. The transformation is included in Article 74 and following regulations and involves the change of the social type of society, but it does not alter its existence or its rights and duties. However, regarding the responsibility of the partners, it will have two moments depending on whether they are operations before or after the transformation. In other words, the partners' liability will not be modified with respect to the acts prior to the transformation, unless otherwise agreed upon between them and with creditors. In the case of leaving partners due to the exercise of the right to withdrawal, their responsibility toward third parties shall not be modified until the transformation agreement is registered and, in that case, during the time that elapses from the exercise of the right to withdrawal until the transformation registration, the administrators, the corporation and the partners with unlimited liability will jointly guarantee the receivers for the social duties adopted in that period.

434. In order to carry out the transformation, there must be a unanimous agreement of the partners, unless otherwise agreed upon for some corporate types (if this shall happen, dissenting and absent partners will have the right to withdrawal); a special balance must be prepared, closed on a date not exceeding one month after the transformation agreement and made available to the partners at the registered office with not less than fifteen days before said agreement. The same established majorities are required for the approval of the balances; concession by the competent bodies of the act instructing the transformation and the concurrence of the new grantors, with documentary proof of the leaving members, of the capital they represent and compliance with the formalities of the new corporate type adopted; publication for one day in the journal of legal publications corresponding to the registered office and its branches: the date of the social resolution that approved the transformation, the date of the transformation instrument, the former name of the company or the corporate name and the new one adopted; what is more, its identity ought to be indubitable in reference to the company being transformed, the partners that are withdrawn or incorporated and the capital they represent and when the transformation affects the data referred to in Article 10, paragraph a), points 4–10, the publication must determine it; register the instrument with a copy of the balance signed in the R.P of Commerce and other corresponding records in accordance with the type of company due to the nature of the assets that comprise the assets and its levies.

435. In addition to this, as long as the transformation agreement is not registered, it can be left without effect; although if it has already been published, the revocation must also be issued. The agreement may also expire if it is not registered within a three-month term after its conclusion unless the delay corresponds to the registration procedures themselves. Any breach of the procedure provided for this purpose makes the administrators jointly and unlimitedly liable.

II. Fusion

436. The merger is conceptualized in Article 82 (LGS) where the rule states that “There is a merger when two or more companies are dissolved without liquidation, to constitute a new one, or when an existing one incorporates one or some others, which without liquidation are dissolved.”

437. The concept provides the two patterns of merger, that is to say, one in which societies dissolve and constitute a new company (merger itself), or when one company absorbs another or others (merger by absorption). Once the merger has been carried out, the merger agreement has been registered and the resulting corporate contract (new contract or capital increase of the absorbing company) has been established, the transfer of equity (rights and obligations) of the merged company to the new entity or the absorbing entity proceeds.

438. The merger requires prior precepts to be observed and they are listed in Article 83 of the LGS as follows: (1) the subscription of a prior merger commitment that sets forth the merits and purposes of the merger, the preparation of special merger balances of each company using homogeneous bases with trustees' reports where appropriate, the relationship of change of the social participations, the preparation of a draft contract or statute of the absorbing company according to the case, the limitations that the societies agree upon in the respective administration of their businesses and the guarantee they establish for the fulfillment of a normal business operation in their management during the period that elapses until the merger is registered; (2) the approval of the prior commitment and merger of the special balances by the companies participating in the merger with the necessary requirements for the modification of the social contract or statute; (3) the publication for three days of a notice in the newspaper of legal publications of the jurisdiction of each company and in one of the newspapers of greater general circulation in the Republic, which must have the following data: the company name or denomination, the head office and registration data in the R.P of Commerce of each of the companies, the capital of the new company or the amount of the increase of the share capital of the incorporating company, the valuation of the assets and liabilities of the merging companies with indication of the date to which it refers, the company name or denomination, the type and domicile agreed upon for the company to be constituted, and the dates of the previous merger commitment and the social resolutions approving it.

439. In addition to this, the advertising duties are established for the purpose of enabling opposition by creditors within fifteen days of the last publication; however, this does not stop the merger process but does allow creditors to be disinterested or seek judicial seizure in the guarantee of their credits.

440. Once the term has elapsed without oppositions or once these are resolved in the aforementioned manners, a definitive merger agreement is adopted, which includes: the social resolutions approving the merger; the list of partners who exercise the right to withdrawal and the capital they represent in each company; the payroll of the creditors who, having opposed them, have been guaranteed and of those who have obtained judicial seizure together with a list of the disinterested creditors, as well as of the special balance sheets and of a consolidated balance sheet of the merging companies.

441. Once the agreement has been signed, in the case of a new company, the merger and its new statute must be registered in the R.P; this is competence of the administration body of the new company that assumes the representation of the dissolved companies until the end of the procedure and that must, in turn, relate this registration to the registration number of the merged companies requesting the cancelation of the latter for the benefit of the new company. In the case of an absorbing company, the aforementioned provisions are also applied to the administration and representation of the absorbed ones, and, for the rest, the formalities established for the amendment of the statute and its consequent reflection in the share capital must be observed; then the cancelation of the registration numbers corresponding to dissolved and absorbed companies shall proceed. All this must be carried out apart from the enrollments corresponding to the special registers according to the nature of the goods that are transferred to the new or absorbing company.

442. What is more, it is possible to emphasize that the merger agreement can be revoked or left without effect until the final agreement has been granted or all the approving resolutions have not been adopted within three months since the preliminary agreement; also, the companies involved can prosecute its cancelation judicially. Similarly, in those cases in which we must reach a consensus in the corporate will for the merger agreement (express agreement in partnerships and majorities arranged for, SRL, SAS and SAU, S.A.), dissenting or absent partners shall have the right to withdrawal.

A. *Controlling, Controlled and Related Companies*

443. There are different assumptions to consider and whose regulation corresponds to different systems.

444. To begin with, it is worth highlighting the intercorporate interests recognized by the LGS which do not imply a full acquisition of the participatory package of a company but a partial acquisition, so that control of a company is acquired or either an active participation without control or, to a lesser extent, a passive participation is held.

445. In the first case, a company is controlling when it owns a share in the share capital, directly or indirectly (granted by a company in turn controlled by it) which gives it the control of the entity's will. This situation is known as internal law control. However, it may happen that society participates in another even if it does not have the majority of votes as in the previous case, but in fact, and for various circumstances, it controls it, which is defined as an internal factual control. Finally, it is also possible that a society which does not participate in another one exerts a dominant influence over it as a result of having special bonds with it. The latter implies an external factual control and it is a recurrent issue in the marketing contracts (franchise, distribution, concession, agency and supply contracts, etc.). In Argentina, the external law control by which a company submits its ad referendum decisions to another according to an express agreement is prohibited.

446. In the second case, where there is no longer a control, precepts of related companies are those in which a company participates in more than 10% of the capital of another; in case of exceeding 25% of the capital, the investee company must be informed about it.

B. *Restrictions on Mergers and Takeovers*

447. Furthermore, prohibitions or restrictions on mergers come from the system of defense of competition provided by Law No. 27,442.

448. Said normative compilation, in its seventh article, defines economic concentration as taking control of one or more companies through the following: a merger between companies; the transfer of goodwill; the acquisition of participatory ownership or any right or the exercise of a substantial influence that grants control of decision-making; any agreement that transfers in fact or legal manner to a person or economic group the company assets or provides decisive influence in the adoption of decisions of ordinary or extraordinary administration of a company; any of the aforementioned acts that imply the acquisition of substantial influence in the competitive strategy of a company.

449. Thus, the following article of the aforementioned legislative body prohibits economic concentrations whose purpose or effect is or may be to restrict or distort competition, so that it may be detrimental to the general economic interest, and the ninth article establishes that, when the total business volume of the group of companies affected in the concentrations is equivalent to or greater than 100 million mobile units (whose value in legal tender will be set annually by the Court of Defense Competence and that is obtained from the sale of products, the provision of services performed, and the direct subsidies received by the companies affected during the last fiscal year that correspond to their ordinary activities, after deduction of sales discounts, as well as the value added tax and other taxes directly related to turnover); besides, such acts shall be notified prior to their improvements or the taking of the control, whichever occurs first, to the national competition authority or to the regulatory entity of the particular activity (cases in which the affected service is subject to economic regulation of the National State). They will only have effect once authorized by the Court of Competence Defense expressly or tacitly due to its silence after the legal deadlines have elapsed (45–120 days since all the information was submitted); what is more, the parties involved are subject to be fined in case of failure to request authorization and the acts thus performed must be revoked and their effects shall be removed. The calculation of the turnover will be carried out considering the controlling companies and those whose control has been modified and their controlled companies.

450. Similarly, the companies intervening in a future concentration may consult the Court of Competence Defense requesting an advisory opinion so that it decides on whether a concentration can be placed or not in the terms of the seventh article and the following regulations. The court's resolution shall be unquestionable.

451. In reference to this, we must emphasize that the following assumptions should not be notified: acquisitions of companies of which the buyer already owned more than 50% of the shares, provided that this does not imply a change in the nature of the control; the acquisition of bonds, debentures, non-voting shares or corporate debt securities; the acquisition of a single company by a single foreign company that does not previously own assets or shares of other companies in Argentina and whose exports to Argentina would not have been significant, customary and frequent during the last thirty-six months; the acquisitions of companies that have not registered activity in the country in the last year, unless the main activities of the object company and the acquiring company were coincident; etc.

III. Cleavage

452. Regarding the division, Article 88 (LGS) provides that there is a split in three cases, namely: when a company without dissolving allocates part of its assets to merge with existing societies or to participate with them in the creation of a new society; when an undissolved company allocates part of its assets to set up one or more new companies; and when a company is dissolved without being liquidated to establish new companies with all of its assets. The regulation of this principle is foreseen by Article 88 and following regulations of the LGS.

453. The assumptions to carry out a split in division-merger cases are those established for the latter and which we have already referred to. However, in the rest of the cases, the premises to be observed are the following: the approval of the division and the reform of the contract or statute of the company to be divided, if applicable, with the attributions of social parties or shares and proportions to the spin-off company or its partners or shareholders; the approval of a special balance for this purpose that must not be older than three months, all with identical necessary requirements already indicated for the modification of the social contract or the statute in the case of merger. Likewise, edicts must be published for three days to enable the opposition of third parties in the same terms of the merger; what is more, said publications must include the following: the company name or company name that is divided; the valuation of assets and liabilities of the company at a certain date and the valuation of the assets and liabilities that constitute the split assets.

454. Furthermore, as we have indicated in the merger, dissenting or absent members will have the right to withdrawal.

§8. Holding Companies and Subsidiaries

455. In relation to holding companies, subsidiaries and branches, having dealt with these assumptions in the different sections intended for the restructuring of the company, concentration and companies incorporated abroad, we refer, in the interest of brevity, to the aforementioned regarding each of the referred topics that have already been thoroughly dealt with.

§9. Taxation of Corporations and Shareholders

456. In this sense, companies pay from 25% to 35%, onwards, for income tax and this frees the partners from paying them at the time of receiving the dividends since they have already been charged to the company. Likewise, with respect to the increase in the value of the shares of partners that is proportional to the capital growth of the entity, the income tax that affects them is settled at the time of the transfer of the shares and is calculated on the highest value (15% with respect to the highest value, except in the case of shares in listed companies). Stocks are not covered by the personal property tax.

Finally, loans to partners by the company entail, in the case of public limited companies, a fictitious interest that does not admit evidence to the contrary and generates supposed profits for which the company will be affected by taxes. In the case of limited liability companies and personal companies, a loan from the company to the partner is allowed without interest.

Chapter 2. Closed Corporation: Private Company—Limited Liability Company

§1. Closed Corporation

457. Most of the characteristics of the closed company were indicated at the time of developing the big corporation, content to which we refer, reiterating the caveat that the closed company, unlike the big corporation, is not included in Article 299 and, therefore, it presents the following notes: it can be constituted for a sole proprietorship; it can omit having an auditor (in which case it must appoint an alternate director); it can establish statutory restrictions on the transfer of shares (but cannot prohibit the transfer) such as the right of first refusal; may establish, by statute, pursuant to the terms of Article 89 of Law 19,550, causes of partial resolution (e.g., upon the death of a shareholder); it can hold a board of directors of one or two members; it can only increase the capital by ordinary meeting and only once up to five times if it is agreed in the statute, otherwise, or in the rest of the cases, it must do so by extraordinary meeting; and it is not under the orbit of control of the National Securities Commission, but of the IGJ.

458. As we said, closed SAs are not those that are simply not listed on the stock exchange, but in this category are all those that, in their bylaws, do not allow the free transferability of the shares but establish a series of limitations. That is to say, however, that open companies are those that do not limit the transfer of shares, whether they are listed or not on the stock market.

459. In turn, this society accepts a subtype which is the sole proprietorship. It is the only corporate type of the 19,550 Company Law that allows the sole shareholder society, but it does have a limitation: the impossibility for that company to constitute another sole proprietorship. With the enactment of Law 27,349 to support entrepreneurial capital, another corporate type was added: the Simplified SAS that allows the constitution of a sole proprietorship and that cannot, in turn, in the case of being a sole proprietorship, constitute another sole proprietorship whether it is a Simplified SAS or a sole proprietorship.

§2. Limited Liability Company

460. As has previously been mentioned, the SRL was introduced into Argentina by law in the 1930s of the twentieth century, showing characteristics of a mixed or intermediate type between partnerships and capital societies. As a preliminary, we must say that this can be derived from certain features of the type such as the exclusion of the partner for righteous cause; the partial resolution due to a member's death; the duty of non-competition of the partners; the joint and several guarantees of the partners for the due integration of the contributions to the company; the limit of the number of partners; the possibility of establishing limitations on the transfers of the entity's participation and the particularities provided for the case of their forced executions; the possibility of making decisions concerning the society because of consultations or communications and the limit in decision-making that must be determined by the agreement of more than one partner regardless of whether one of them has an absolute majority of the share capital; the limitation of liability to the subscribed capital and the admission only of contributions consisting of duties to be given; etc.

461. In reference to the study of the social type, established in the LGS (Articles 142–162), it is worth mentioning that it has a company name and that it can include the name of one or more partners, accompanied by the reference "sociedad de responsabilidad limitada" (SRL) or its abbreviation "SRL" (LLC in English). As we have been referring to, the omission to indicate the social type makes the subscriber jointly and severally liable to the company for the obligations thus contracted.

462. What is more, it is a social type whose capital is divided into quotas, which must have a value of ARS 10 or their multiples, but all quotas are worth just the same and give the right to one vote. The entity can be constituted by a public or private instrument with certified signatures and must be registered in the R.P; failure to do so will be included in section IV already analyzed for breaching that formal registry duty.

463. The partners, who cannot amount to more than fifty, contribute to the company duties to be given that they subscribe in full at the time of their constitution and that they can, in the case of obligations of giving sums of money, integrate them in a 25% to the constituent time and the remaining balance within a period of two years. In the event that the contributions are duties to give goods, they must be fully provided at the time of incorporation; they must be provided in property and be susceptible to legal resolution. The partners jointly and severally guarantee third parties the effective provision of the subscribed contributions and the declared value of the integrated contributions.

464. Likewise, the transferability of social quotas cannot be prohibited, but it must be limited. This occurs through the preferential and estimate rights, cases in which the transmissibility will be determined by the previous offer that the rest of the partners will have to make the partner that wishes to transfer his or her shares or by the possibility of submitting to the unanimous decision or majority the possible admission of a third party by the transfer of the social shares, respectively. In all cases where these limitations are stipulated in the partnership agreement, the procedure must also be established in which these rights must be exercised within a maximum period of thirty days from when the selling partner is informed about the data of the potential buyer together with the purchase price established. However, if there are differences between the company or partners and the selling partner with respect to the purchase price of the shares, they may object to it and urge its judicial review through experts; this process shall be borne by the party whose alleged price is lower than the price that experts finally determine.

465. In reference to this possibility that the partners have to establish limits to the free transferability of shares, when these have been arranged and are ready to be executed by third-party creditors of the partner, there will be no simple auction procedure; instead, the company will be notified about the imminent auction fifteen days in advance so that the creditor, debtor partner and society try to reach an agreement; failure to do so, it will result in an auction. Notwithstanding the foregoing, once the auction has been carried out, the grantee will not be admitted as a full member of the company, but this effect is suspended for a period of ten days in order that the company or a third party presented by it, or a partner, acquire the shares at the price determined at auction through their deposit and thus prevent the admission of an unknown third party from the company. If this does not happen, then the third party that has acquired it at auction becomes a member of the contract as a partner. Likewise, in the case of a partner's death, there is disagreement in the doctrine as to whether or not this results in the partial resolution of the contract if it does not establish anything about it. Our conclusion is negative since Article 90 does not mention the SRL in cases in which a partner's death results in partial resolution (only mentions the cases of the collective society, the simple limited partnership and capital and industry society). Thus, the death of a member does not cause partial resolution and the heirs may assume the status of partners if they wish to do so. However, if the contract establishes the incorporation of heirs, they will become part of it but may assign their shares and during the first three months the pacts that limit the transferability of the participations will not be applied.

466. Social organisms in the SRL are named as follows: administration, management; governmental body, meeting of partners; and audit, syndication or supervisory board, the latter being an optional body unless the company has a capital exceeding ARS 50,000,000.

467. Regarding the management, we must point out that it may be single or plural management and may be formed by partners or third parties. In the second case of plural management, different management functions may be established for each manager or a joint administration (formed by all of them) or collegiate (more than one partner) can be established or it can be indistinct. If the contract does not establish anything, this last case is considered verified. The sort of organization of management is not indifferent in terms of responsibility, since if there is allocation of functions the liability for the proper exercise of the same will fall on the one who was appointed to carry them out and, also, although its performance is imposed to more than one administrator, the judge may determine different degrees of responsibility based on the participation of each one in the ratified acts.

468. Subsequently, in the same terms as those previously referred to regarding the revocability of the positions of administrator, managers may be removed with no apparent reason by the majority of capital attending the meeting established for that purpose, unless otherwise agreed on, and, likewise, when the removal of the manager has been a stated condition to contract a partnership, dissenting partners will be entitled to a withdrawal.

469. Besides, in the case of established plural management, representation may be individual or plural. The company is bound by the representatives acting in that capacity as long as the acts in question are not notoriously different from the corporate purpose. When a regime of plural representation is established by the managers, it can be organized in an indistinct way where all of them can individually represent society, or collegiate where more than one must act to do it according to the established number, or joint where everyone must act so that the entity is bound. The infringement of this regime, as previously stated in the other types, determines as a consequence that the company will not be bound in the particular act, except in the case of subscription of securities, contracts in forms, adhesion contracts and distance contracts. In these cases, the solution of the law of obliging the company, although it does not have the conditions of representation established in the social contract, is imposed due to the state of defenselessness that the contracting third party presents in the established cases. In addition, all those who have exceeded their representative capacities will be liable for the damages that these acts could cause to the entity.

470. Regarding auditing, it is not advisable to refer to this section since the same rules apply to the SAS, so we will be dealing with this while analyzing that social type.

471. As for the governing body, the resolutions concerning the society will be adopted after deliberations according to the principles established by the contract provided that their authenticity is guaranteed. So it can be deliberated through simultaneous consultation conducted by management or a written statement in which all partners express their will. Apart from this, the resolutions may be adopted by means of a meeting of partners constituted in an assembly; in this case, the management shall summon them to the domiciles constituted by them so that they attend it. This case is mandatory for the companies that fall under Article 299, subsequent 2, that is to say, that they possess a capital superior to ARS 50,000,000. In order to change the social contract, if it does not establish anything, the required majority is that representing two-thirds of the share capital and it can be carried out provided that at least there is the agreement of two partners. Notwithstanding the foregoing, the contract may establish another regime and reduce the majority of necessary capital up to an absolute majority limit, although it may not modify the necessary agreement of at least two partners. In cases where it is decided to move the company's address abroad to transform it, merge it, split it, extend it, redirect it, change its purpose, or increase the duties of the company, the dissenting partners will have the right to withdrawal.

§3. Joint-Stock Companies

I. Demands of an Economic, Legal and Social Context

472. As it was exposed in several explanatory opportunities related to the Simplified SAS carried out by those who participated in this legislative initiative, there was a local and international scenario that justified the need to review the corporate offer provided by our LGS No. 19,550 to the entrepreneur. But this was not the only basis on which the proposal was established but, added to this, there were a series of administrative, financial and judicial obstacles that conspired against local and international entrepreneurship in the country.

473. A clear example of this was the 2015/2016 ranking published by the World Bank in terms of "doing business," that is, the facilities offered by a market to set up a business with respect to ratings, installation of services, offers of credits for ventures, etc. On this list, our country was ranked No. 157 on a world scale and No. 10 in the Latin American region. Seen this way, this data does not offer a detail susceptible of valuation but suffice it to say that in the regional detail, Argentina was only ahead of Venezuela and Bolivia (behind Mexico, Chile, Peru, Colombia, Panama, Uruguay, Paraguay, Brazil and Ecuador), or on a global scale, Argentina was behind countries such as Macedonia, Kosovo, Costa Rica, China, Nicaragua, El Salvador, South Africa, Nigeria, Pakistan, Honduras, Indonesia and India.

474. Added to this as another considerable argument, in relation to comparative law there were some close cases such as Colombia, Mexico and Chile, where this phenomenon of the incorporation of the new corporate type with outstanding success had already occurred. It is enough to review the data of the Superintendence of Colombian Companies, from which it is inferred that during 2014, 56,533 Simplified SAS were constituted out of a total of 58,550 companies, that is to say, 96.56%, and, in 2015, another 47,956 did so out of a total of 49,319, respectively, that means that the percentage was increased up to 97.24%.

475. In addition, up to now, the Argentine market offered the entrepreneur or small and medium-sized company, a variety of traditional types such as the SRL and the SL, which were recently joined in 2015 by the simple society, residual or informal located in section IV of the LGS, together with the SAU. In this regard, it is worth mentioning that the Argentine market presents a distortion in relation to the legislative purpose that accepted the different types referred to, inasmuch as there is an abuse in the choice of corporations for small businesses at the expense of the liability limited society to the point of proposing *de lege ferenda* the extension in the application of principles that correspond to the mixed society to those closed but with capital, which mostly take place as closed family corporations (e.g.: activity in competence carried out by the partner, assumption of the partner's heir). Already in the years 1999 and 2000, the IGJ showed striking data as the constitution of 8,949 SRL compared to 13,974 SAs and 4,850 SRLs compared to 5,412 SAs, respectively. Finally, the new regulation for simple, informal or residual societies, although it grants considerable benefits in comparison with the previous regime of de facto or irregular companies (direct opposability, joint responsibility although unlimited, etc.), the truth is that it does not represent a tempting offer for the entrepreneur, and neither does the SAU because of its inclusion in the seventh paragraph of Article 299 of the LGS (minimum capital of single and total integration, compulsory union, permanent State supervision, etc.)

476. What is more, digital development has modified old qualitative and quantitative parameters of the valuation of a company, and intangible assets are currently the most important ones. Thus, as can be seen in the local market, those companies that have digital platforms, databases or computer programs are the best valued. An example of this is the "Mercado Libre" platform, a company valued above YPF or Aerolíneas Argentinas, something that years ago seemed utopian. Another case may be the website "Despegar.com," among others.

477. This reality has had a decisive impact on the market and the legislative systems must contribute to the need to accompany those changes, as the commercial dynamic is certainly increased to extreme levels with technology ready to serve those changes and bureaucratic obstacles go against the competitiveness of a developing country that wishes to have investments.

478. Let us point out that out of all these symptoms, the law supporting entrepreneurial capital has incorporated a new type of society, something that is one of its main features, a novelty that can become decisive when referring to the ending of bureaucracy in project management and that it constitutes the SAS as the rule of the entrepreneurial market as opposed to the other types of exception. Likewise, the regulation has as its goal, the adaptation of the system to the digital development since the information society, even with its weaknesses and constant updating, is more useful and safer for operators in the commercial field. The easy digital development will surely diminish the work of commercial courts, fiscal organisms, lawyers as well as professionals of Economic Sciences, but this is necessary when considering investment benefits and the necessity to *aggiornarse* itself to a global competitive world.

II. Its Characteristics

479. First of all when regarding the SAS, it must be remarked they do consider the importance of the autonomy of the will in a changing market and that presents numerous challenges for the entrepreneur; besides, we must also highlight the following features: (a) it constitutes a new type of society by actions independent of those preexisting (it is not a subtype of the SL or of the limited partnership by shares); (b) the small and medium-scale enterprises are its main goal (although its use and scope are unpredictable); and (c) that has been created apart from the LGS, as it arises from Articles 33–62 (Law 27,349) of Support of Entrepreneurial Capital.

III. The Act of Incorporation and the Constitutive Instrument

480. The SAS can be constituted as a sole proprietorship, but it can also do so in the event that the founder is a human being, in such a way that he/she is the only person who participates in the social organisms. This means that, by dispensing with compulsory union, the SAS can find the same entity in the administration and government bodies, thus being a true one-member society in all respects, unlike what happens to the SAU that imposes necessarily the private supervising body. In the latter case, although the reform of Law 27,290 and in accordance with its organisms, it can have just a sole entity, the truth is that considering the organisms in general, there will be at least two people since there is a requirement of unionism.

481. Likewise, the governing body may be composed of one or more human beings or legal entities, but in the case of a sole proprietorship, it cannot be constituted by another sole proprietorship (SAU or SAS—with one proprietorship). This limitation of Article 34 is consistent with the last paragraph of Article 1 of Law 19,550 but does not refer to the type of society but it refers to the sole shareholder, so an SAS with a plurality of partners can constitute both a one-member SAS or an SAU.

482. Now, here the problem of the one-member society arises when its partner is, in turn, a sole proprietorship. We believe that the same position used at the time for SRL that has become a sole proprietorship should be used and so, although the SAS cannot be constituted by another sole proprietorship, the fact that some circumstances make that situation occur and it becomes a sole proprietorship company, it will not lead to its dissolution if the entity is economically and socially viable, for it will be acknowledged as part of section IV of the LGS. This is consistent with the current wording of Articles 94 and 100 of that legal body.

483. Regarding the sole proprietorship and the incidence that this assumption has regarding the debate on the legal nature of the contract as a plurilateral organization, we ought to remark that we adhere to the position which does not change that feature because, even when the act arises from a unilateral declaration of will and not of the agreement of two or more persons, this does not prevent new partners from being incorporated into the contract in the future; consequently, it still holds its nature as a plurilateral organization contract.

484. Apart from this, as for the controlling partner, it cannot fall in a company included in Article 299 of LGS paragraphs: (1) (they make a public offering of shares or debentures); (2) (have a capital of more than ARS 10 million); (3) (are of mixed economy or are included in section VI); (4) (carry out capitalization, savings or in any other way require money or securities from the public with promises of rendering services or future benefits); (5) (exploit concessions or public services); and (6) SAU. In other words, in this respect, as it is logical, the SAU cannot be a sole shareholder of an SAS, but also, it cannot be a controller either. The nonobservance of these limits without transforming the type or changing the control makes the responsibility of the partners joint and unlimited.

485. As for the constitutive instrument, which is not called a contract or statute (Article 36), although the law refers to the second (Article 59, e.g.,), the form established by the legal regime is that of a public or private instrument with certified signatures, and the certification can be granted by a banking, judicial or registry authority; also, it can be issued by a notary public or even by digital means. This variety provided to the entrepreneur is of total interest and will be accepted in a good way since the current varied means have been noted so as to subscribe documents and these alternatives do not imply a decrease in security that should prevail. In this way, the volume will be directly related to the needs of the market and there are no bureaucratic excuses for not carrying out the constitutive contract as a tool that structures the business.

IV. Limitations

486. The SAS cannot make a public offering of shares under the terms of Article 299, paragraph 1 (LGS), but can access and participate in the Collective Financing Systems—SFC—of Article 32 of Law 27,349, offering participations in search for investors (Article 24, paragraph 1), an activity that will also have the National Securities Commission as the enforcement authority (Article 22). In this regard, the SFCs will be subject to the principles of transparency, diligence, objectivity and, in accordance with the standard of good business order, they are subject to the duties imposed by specific legislation.

487. In relation to what we have referred to, the mechanism of "crowdfunding" is important; by means of this mechanism, the entrepreneur presents his project or business idea to an online platform of collective financing (such as Kickstarter, Indiegogo, Seedinvest—investments—Ideame; BRAINSTORMING, Crowdfunding Argentine Real Estate, Crowdium—inmobiliario—Club Kick-Off—for soccer clubs—among others), applying to be financed by third parties.

488. Another limit of undisputed application, because of its compatibility with this microsystem and because it is of public interest, is the regime of imputation of the unenforceability of the legal entity included in the third section of Article 54 of the LGS. That is to say that in the event that the company's actions involve extra-corporate purposes or constitute a mere resource to infringe the law, public order or good faith, or to interfere with the rights of third parties, the consequences of their actions will be directly imputed to the partners or controllers that made them possible, who will be jointly and severally liable for the damages caused.

V. Social Capital

489. (a) Minimum capital: At the time of incorporation of the company, the minimum capital required by law is twice the living minimum adjustable salary (Article 40). Today it would be, in Argentinian pesos, the amount of ARS 66,000 approximately.

490. Establishing a capital in these conditions brings up some questions that modify the traditional model of the 19,550 Law because, on the one hand, since it is a little capital and considering that there is the possibility that this society has a plural purpose it breaks the relationship established between the capital and the purpose agreed on as a necessary concept and, on the other hand, it determines a dynamic reference for the calculation of capital that does not need revision in the passing of time as a consequence of the fluctuations of the economy, inflation, etc.

491. Besides, the intangibility and immutability of the share capital are not modified, since at the time of incorporation the initial capital is consolidated and the dynamic reference should not be observed subsequently because of experimenting with successive variations, but only for those who set up new companies, but not with respect to those already constituted.

492. In reference to what we have previously analyzed, regarding the relationship between the purpose and capital that comes from the concept of society regarding the need to make contributions to apply them to the production or exchange of goods and services, as provided in the first article of the LGS, we reinforce the idea that this new type of company ends at least with the need for a direct relationship since it allows the possibility of providing a multiple or plural purpose and the establishment of a capital equivalent to twice the adjustable minimum living wage.

493. Currently, we can see that there is a certain minimum capital for SAS and sole proprietorship corporations, which amounts to ARS 100,000 and, in the case of the latter, it must be provided totally at the time of the founding act. What is more, with respect to SRLs, some courts in Cordoba require the capital to amount up to at least half of the capital provided for SAs, that is to say, ARS 50,000.

494. As an example of what is referred to in the previous section, cite general Resolution No. 8/2016 of the IGJ which states three arguments to support the validity of the relationship between the purpose and the capital: (a) Background: Article 68, paragraph 2, Resolution No. 7/2015 ("As a guideline for registration, in limited liability companies a minimum of representative capital of thirty percent (30%) of the capital stock required for public limited companies will be demanded as established in Article 186 of Law 19,550"); (b) "That the profuse legislation of the General Companies Act demonstrates the intention of the legislator to regulate different aspects related to social capital, however the General Companies Act does not establish a minimum capital for corporate types different from the Limited Company (SA)"; (c) "That with respect to the amount of the share capital, the absence of objective parameters to assess its sufficiency a priori could lead to arbitrariness that the comptroller's authority should avoid (it is undeniable that the social capital must be in accordance with the scope and nature of the corporate purpose that wishes to be achieved)." All this, as the SAS has been established would be forgotten. Even this outcome should occur with respect to SRL, all in order to avoid arbitrary discrimination.

495. (b) Role of Capital: Another issue that arises because of this minimum capital and which is almost symbolic is the old discussion on the role of guarantee of corporate capital. From a modern perspective, it has been argued that capital currently constitutes the framework for the participation of partners in society, but it is not a guarantee with respect to third parties, since the latter are interested in the company's equity at the time of contracting with it. When a financial institution decides to grant a loan to a company, it does so considering its financial statements, and the guarantees offered, and not according to the amount of its capital; besides, the external financing mechanisms are the most used by companies for their advantages to have access to credit. Apart from this, we should mention the importance that capital holds even today through the rule of Article 94, paragraph 5; and also, Articles 96 and 99, second paragraph, of the LGS.

496. (c) Reimbursement of Capital: Likewise, with respect to the repayment of capital, the SAS has a considerable advantage by supporting the idea of the entrepreneurial business above the importance of the initial capital and in coherence with what has previously been expressed, not only because the minimum capital required is almost symbolic but, beyond that and for the case that the contribution is money, also it allows, the same as the rest of the social types (with the exception of the SAU), the reimbursement of 25% when it is set up and the remaining balance within a period of two years. As a novelty, it is established that the constitution expenses (fees and other administrative expenses) are regarded as payments on account of the reimbursement.

497. Regarding the non-monetary contributions, the payment must be total at the time of setting up the company and the valuation may be determined voluntarily by the partners according to the criterion supported by them or by the market price commonly used and third parties may challenge it within five years of the execution for the case of bankruptcy or insolvency, although this resource does not proceed when the valuation has been in court. The valuation mechanism should expressly arise from the financial statements (Article 42).

498. Another particular characteristic of the Simplified SAS is the solidarity and unlimited guarantee of the partners for the integration of the capital, a criterion established according to the greater similarity that the type shows with the SRL against the Limited Company (SA).

499. (d) Capital Increase: The increase of the social capital is totally free according to the will following the criteria established in the constituent instrument, and even the creation of different types of share rights and different premiums may take place in order to concentrate on the importance of the investor; what is more, it can also be established in the original act that the increase should not be published or registered when it does not exceed 50% of the capital.

500. (e) Irrevocable Contributions: The irrevocable contributions on account of future issuance of shares will keep that character in the net worth up to twenty-four months from the date on which the administration organism manifests its acceptance, an act that must take place within fifteen days to count from the partial or total income of the sums corresponding to the contribution. After the twenty-four months without capitalization, the sums will be placed in social liabilities. The Law of Support for Entrepreneurial Capital establishes an intermediate term for the Simplified SAS with respect to the capitalization of irrevocable contributions, a term that lies between an undefined period as established by Law 19,550 and a fixed term of shorter duration determined by Resolution No. 7/2015 of the IGJ for the companies by actions. This last regulatory body establishes in Articles 103 and 315 that the assembly must expressly decide on the capitalization of said contributions within the fiscal year in which the contributions have been accepted by the administrative body; therefore, failure to deal with this subject matter or if it is dealt with extemporaneously or the rejection of the capitalization of the same one will leave its reimbursement unimpeded.

501. (f) Accessory Benefits: Services may be agreed upon or provided as accessory services by partners, administrators or third-party providers; in all cases, the nature, extent, manner and compensation shall be established as well as the penalties for non-compliance and the alternative methods of integration in case the rendering of the benefit becomes impossible. The valuation of the contributions can be established in the constitutive instrument justifying its background or by subsequent unanimous resolution of the partners, as well as by the determination of experts appointed unanimously by them. Likewise, the subsequent modification of the benefit is subject to the approval of the obliged person and of the entire group of partners.

502. (g) Division of Capital: The capital is divided into shares that must be issued or, otherwise, the company must keep a record book of shares supporting the balance of account receipts and lack of issuance.

503. In addition, actions of different classes that establish equal or different political and economic rights may be created, differentiating themselves from the parameters established by Article 216 of the LGS.

504. Likewise, the stock splits are registered in a register of shares in which all personal or real rights and other restrictions or prohibitions that affect them must be recorded, and must also be transcribed in the title for the case of issued shares and in the receipts issued for the case of book-entry shares. We must also remark that forms of negotiation or transfer of shares can be established in the constitutive instrument, this act can be subject to approval by the shareholders' meeting, and even any transfer of the whole or of some kinds of shares may be prohibited for a period of no more than ten years provided that this decision is taken for the entire share capital.

505. Article 48 concludes in the last paragraph that any negotiation or transfer that does not comply with the provisions of the instrument of incorporation will be of no value. As regards this issue, we understand this regulation is incorrect because the act will be unenforceable to society and partners, but valid between parties if the third party has been carried out in good faith. Thus, the partner who negotiated or transferred the participation breaching the provisions of the constitutive instrument or subsequent resolutions of the partners' meeting will be liable for damages that may be attempted by the third party that has acquired it and has been harmed.

VI. Company's Purpose or Object

506. One of the innovations that can be observed in the corporate purpose is that of the type with respect to the traditional regime of societies, inasmuch as this rule is set aside from the assumption of precision and determination rigorously conceived with respect to the object according to Articles 11, paragraph 3, of the LGS and 156 of the CCCN, to give rise to the possibility of establishing a plural or multiple company purpose which includes activities that are not related to each other, considering the entrepreneurial feature that does not recognize limits, so this is an innovation that deserves to be highlighted.[72] We must point out that we believe that ultimately the purpose will be determined in the wording, although it will not necessarily be the only one, it will possibly be plural, so it can be argued that the requirements set forth by the LGS and the CCCN are observed in this respect.

507. A precedent can be found in Resolution No. 8/2016 of the IGJ that modifies Article 67 of Resolution No. 7/2015, which established that the object must be described in a concrete manner and specify "the activities that will contribute to its achievement, and that the entity actually intends to carry out." This modification for some doctrine supposed the suppression of the demand of a single object.[73] While it is true that the wording of the resolution can generate this idea, we believe that it is now that the single object for this particular case of the SAS has been deleted, as it has been revoked by a special law (and it has not been revoked by a regulation) that establishes the possibility of absence of connection among the activities that make up the object, turning it plural.

508. Currently, the Inspection of Legal Entities of Cordoba (Inspección de Persona Jurídica (IPJ)) has a series of models of social objects that, if entrepreneurs incorporate them into the constituent instrument without modifications, the inspection as qualifying response will approve the constitution of the entity without further processing. Until now, the objects of transportation, real estate, financial, construction, agricultural, computing, gastronomic, tourism, and others are included in a plural object preestablished by the IPJ.

509. The plural object preestablished by the comptroller's organism is of great importance to ensure the broad scope of action of the legal entity in the entrepreneurial field and the speed of the constitutive process that appears as one of the SAS's characteristics.

510. The multiple or plural object is an opportune conversion variable for the entrepreneur and it is therefore worthwhile to critically analyze the 2020 resolutions of the IGJ, in accordance with the following reflection.

72. O.J. Marzorati, *La sociedad anónima simplificada. ¿Será una realidad?*, AR/DOC/3617/2016.

73. M.C. López Linetti, *El objeto social: la supresión del objeto único a la luz de la Res. Gral. IGJ 8/2016,* XIII Congreso Argentino de Derecho Societario, pp. 228 a 233.

511. Perhaps the virtue of an institute and of freedom stands out in times of pressure. Perhaps, in the face of paralyzing reality, creativity and entrepreneurship stand out as the foundations of a poor country with dreams of a prosperous future.

512. Productive minds only need legal instruments and legal places to shine, instruments to which we must assign their value or importance, which is that of a mere tool. Legal instruments are not an end in themselves; they do not exhaust the horizon but simply constitute a means to catapult the brilliance of those who use them at different times and channel the resources of those who wish to support them.

513. Having said this, in accordance with the title of this chapter, we raise two issues or questions that we will try to answer: (1) Does the multiple object comprise all lawful activity? And also, is it a proven instrument for overcoming the economic pandemic? The answer lies in the primacy of reality and, therefore, it is YES, although Article 36, paragraph 4, of the LACE, requires clarity and precision in the activities; (2) Are the concepts of businessman and entrepreneur synonymous? The answer is YES and NO at the same time. Personally speaking, I do believe every businessman is an entrepreneur, but perhaps not every entrepreneur is a businessman. The latter comes from the fact that the businessman always has entrepreneurial initiative and is reactivating his desire to expand, diversify and multiply through his ventures, while the entrepreneur often delegates the generation and management of resources to the businessman so that he can fully devote himself to developing his idea while counting on the latter's support.

514. Currently, the multiple object has received doctrinal attacks and some also regulatory, even today there will be no shortage of people who say that it is used in abuse to request authorization of excepted activity and circulate during the time of isolation. This graphic expression that does not deserve attention in the assumption does deserve a reflection as a description of a position in front of the institutes whose analysis starts from the pathology without highlighting that it is only that since the rule is healthy. It is healthy that in a pendular, uncertain, unstable and high-risk country, capital can be invested in versatile societies that take up the demands of the market and seek to create blue oceans. We take an institute of North American law (e.g., Laws Types of SRL and Soc. Capital of the USA—ULLCA and RMBC[74]—Delaware legislation DGCL[75]) applied in a country with some certainties and also with a desire for permanent innovation, although due to its flexibility seems tailored to our economic needs because the reconversion and diversification of the entrepreneur in our country is an imperative for survival. Notwithstanding

74. Section 112 of the ULLCA allows the formation of a company to carry out any lawful object, therefore the company enjoys the great possibility of entering into business and carrying out activities; s. 2.02 of the RMBC establishes that the inclusion of the corporate purpose in the articles of incorporation is unnecessary and it has been interpreted that, in case of silence, it is comprehensive of any lawful activity.

75. Articles 101 and 102 of the DGCL establish that the company may be incorporated to develop any lawful purpose or objective.

this, the institute has been accepted in comparative law, applying it to the most varied realities (Mexico, Colombia, France, etc.).[76] It is not even true that Europe has turned its back on a continental level to the institute of the plural object since, if we are to what is established by the EU Regulation 2157/2001, which in Article 15 does not establish anything particular in relation to the corporate purpose for the European SAU, it determines a reference in this regard to the material norm of the country of the registered office. In the event that country is the United Kingdom (beyond the current transition due to the activation of Brexit), we will be faced with the possibility of an undetermined object that authorizes the entity to carry out any legal activity and this must be recognized by the rest of the members of the union.

515. It is not true, however, that Europe has turned its back on the institute of the plural object on a continental level, since, if we look at the provisions of EU Regulation 2157/2001, Article 15 although it does not establish anything specific in relation to the corporate purpose for the European Company, determines a reference in this respect to the substantive rule of the country of the registered office. In the event that this country is the United Kingdom (beyond the current transition due to the activation of Brexit), we will be faced with the possibility of an indeterminate object that authorizes the entity to carry out any lawful activity and this must be recognized by the rest of the members of the union.

516. Apart from this, if we believe that the single object protects the partners, then let them decide whether to invest in a company with a multiple object. It has been said that the multiple object is neither precise nor determined, but it is indeed precise; however, it is comprehensive. The only limit to the multiple purpose with regard to the activities included is Article 279 of the CCCN[77] (that they are possible, lawful, not harmful, and that they respect human dignity, morals, public order and good customs).

517. However, what if the object were blank, authorizing any lawful activity? It would be imprecise and indeterminate, in breach of Article 36, paragraph 4, as well. The question is, what changes with respect to the multiple object currently written in the pre-qualified forms were established by the administrative bodies? Does the limitation of a single purpose apply when the LACE expressly authorizes a plural purpose? Moreover, what would be the harm of agreeing on a company with a very broad object as long as it is lawful? None. The LACE, through the establishment of the plural object, has put aside the theory of specialty with regard to the object, making it possible to provide the administrator with the volume of business necessary to maximize the productivity and performance capacity of the entity. By disregarding this theory, LACE is part of the most modern trends[78] that are moving towards the disappearance of the corporate purpose as an essential constitutive element and

---

76. Colombian legislation establishes in Art. 5, subs. 5, the possibility of choosing a determined or undetermined object, according to convenience and necessity; French legislation of 1994; Mexican legislation of 2016; etc.
77. A. Ramirez, *Simplified Joint-Stock Company*, Astrea, BS AS, 2019, p. 146.
78. F. Reyes Villamizar, *Corporate Law in the United States and the European Union*, Legis. Bogota, 2013.

proposes the equating of the corporate body with the individual.[79] Furthermore, if one wanted to be conservative and take the General Societies Act as a reference, which would not be appropriate due to the priority application of the microsystem (Article 150, CCCN and Article 33 LACE), it is not entirely appropriate to affirm the impossibility of a comprehensive object or purpose. This is because the de facto company, as recognized by the General Societies Act, can include an unwritten object, which can be varied from the factual aspect.

518. In addition to this, it must be pointed out that the relationship between object and capital in terms of the production function has clearly been broken, as inventiveness and the infinite possibilities of financing have destroyed this relationship.

519. Continuing with this adequacy test carried out by the administrative staff is derisory today, and it is at least worth thinking about whether there is anyone better than the founders to know the necessary initial financial injection.

520. What is more, the question arises as to whether operators need freedom or guardianship. Freedom under responsibility requires maturity and considering the individual as the master of his or her own reality, as he or she voluntarily decides to prolong or modify it. With that premise as a guiding principle, let investors decide where to invest their money and who will control it; let third parties decide whether they want to contract with a multiple-purpose company with a wide variety of economic units or not, and let us not think of pathology as the only truth. An attempt is made at all times to protect a supposedly unprotected subject (third parties, minorities, etc.) as if they had not consented to their realities and wagered on them conscientiously, or as if they did not have the necessary means to make sure before contracting.

521. In this excessively interventionist context, the questions would be: Isn't more harm done than is to be avoided? Isn't the market more contracted and investment driven out than the harm prevented? Which is the greatest harm? If we are so guaranteed, why has reality given us its back? Do we want to have everything under control and regulated beforehand into stereotypes and thus kill creativity? Are we afraid of the unknown?

522. The pluralistic purpose designed for the coexistence or discontinuity of several economic units that support each other according to reciprocal circumstantial surpluses and deficits can avoid or at least postpone the company's end. Is it not in the interest of shareholders and creditors for a company to be able to reconvert itself when facing measures or realities that affect a sector of the economy and even eliminate the dissolution hypothesis of impossibility of fulfilling the purpose? These possibilities allow the entrepreneur to try multiple ways to escape before going into bankruptcy. This is conceivable.

79. S. Balbin, *Simplified Joint-Stock Company*, Cathedra Juridica, BS AS 2019, p. 64.

523. I clearly understand that this is the moment to acknowledge all that creativity can achieve when facing this economic pandemic so as to help and support the company which is able to keep the jobs and keeps on generating wealth thanks to its versatility. Just turn on the news and you will see an overflow of news related to companies that have modified their business model and have turned to meet the market's needs in this undefined pandemic scenario. Do we need more proof? Although Argentina is not living under a pandemic, it is living under uncertainty, and instability, without a guiding light and with an unsustainable development that swings back and forth depending on the circumstances and, sometimes, against them. It is enough to look at the obstacles of all kinds imposed on the companies of food distribution technology, applications that should then be highly valued in these times as they enable us to feed ourselves, trade, etc., by bringing demand and supply closer together during isolation.

524. Furthermore, reprehensible conducts already have all the repressive and sanctioning set of penalties of common law, applicable without doubt to any case in which the vehicle is the Simplified Joint-Stock Company (SAS) or any other. Our environment does not owe its decadence to the Simplified SAS and, hence let us not take away the attributes of these companies by trying to make them look like other companies, because they are not. Let our community decide in each case whether to take or leave the tool, and let us regard our citizens as capable and mature, since guardianship does not always protect, perhaps we should think that, when it does not educate, it sometimes spoils.

525. To conclude, we note that these postulates and reflections are due to certain unconstitutional resolutions issued by the IGJ in the Autonomous City of Buenos Aires, which we transcribe below. Thus, by means of General Resolution No. 5/2020, General Resolution No. 8/2016 was repealed in its entirety and provided as follows.

526. Article 67, Resolution No. 5/2020: "The corporate purpose must be set out in a precise and determined manner by means of a concrete and specific description of the activities that will contribute to its effective achievement. The inclusion of other activities, also described in a precise and determined manner, is admissible only if they are related, accessory and/or complementary to the activities that lead to the development of the corporate purpose. The incorporation of companies or amendments to the corporate purpose that contemplate the presentation of a multiple purpose shall not be allowed, without prejudice to the related, accessory and/or complementary activities under the terms of this article and with the exception of those corporate purposes registered prior to the entry into force of General Resolution (General Inspection of Justice) 7/2005. The set of activities described must bear a reasonable relation to the company's share capital."

527. The corporate purpose of a Simplified SAS with multiple purpose, according to the pro forma modalities that have been used, complies with the precision and determination requirement, although the nature of the multiple purpose is precisely the diversity of unconnected activities included. Thus, the IGJ unconstitutionally modifies Law 27,349 (Article 36, paragraph 4) by not regulating it at all but simply contradicting it and altering its spirit (Article 99, paragraphs 2 and 3 of the NC).

528. Article 68, Resolution No. 5/2020: "The General Inspectorate of Justice shall require an initial share capital figure higher than that fixed in the constitutive act, even in the constitution of companies by shares with the minimum figure of Article 186, first paragraph, Law 19,550, or of Article 40 Law 27,349, if it notices that, by virtue of the nature or characteristics of the activities included in the corporate purpose, the capital is manifestly inadequate."

529. Naturally, by prohibiting the multiple purpose, the IGJ removed a problem by avoiding, under its anachronistic view, having to quantify the desirable capital to carry out such an object. At the very least, perhaps, although reprehensible, it was more logical to ask for a business plan, financing plan, crowdfunding alternatives, possible investment rounds with repayable or convertible funds, etc., rather than continuing to assign a productive function to the capital that has been lost in practice. Who is the IGJ to tell companies how to finance themselves and third parties how to invest? The function of guaranteeing capital is fulfilled, as a duty of equity balance, with ARS 1 as a retention figure. In view of the imbalance and consequent production of a dissolution cause, liability actions are triggered with respect to the administrators and partners who endorse it for the risk created and the damage produced, in accordance with Article 99 and subsequent articles of the General Societies Act. There is no more risk, no more lack of protection, no more need for protection. It is only necessary to educate the sovereign in responsibility and understanding of the commitments it assumes so that it can assess the risks with immediacy, transparency and maturity, nothing more. It is true that those who diversify can accumulate wealth, but in doing so they generate business units that in turn mobilize the economy and generate countless jobs. Let us encourage the multiplication of talents as the biblical text says, let us support the generators of ideas and wealth, and let us accompany them, knowing that we are the legal operators and vehicles for them, for we are not an end in ourselves. We do redistribute or request the redistribution of what others produce. Let us be wise and fair in doing so without taking a leading role that the new world has ceded to the great creative or entrepreneurial generators of resources.

VII. Simplification of Procedures

530. The simplification of procedures constitutes, perhaps, one of the most important contributions of this new type of company and the law of support for entrepreneurial capital. It would seem really inconvenient to describe in this way the simple fact of digitalizing the process and turning it automatic, but for the entrepreneur who needs the instrument and the legal entity in full with all its effects immediately, the administrative and judicial bureaucracy can be very tiresome. It is worth saying that in Córdoba the procedures can take at least five months in the courts for the SRL and up to one year in IPJ for the Limited Company (SA), according to each case, something that clearly implies a deficiency of the instrumentation against the commercial dynamic. In this sense, we should remark that the IPJ of Córdoba has echoed the innovative impulse and has now instrumented and digitized model types for the Limited Company (SA) (constitution of Express Stock Company), making it possible to be established with greater speed.

531. In reference to the SAS, the simplified procedure supposes a duty of compatibility of the control organisms (IGJ and IPJ) with the provisions of Law 27,349 in its Articles 38, 60, and subsequent. Thus, the signature certification can be verified through the digital signature according to the terms of Article 288 of the CCCN for instruments generated by electronic means, according to which this modality undoubtedly ensures the authorship and integrity of the document. Likewise, the constitutive instrument prepared by electronic means using a standard model through the platforms provided for this purpose must be registered within twenty-four hours of its presentation (Article 38).

532. Regarding the registration of the company in AFIP, after the instrument is registered in the R.P, the registration will be carried out in a twenty-four-hour period and without the need to immediately prove the domicile established, but within a period of twelve subsequent months. From the above mentioned, it is clear that there is no bureaucratic process; besides, the partners living abroad will be granted an identification password within a term not exceeding twenty-four hours. Once these acts have been carried out (they should not take more than forty-eight hours), with the constituent instrument together with the Individual Taxpayer Identification Number (CUIT), the opening of a bank account can be requested to start operating. As it can be seen, in these cases, the society hardly spends a few hours under the condition of being set up, so the rules of this regime will be scarcely implemented.

VIII. Corporate Organization

533. The SAS brings with them the notion of a true contracting society since the autonomy of the will finds few limits as previously enumerated. It has been cataloged as a *Taylor-made* suit by operators; what is more, the law has tried to provide them with a totally versatile and flexible tool that allows them to fit their needs and projects. The English expression that is usually used is "to fit" and is totally appropriate for the case since the features of the type are that the entrepreneurial project will not only fit into a predetermined mold but it is also the mold that will be adjusted to the project through contractual freedom.

534. Besides, freedom will have its limit in the imperative regulations and those of public order acknowledged not only in this microsystem but also in the LGS and in the CCCN. As examples, we can cite Articles 13, 18–20, 245 last paragraph, etc., of the LGS.

A. Governing Body

535. The governing body is composed of a group of partners and it has certain characteristics compatible with the new technologies. Thus, resolutions can be adopted through simultaneous consultations that must be answered within ten days of being taken, or resolved the matters put into consideration through a partners' meeting that may take place at the headquarters or in another place; in addition, the partners can attend the meeting either personally or from a distance using electronic means that allow simultaneous communications and a record must be implemented by the administrator or legal representative establishing the decision, the means used, and glossing the endorsement records. In this way, the SAS adopted this innovation that had already been adopted by Article 158, paragraph a, of the new CCCN.

536. Likewise, and also following the criteria adopted by the CCCN, regarding the call (Article 158, paragraph b), the partners' meeting may be self-convened provided that the total share capital is present and decisions are adopted unanimously in its agenda (Article 49, in fine).

537. In the case of the sole shareholder, in order to keep the existing division between his/her personal interest and that of the legal entity, it is essential that the decisions of the body must be registered in a record.

B. Administration Organ

538. The administrative body does not hold a denomination as the government organism does; consequently, the parties will determine the denomination it will have as management or directory or simply administration and will be composed of one or more administrators (whether they are partners or not), and at least one of them must have a real domicile in Argentina. For these purposes, we understand that the criterion of domicile and residence are synonymous.

539. In addition, the duration of the position may be determined or undetermined and, in the case when the company dispenses with the supervising body, it must have a substitute administrator.

540. Regarding its operation, the meetings of the organism can be carried out in the same way as referred to the governing body, in other words, personally or remotely using electronic means; what is more, the members can also self-convene when all administrators are present; besides, in the latter case (and unlike the partners' meeting for the self-convened), they are able to resolve all the topics in the agenda by a majority.

541. Finally, regarding the responsibility of the administrators, it coincides with the system established for the SRL following mainly the provisions of Article 157 and its remission to Article 274 of the LGS for the case that it is a collegiate body, that is to say, that the members of the administration shall be liable individually or jointly according to the form of organization, regulation of operation and regime of action established.

C. Audit Organ

542. The inclusion of this body in the constitutive instrument is optional, with the possibility of establishing both a receivership and a supervisory board; besides, these organisms will be subject to the LGS regime in matters of competencies, functions and responsibilities. This option is a clear advantage over the SAU.

IX. Books, Records and Digital Documents

543. Another innovation of the corporate type (linked directly to the new digital realities) is their bookkeeping method and the way they show the accounting information to the supervising organisms.

544. Thus, with respect to the information required by the National Treasury, the AFIP will determine its content, making it compatible with the regime established by the LGS and the technical resolutions of the professional Economic Science councils, establishing the manner and generating the relevant digital applications for the loading of documentation and abbreviated information.

545. SAS' mandatory digital records which must be identified by electronic means before the R.P are five, namely: minute book, stock registry book, daily book and inventory book and balance sheets. Similarly, Public Registries may implement the use of digital media or arrange a website for the uploading of the required information and that shall have a controller regime established for this purpose, all in order to replace the use of the indicated registers.

546. From the aforementioned, it is assumed that the only book that was not allowed to be taken by mechanical means (i.e., to say the one of inventory and balance) can now be recorded in digital records for this type of company. This implies a challenge in terms of certification of financial statements and the obtaining of a visa by the professional councils of Economic Sciences, all of which must be adjusted to the new needs.

547. With respect to the modifications of the constitutive instrument and the granting of powers or other analogous documents, they may be authorized through the use of an electronic notarial protocol and by means of a digital signature, and must then be registered exclusively in an electronic manner in the R.P. In this case, the document shall have a digital signature and, if the documents are made in a similar manner with a holographic signature, they must be previously scanned and then uploaded in the system.

548. To load the information before the public administration, the first step is to use the HASH methodology, which will take place by downloading an application prepared by the Ministry of Modernization of the nation. In this way, once the document containing the information has been drafted and saved in PDF format, it must be linked to the HASH that is inserted in the form downloaded for the particular procedure, so that the system then sends the HASH code to the database *Block Chain* data that generates a digital receipt.

549. The HASH methodology consists of a cryptography system that represents in a compact manner a file or data set under an alphanumeric code. The system uses algorithms that ensure that the response (or *HASH)* will make it impossible to know the data which have been entered since it is a unidirectional function that will allow detecting any change in the document.

550. Apart from this, the *Block Chain* database consists of a shared database that includes interconnected databases and which, as referred to in the previous paragraph with respect to the *HASH*, provides due reserve of the information entered; also, it does not allow the modification of the inserted data without being verified.

551. The digital environment brings about numerous benefits for the security, confidentiality and inviolability of information, as well as its immutability. This is so because any modification made leaves a mark. At the same time, it is a system that allows a considerable reduction of expenses both for structures of all kinds and environmental ones.

X. Transformation

552. As stipulated in Article 61 of the law to support entrepreneurial capital, all the companies accepted by Law 19,550 can be transformed into SAS. Let us remark that the regulation establishes that Public Registries shall have to regulate the changing process of the entity; consequently, the regulations of the LGS will not be applicable in this respect, with the provision that the regulation stipulates otherwise.

XI. Employment Contract Law

553. Interestingly, Article 62 (Law 27,349) establishes that the provisions of Law 20,744 and, in particular, Articles 29–31 will apply to the SAS. The aforementioned rules provide for joint and several liability in the cases of contracting through a third party or by cession of space for exploitation, also, when there are subcontracting cases, or in the cases of group of companies where there have been fraudulent facts or when there is a risky management the principle enunciated is unacceptable. Labor Law is of public policy, for it will always be applicable and that is why this regulation should not be analyzed and its inclusion is not understood.

XII. Normative Priority

554. The normative priority system admits, according to what is established by Law 27,349, a duality of implementation according to whether it is the general regime of the type or, particularly, of the rules related to the corporate bodies. For a better understanding, we elaborate a chart to establish the order of priority according to the cases expressed, namely:

(a) General Regime: imperative regulations of Law 27,349, of the LGS and of the CCCN; autonomy of the will; supplementary regulations of Law 27,349, LGS and CCCN.
(b) Organisms: mandatory norms of Law 27,349, the LGS and the CCCN, autonomy of the will, supplementary norms of Law 27,349, of the SRL, LGS and CCCN.

555. It is notorious the relationship of this company with the LLC whose rules are applied collaterally as regards organisms, although it is an SAS, that is why it has been well qualified as a hybrid by the doctrine.[80]

556. Now, beyond the similarity to the SRL in some features regarding the organisms, it seems to us correct to point out that in the SAS the activity in competition for the partners is not prohibited, especially if they are a plural or multiple purpose SAS, and the exclusion sanction of the partner is not applied since he/she is considered to be an investor that is why there is a decrease of the personal factor in this particular type, so it is able to search for investors even in secondary markets that can take risks to develop an idea and with the last aim to enjoy the benefits of success that will be transferred to the value of social participation.

XIII. Alternative Conflict Resolution

557. Finally, as determined by the commercial dynamics and entrepreneurial vertigo, the resolutions of social conflicts that can arise should, in the first place, try to be resolved in an amicable way through the use of internal mechanisms and, in the case of a negative result, may be solved by either State or private judges. We also believe that the second option of judges, whether in ad hoc or institutional arbitrations, will prevail in practice, based on the greater compatibility of this private regime of administration of justice with the urgent needs of these types of ventures.

XIV. Some Conclusions on Simplified Joint-Stock Companies

558. It is appropriate to establish the alienation (insensitivity) of the Simplified Joint-Stock Companies with respect to Chapter II of the General Societies Act, as it

80. O.J. Marzorati, *La sociedad anónima simplificada, ¿Será una realidad?,* AR/DOC/3617/2016.

arises from an independent microsystem that only refers to the second chapter in the organic part of the SRL and in a subsidiary manner. The special legislation has its own objectives and principles, as it also exhorts us to free ourselves from the compelling corporate and the inflexibility of the General Societies Act, although freedom does not imply licentiousness, and the limits common to all legal acts in the exercise of the will autonomy (such as duty not to harm, good faith, public order, abuse of law and, in particular, the unenforceability of the legal entity) must be observed at all times. Thus, the mandatory rules of the General Societies Act would be available in the Simplified Joint-Stock Companies if provided in its constitutive instrument (Article 150 National Civil and Commercial Code—suppositions of Article 13, General Societies Act—except for those of national and international public order, General Societies Act—in my opinion—Article 18 or 124).

559. In the same way, we do believe that the Simplified Joint-Stock Companies are a tool of good use for constituents and subsequent members who are considered capable, mature and responsible, and the State should not intervene in the will autonomy of private individuals through excessive interference. In this order, it is, as has already been stated, a tailor-made type that takes into account the new trends in comparative law on the subject and which makes the type compatible with the flexible and ephemeral nature of exponential growth as characteristic features of the information society, tailored to the business according to its needs or as required by investors in initial stages or future times or as required by the uses of the investment market in the area. The autonomy of will implies self-determination as it materializes the natural and subjective right of Article 14 of the NC to associate for useful purposes (with the limits indicated), occupying the third place in the normative priority (order: (a) Imperative Regulation LACE; (b) Imperative Regulation; (c) National Civil and Commercial Code; (d) Autonomy of Will; (e) Supplementary Regulation LACE; and (f) Regulations of the General Societies Act—Limited Liability Company p/ org. and the rest-); Article 141 and subsequent articles of the National Civil and Commercial Code.

560. To conclude, in view of the freedom that prevails in the microsystem, we have no objections to listing some of the viable clauses that, in our opinion and as we have discussed with friendly colleagues (particularly with Ricardo Cony Etchart), can be included in a Simplified Joint-Stock Companies statute. These are, among others, the assignment of voting rights to the pledgee; early waiver of the right to receive dividends (gained through the resale of shares for a higher value of the company); early dividends or dividends with interest or as a result of special balances; restitution of contributions with premium or rewards; agreement to fix the price of shares far from the real value to be executed by another shareholder and acquirer; payment of dividends to an investor whether there are profits or not; golden shares; suppression of the rights of accretion and/or preferential subscription; share dilution agreement with recess or "exit" option; obligation of permanence or vesting of shares; issuance of shares above or below par; possibility of including para-corporate agreements in the instrument of incorporation for their enforceability (Article 36, paragraph 9); etc.

Part II. Partnerships

Chapter 1. Different Types (Legal Personalities, Liabilities, Contribution, Profits, Management, Transferability of Partnership Interests)

561. Once the general guidelines of Law 19,550 are developed in the initial chapters, we should concentrate in this section on the partnership company types.

§1. Companies of Section IV

562. Thus, it has a fourth section in the first chapter (Articles 21–26), established for all those atypical or typical societies that omit necessary requirements or necessary constitutive presuppositions, which have been denominated as informal, simple or residual societies by the doctrine. This section which we could even consider a new open type of society denotes certain consequences for the societies established there such as the regime of direct opposability, that is to say, that the entity can oppose those who have been linked to the society or know about their existence and cannot oppose *erga omnes* since they lack registration and consequently, the total absence of registration publicity.

563. Direct opposability affects not only the possibility of claiming the existence of a society that can be proved by any means of proof but also the composition of its bodies and their representation so that it is liable. Thus, the contractual provisions regarding representation are opposable between partners but as regards third parties any partner represents the company, unless otherwise agreed upon to have been known by the third party at the initial time of the legal relationship.

564. Likewise, the partners' responsibility, except for three specifically foreseen exceptions, is joint and unlimited, although subsidiary, that is to say, once the social patrimony has been auctioned in its totality and when there are some pending duties, each member is liable for an equal share personally and with all his assets (the debt is divided by the number of partners). Apart from this general criterion, there are three cases in which the partners are responsible jointly and severally. This arises from the contract itself when the partners have agreed to that responsibility, or, when, although there is no agreement in the contract, they have assumed responsibility for the third party, or, finally, when the non-registered adopted type has, as a result, such a liability (for instance, a collective non-registered society).

565. Furthermore, with respect to the ownership of property subject to registration, the company can have its ownership on condition that the written contract with certified signatures (if it exists) is submitted to the special registry and, if it does not exist, a written statement with the same formality should be submitted in which the partners declare the existence of the informal society and its composition.

566. Finally, the precarious status of the company in the fourth section that shows formal faults or typical omissions at the constituent time can be overcome through the process of rectification when partners reach a unanimous agreement or even by a judicial rectification ordained by a judge, without implying those situations an aggravation of the responsibility of the dissenting partners who will have the right to withdraw from the company. Finally, when the company does not have a term of duration or when the term is due, any partner may request its liquidation, which will have a definitive effect ninety days after being informed to the other partners. During this period, the latter may pay the corresponding part to the member who requires it if they wish to continue in the entity and not liquidate it.

§2. Collective Society

567. The collective society has been regulated by Argentine Law from the time of the enactment of the first Commercial Code (1862), in which the social signature was equivalent to the signature of each one of the partners that were jointly and severally bound (Articles 454 and 455), implying the declaration in bankruptcy of the company also that of its partners (Article 1530). Then, with the sanction of the 1889 Commercial Code, this principle was kept until the enactment of the 19,550 Law of Commercial Companies in 1972 and the subsequent amendments until the most recent in 2015 (Law 26,994).

568. The current regime of the collective society retains the characteristics of the type, taking into account the great importance of the partner as a contract *intuito personae*, although plurilateral and of an organization with links and juxtaposed interests unlike what happens in the exchange contracts. This characteristic note is reflected in solutions such as the partial resolution of the contract due to a partner's death, unanimous decisions, unless otherwise agreed on and the prohibition of the partners from competing with the society under warning of exclusion and compensation for damage, etc.

569. Thus, Articles 125–133 of the law establish the typical beliefs and the organic functioning of this society, which, as we have already mentioned before, presents features that characterize it. So the company can be called by fictitious names or company names (name of the partner or partners; in the first case, the words "and company" must be added), followed by the reference "collective partnership" or the acronym "S.C."

570. The partners are jointly and unlimitedly liable, in a subsidiary manner, once the social assets have been auctioned. If the contract is agreed to another responsibility, the latter is not opposable to third parties, without prejudice to internal relations between partners.

571. Likewise, to be modified, the contract needs the unanimous agreement of the partners, unless otherwise agreed upon, which will have as a limit the absolute majority of assets. Any other decision that does not imply modification of the constituent instrument is adopted by that majority.

572. Furthermore, the management of the company will be organized in accordance with the terms of the constitutive contract, and the administrators may be removed without any cause by the decision of the absolute majority of capital at any time unless otherwise provided. If in the contract a righteous cause for the removal is agreed on, the administrators will retain their position until a final judicial decision and, if the latter is established by the cessation order, the dissenting partners will have the right to withdrawal. Similarly, the administrator may resign at any time, provided that the resignation is not taken suddenly or causes harm to the entity; otherwise, it will be liable for the damages caused. To conclude, in the absence of provisions in the contract related to the organization of the administrative body and the regime of representation, any partner will administer and represent the company in an indistinct manner.

573. Let us remark that the society will be liable when its representatives behave as such on condition that their deeds are not different from the social purpose. When a regime of plural representation is established by the administrators, it can be organized in an indistinct manner so that all the administrators can individually represent the company, or collegiate where more than one representative must act so as to do it according to the established number, or joint where everyone must act so that the society is bound by the representatives. As a consequence, the infringement of this regime results in the company not being bound in the particular act, except in the case of subscription of securities, contracts established according to the law, adhesion contracts and distance contracts. In these cases, the solution provided by the law is that the company is liable in spite of the conditions of representation accorded in the social contract not being determined, this is so due to the state of defenselessness that the contracting third party definitely presents in the established cases. What is more, those who exceeded their representative capacity will certainly have internal responsibility for the damages that could result for the entity as a consequence of such acts.

§3. Limited Simple Partnership

574. The limited partnership is another particular type that the 19,550 LGS has in its Chapter 2, Articles 132–140. In this social type, there are two categories of partners: general partners and limited partners. The former can manage and represent society in solitude or with third parties and, as regards their duties, they are liable as the partners of the collective society; this is in solidarity and unlimited, although subsidiary manner. Besides, the limited partners are forbidden the possibility of managing the company and their responsibility is up to the subscribed capital, which can only consist of contractual obligations. Notwithstanding the foregoing, if these partners interfere in administrative acts, the responsibility of those who do so will be of the same order as that of the joint partners for those acts or for all acts if they do so regularly unless these circumstances are expressly authorized and required by law since the fulfillment of a legal obligation, it is clear that it does not constitute any act of infringement. This last assumption arises in cases in which all the limited partners are unable to administer due to causes set forth in the law (bankruptcy, public tender, death, disability or disqualification), cases in which the limited partner must assume, due to the urgency, the administration of those acts that do not admit any delays and without aggravating their responsibility according to their category of partner while that situation is solved within a maximum term of three months. Furthermore, the prohibition to administer to the limited partner does not include the acts of inspection, verification, examination, surveillance, opinion and advice, all of which are expressly permitted.

575. The company shall have a name or company name with the addition of a limited partnership or its abbreviation. The non-clarification of the social type by means of the aforementioned addition will make the signer jointly and severally liable to the company. The corporate name can only be composed of the name of the joint partners either in their totality or of some of them adding "and company" or its abbreviation "cía."

576. However, for the regime of administration and representation that will be exercised by the limited partners, the provisions of the collective societies apply; that means that first, the provisions of the social contract must be followed and, if nothing is expressed, any partner may administer and represent the company in an indistinct manner. Likewise, the administrators may be removed without any reason at any time with the vote of the absolute majority of the capital, including the limited partners, unless otherwise provided. If in the contract a righteous cause for the removal is agreed on, the administrators will retain their position until a final judicial decision and, if the latter determines the cessation order, the dissenting partners will have the right to withdrawal. Similarly, the administrator may at any time waive his or her position, provided that the resignation is not inopportune or causes any harm to the entity; otherwise, he or she will be liable for the damages caused.

577. The company is bound by the representatives acting in that capacity as long as the acts in question are not notoriously different from the corporate purpose. When a regime of plural representation is established by the administrators, it can be organized in an indistinct way in which all the administrators can individually represent the company, or collegiate where more than one must act to do it according to the established number or joint where everyone must act so that the entity is bound. The infringement of this regime determines as a consequence that the company will not be bound in the particular act, except in the case of subscription of securities, contract forms, adhesion contracts and distance contracts. In these cases, the company is obliged despite the fact the necessary conditions of representation provided by the social contract are not presented in the case, due to the defenselessness of the contracting third party although this generates internal responsibility of whoever has exceeded its representative scope.

578. Furthermore, the decisions concerning the society are taken by the limited partners who are commanded by an absolute majority of capital, except in the case of appointment and removal of administrators as well as the treatment of the financial statements in which the limited partners participate. For the reform of the social contract, the same collective society regime is applied considering only the limited partners, that is to say, that they will resolve unanimously or by an absolute majority if the social contract expressly establishes it.

579. Finally, it is worth mentioning that the death of a member brings with it the termination of the contract regarding the participation of the deceased and, in the case of a simple limited partnership of two partners, the surviving partner will have three months to rectify the situation and reestablish the double category of partners, adding at least one other partner; otherwise, the company will become in full right into a sole proprietorship.

§4. Capital and Industry Company

580. The Capital and Industry Company constitutes the third social type of personal character that regulates the LGS in its Articles 141–145. Once more, there are two categories of partners: a capitalist partner and another industrial partner, but, unlike the limited simple partnership, none of them is prohibited from administering it, only third parties are prohibited from doing so. As previously stated, the company is obliged by the representatives acting in that capacity so long as the acts in question are not notoriously different from the corporate purpose. When a regime of plural representation is established by the administrators, it can be organized in an indistinct manner where all the administrators can individually represent the company, or collegiate where more than one must act to do it according to the established number, or joint where everyone must act so that the entity is bound. The infringement of this regime determines as a consequence that the company will not be bound in the particular act, except in the case of subscription of securities, contracts in forms, adhesion contracts and distance contracts. In these cases, the solution of the law of obliging the company, although it does not have the conditions of representation established in the social contract, is imposed attentively to the state of defenselessness that the contracting third party presents in the established cases. What is more, those who have exceeded their representative powers will be liable for the damages caused to the entity.

581. The company may have a company name or a corporate name, always adding capital and industry or its abbreviation; otherwise, its omission makes the subscriber jointly and severally liable regarding the entity for the obligations thus contracted. In the case that a company name is used, it must be formed only by the capitalist partners, by either all of them or some with the addition "and company" or its abbreviation "cía."

582. However, regarding the responsibility, the capitalist partners are liable as the partners of the collective society, this is solidarily and unlimitedly although in a subsidiary form, while the industrial partner is responsible up to the limit of the profits that have not been perceived. In order to determine the profits that the industrial partner must receive, the social contract will be in charge of establishing this; failure to do so will be determined judicially.

583. However, in order to determine the extent of the liability of the latter, the accrual criterion must be kept in mind, but not what has been perceived, that is to say, from the moment when the right to receive the profits has been granted, unlike the criterion of the perceived that would be the case of the effective reception of them.

584. At present, this social type is in disuse by the market, since this concept has been affected by the labor regime that has often regarded it as an existing concealed employment relationship between the partner that provides financial capital or securities and the one who contributes with his work or science.

585. In connection with the description of the social type, it is worth mentioning that all the partners participate in the resolutions of the entity that will be adopted unanimously or by absolute majority of capital if this is established in the contract and, for the latter case, the industrial partners will count with the same number of votes as the capitalist that has provided less.

586. Finally, as previously mentioned with respect to the limited simple partnership, the death of a partner brings about the termination of the contract with respect to the participation of the deceased, and in the case of a company of capital and industry of two partners, the surviving partner will have three months to redirect the situation and reestablish the double category of partners, adding at least one other partner; otherwise, the company will become in full right a sole proprietorship. This resolution is established by Article 94*bis* for these companies that have two categories of partners but, unfortunately, do not include the SC or the SRL that should have the same solution in the case of partial resolutions concerning deaths that they will leave them with only one partner.

587. Finally, regarding the dissolution and liquidation of partnerships, we refer to what was developed in the dissolution and liquidation points at the time of dealing with the big corporation, as those provisions of the general part of the law apply also to them.

Part III. Complementary Issues

§1. The Regulatory Priority System from a Corporate Perspective

588. The legal system as a whole comprises general systems and microsystems that complement and complement each other. In the application of convergent precepts, compatibility clauses must necessarily be observed, which constitute a guideline ensuring the coherence of the system understood as a complex whole. To this effect, we have taken as a source of study some assumptions through which we relate these concepts.

Preliminary Analysis

589. The national private law system can be seen as a comprehensive legal ecosystem of a fundamental or general system, the Civil and Commercial Code (CCCN), and microsystems or special regimes that revolve around it and converge in its application. It happens that, in view of the application of converging regimes, whether of a general-special or a special-special convergence, the compatibility clauses of the regimes must necessarily be observed and, in short, those that arise from the CCCN must be observed.

590. By way of illustration as a basis for the approach and going into the particular, there is usually some turbulence in the doctrine at the time of determining what would be the special law applicable to cases such as that of a bankrupt company or the application of the mandatory rules of the General Law of Corporations to simplified joint stock companies. We will deal with these two particular cases to support the analysis, regardless of the fact that the arguments can be exported to other scenarios of the same nature.

Analysis

591. Articles 150 and 963 of the general body of law provide a criterion of compatibility between the systems and establish the order of priority according to which the precepts are applied in the following excluding order: the mandatory rule of the microsystem; the mandatory rule of the general body, the autonomy of will; the supplementary rule of the microsystem; and, lastly, the default rule of the general body of law.

592. Having listed the priority, it is appropriate to ask: 1. What special regime governs a bankrupt company?; 2. Are the mandatory rules of Law 19550 applicable to simplified joint stock companies (SAS)?; 3. Can convergent regimes be applied harmoniously?

593. With respect to the first question, perhaps the answer should be constructed by establishing application criteria to resolve the plurality of cases in which convergent applications of the two related microsystems, bankruptcy and corporate, would be activated.

594. In attempting to reach these horizons, we advance the criterion that the specificity of corporate law and, particularly its mandatory rules, is not displaced by bankruptcy law, whose preventive system is accessed freely or through conversion, as a protective shield. In other words, there is complementation, the latter being developed through the establishment of a procedural system and establishing limitations to corporate operations imposed by the same *ad referendum* of judicial authorizations. Thus, in each case, the matter must establish compatibility in the application of one regime or the other, all in accordance with Article 150 of the CCCN. In principle, we do not notice mandatory provisions of the bankruptcy law, procedural and dispositive, that alter the mandatory provisions of the corporate law, such as the maintenance of the nature of the corporate business, even in sole proprietorships, or the protection of third parties, apart from preventing direct actions against the corporate assets.

595. However, there has been much debate on the applicability of Law 19550 to the simplified joint stock companies (SAS) and the limitations that may or may not derive from the General Law of Corporations with respect to them. Article 33 of Law 27349 for the Support of Entrepreneurial Capital (LACE) provides that "..... In addition, the provisions of the General Corporations Law, 19.550, as amended in 1984, shall be applicable insofar as can be reconciled with those of this law". The regulation is quite clear in stating that the special law is Law 27349 for the Support of Entrepreneurial Capital and, by reference to the latter, the General Law of Corporations applies insofar as it is compatible. There is no alternative reading in this respect under the terms of Article 150 of the CCCN, according to which the following excluding order of application applies: mandatory rules of Law 27349 for the Support of Entrepreneurial Capital; mandatory rules of the CCCN; constitutive instrument; Chapter 1 of the General Law of Corporations with respect to general matters and the LLP regime with respect to corporate bodies (cf. Article 49 of the LACE); and supplementary rules of the CCCN.

596. Articles 55 and 56 of the LACE also expressly refer to the mandatory rules of corporate law in matters of grounds for dissolution, remediation, liability, condition of viability and liquidation stage (Articles 84 et seq. of the General Law of Corporations). We understand that, despite the clarity of Article 33 of Law 27349 for the Support of Entrepreneurial Capital mentioned above, the debate has arisen due to the need for part of the doctrine to ensure a certain balance in the partners' rights with respect to simplified joint stock companies. Thus, it has been proposed in numerous dissertations and academic articles, as well as in resolutions of control agencies, that not only the mandatory rules of the general part of the Corporations Law but also those unavoidable rules that regulate corporations, should be applied to simplified joint stock companies. Regarding this second point, we believe that it is not appropriate to extend the regime of a different type to simplified joint stock companies without a referral rule, since there is none and, in fact, as mentioned above, in the matter of agencies, Law 27349 for the Support of Entrepreneurial Capital applies the LLC regime (Article 49) and not that of stock companies. This is unobjectionable and has been the reason for the presentation of a bill that has been approved by the Senate, which proposes to extend the stock company regime to simplified joint stock companies, a criterion that we do not share.

597. However, a greater objection arises when it comes to stating that certain rules of the first chapter of the General Corporations Law, such as Article 13, are not applicable, insofar as it is a rule that includes the ideas and forces that structure a company. We do however believe that even Article 13 is of subsidiary application in simplified joint stock companies, that is to say, it is a fourth-order rule in the normative priority that prevails only for the cases in which its sections are not expressly or tacitly repealed by the autonomy of the will in the terms of the particular constitutive instrument. It should not be overlooked that the private rights of the constituents are preserved and are entirely waivable at any time (*ab initio* or at the time of exercise) and that the community of risks, for example, can adopt the most varied manifestations according to current business schemes. It is for all these reasons that one should opt for the feasibility of the derogation by means of a constitutive instrument of any mandatory rule of the General Law of Corporations, such as the cases of Article 13 thereof, the preferential subscription right, the issue of shares under par, etc. All this can be agreed upon in a simplified joint stock company, provided that there is no breach of the duties of good faith, lawfulness of the activity, regular exercise of rights, avoiding abuses, etc.

Conclusions

598. The two cases taken as a basis for analysis cannot be subject to homogeneous criteria because, in one case, the regimes are entirely convergent and a reasoning must be constructed to make them compatible in accordance with the established normative priority criteria. Now, in the second case, the relationship between Law 27349 for the Support of Entrepreneurial Capital and the General Law of Corporations, the special law itself (LACE) determines when and how the LGS will be applied, thus making its precepts less mandatory, except—undoubtedly—for the existence of first-degree criminality, that is to say, of a corporate business, which is obvious. To sum up, we believe we have made clear the compatibility of the converging legal regimes in the two broad cases assumed.

§2. The Current Function if the *Ius Mercatorum* in a Global Market

599. Globalization has reached its highest expression with digitalization, which has led to the establishment of contracting and regulatory standards not only at the international trade level but also at the domestic level. Thus, we are currently witnessing a sort of common language in organizational and transactional matters from the perspective of private law, based on the autonomy of will, good faith and the dialogue of sources, as well as on the need for prompt responses in the resolution of conflicts to provide certainty and efficiency to operators. Simplified Joint Stock Companies (SAS) are an example of this since they are an open and contractual type of company—within the system of personified organizational relationships—incorporated into our system to enable the reception of those evolutionary advantages that modern corporate law has experienced throughout the world.

Introduction

600. In these times, a comprehensive assessment of commercial or mercantile law from a universal perspective is inevitable. In this sense, whether it can be claimed that we have returned to the main source, *ius mercatorum*, should be reviewed.

Unlike other times, where the *lex mercatoria* prevailed with greater force in delimited territories and in the hands of very singular operators, in the current new world order, borders are no longer in force, as a result of a unified global market driven by an international community that proposes economic integration (integration agreements), deregulation and consequent harmonization of residual law (UNIDROIT, etc.), and the gradual elimination of tariff barriers to international trade (Marrakech agreements of 1994, WTO).

601. We are facing a global market where inefficient production and/or service is discarded to give way to the exponential growth of comparative advantages (economic and legal) and thus seek a single global market that fosters competition and transnational business.

602. We are witnessing, in this order, the offshoring not only of large companies but also of SMEs with global activities. In turn, the vertigo of the immediate installed by habit rests on digitization, standardization in contracting and agile means of conflict resolution. Finally, we understand that autonomy of will gives the law the possibility of consolidating this new *ius mercatorum*, based on the common language of investors, businesspersons, entrepreneurs, consumers and users, all of which allows for the incorporation of mechanisms and harmonized provisions from the most diverse legal families in domestic and transnational usage. This implies that a territorial comparative advantage results not only from the economic or productive resources that take place but also from the exceptional regulatory imperativeness and application of public order and state intervention in any of its manifestations, levels or powers. As it should in the face of unauthorized, illicit financial intermediation, practiced under sophisticated forms and denominations in foreign languages.

Requirements of a Global Market

603. The global market presents not only many challenges but also opportunities by relativizing the negative impact that may result from a hostile nearby environment. Note the Argentinian case where, although the country is in a circular economic crisis, this has in no way hindered the growth of the knowledge economy. On the contrary, the generation of intellectual capital is perhaps inversely proportional to the contraction of the economy. In the agro-exporting and knowledge services exporting sectors, the country is undoubtedly at the forefront and has continued its growth path beyond the complex environment.

604. This has led, even by osmosis, to the sophistication of the corporate and financing structure required by SMEs providing international technology services, but this sophistication has also been made available due to the standardization of certain corporate and contracting engineering, moving away from traditional exchange relationships to generate a system of organizational relationships, whether personified or not, even highly complex.

605. The liberalization of trade (WTO agreements) and the freedom for setting up companies and entrepreneurs (human or legal persons) have led to the stereotyping of businesses in terms of common framework patterns (irrespective of the particularities of the business or activity in question), thus facilitating the construction and understanding of the *jus mercatorum* by operators throughout the world.

Comparable Advantages (Economical and Legal)

606. Offshoring the company aims to take advantage of the territorial benefits and thus achieve the best objectives at the lowest cost from a comprehensive view of the business. But the benefit is not exhausted in the economic exploitation but also in those advantages that a certain legal system can offer. From an economic perspective, the comparative advantage comes from making the most of a country's tax prerogatives, logistics, open economy, lower social charges and the costs of legal mediation, etc., without this involving the validation of cases of economic or social dumping. However, from the legal point of view, the flexible rights that make it possible for companies to be set up without complex barriers and the greater implications of autonomy of will, are attractive to entrepreneurs, businesspersons and investors. It is worth stating, in order to banish any pathological perception that deviates from what we are trying to illustrate, that the advantages or benefits do not include cases of scarce information or collaboration to facilitate money laundering or other white-collar crimes, or merely financial capitalism that does not encourage productive undertakings. Some sectors try to postulate that freedom makes certain territories fertile for the perpetration of crimes, something we do not agree with. In fact, as a result of the harmonization of information systems, data cross-referencing, compliance rules, criminal liability of legal persons, rapid punishment of illegal activity, etc., these sites have been clearly identified and are residual.

607. Finally, the Anglo-Saxon root of the law has been strengthened in international trade, receiving international and national contracts, even in continental European and South American countries, institutes that are typical of those legal families. Autonomy of will, in its various manifestations (creation of private law by incorporating practices and customs or the incorporation of foreign law through conflict autonomy), is the way for the incorporation of proven-quality foreign practices, which makes it possible to break down walls and promote understandings.

Deregulation and Self-Regulation

608. Deregulation and soft law proposals allow for rapid harmonization and standardization in contracting. The interesting thing about the current times is not this, which has been pointed out for a long time now, but how standardization has found incorporation even in domestic contracting. The creative dynamics of commercial contracting are also far superior in their adaptation to the static that can result from a codification of behaviors and their legal responses. Qualified doctrine has claimed, at the time, that "the inadequacies of the commercial legal system in the face of the growth of economic operators and the insufficient sensitivity of its drafters to the phenomenon of the irruption and predominance of industrial activity (today it would be knowledge), which characterizes the current economy, as well as the expansion of what would later be called 'economic law', are only the factual material that accounts for the long-standing process of decoding and anti-coding." Harmonization or standard contracting and deregulation can be clearly seen in different specialties such as corporate law, intellectual property law, domestic and international commercial arbitration, maritime law, etc., with an increase in organizational relationships, whether personified or not.

609. Meanwhile, in the residual regulation that contains the borders to that autonomy of will or the subsidiary solutions in what is not considered in the contracting, harmonization is also sought in the first degree in order to later attempt the uniformization or unification of the international business law. Note the work of UNIDROIT, the Institute for the Unification of Private Law, the Regional Forums, etc., all organizations working on the creation of model laws and legislative guides.

Corporate, Financing and Intangible Asset Engineering

610. In practice, especially with regard to the entrepreneurial ecosystem or start-ups providing technology services or intellectual capital, we are witnessing certain standard models of financing and offshoring, not just productive but also corporate.

In other words, there is an inverse concentration procedure in which the vehicle company may be born before its own parent company. This is so because the intellectual capital is scattered in the southernmost and most remote points of the globe so the idea is born first and is then accompanied in its development by the corporate. Thus, the company created by the founders will not channel the large investments, but perhaps the initial ones coming from state seed funds or from related persons and venture capital provided by angel investors. However, while procuring large investments in series A, B or C, the founding company is displaced from the heart of the business by a holding company established in a territory that has comparative advantages in terms of corporate and investment security. This holding company, which will come to control the founding company, now transformed into a vehicle and a work company, will be the global investor's landing port and will concentrate not only on the investment but also on the exploitation rights on intangible assets of higher value (intellectual capital), which support the business model.

611. In this sense, the entire corporate branching strategy responds to the security of the business, the investment and the projection even of a future sale of the group or controlling stake. The latter is because research and development activity is very costly for companies to promote internally, so lower-cost alternatives are sought (absorbing a start-up that has developed a certain technology, linking with universities for research, etc.).

612. However, if the chosen law or those that are connected with the business recognize it, the incorporation of companies with minimum or non-existent capital with a very broad purpose (e.g., any lawful activity—Argentina requires determination—cf. Articles 11.3 of Law 19550 and 36.4 of Law 27349) and the most varied clauses as we have previews said, such as: *"(i) first refusal provision; (ii) first offer provision; (iii) tag along provision; (iv) drag along provision; (v) vesting provision; (vi) clauses providing for specific rights to appoint directors without such right having to be proportionate to the percentage of shares held by the beneficiary of such right; (vii) clauses providing, in specific cases, for the reduction of the director's liability, by a decision taken by the shareholders by simple majority (e.g., hiring a director to overcome a solvency or similar crisis). (viii) clauses restricting certain activities of the Board of Directors whose performance is subject to the affirmative vote of certain shareholders; (ix) good leaver and bad leaver provisions; (x) buy and sale provision, puts and call provision; (xi) clauses providing for the obligation of certain partners to finance the company, with associated privileges in their favor; (xii) accessory benefits of a financial nature; (xiii) rights of observation and assistance to the management body in favor of partners who are not company directors; (xiv) oversight rights; (xvi) qualified information rights; (xvii) Restrictions to carry out activities in competition, even indirectly; (xviii) temporary prohibition to sell shares; (xix) specific clauses to protect minorities (anti-dilution provisions); (xx) clauses to suspend the payment of dividends based on the needs of the company's financial policy; (xxi) plural purpose; (xxii) setting of quorums and variable majorities by subject matter; (xxiii) Clauses providing for the subscription of preemptive rights; (xxiv) Issuance of shares at a premium in any form agreed upon in connection with a specific business or capitalization round; (xxv) Specific clauses for disqualification of directors; (xxvi) Clauses for the exclusion of partners; (xxvii) Clauses providing for decision-making through consultations, written manifestation, meetings, etc. (xxviii) Clauses for the solution of deadlock situations; etc."* 5. *In this sense, the incorporation by many countries of simplified joint stock companies, which have common legal patterns in the different systems and, to a greater extent, even by those that have incorporated the model law, is particularly important. This type of company shows a modern corporate law, with a strong contractualist imprint that makes it possible to adapt corporate engineering to the business and current winds, making the most of source dialogue. It is worth saying, as we have already stated on other occasions, that the mandatory nature of the LGS is available for SAS, as a subsidiary regime, provided that the duties of legality and non-damage are observed and abuses are avoided.*

613. However, the legal instruments of financing also present certain standardization according to the stage of investment in question, such as FAST (Founder Advisor Standard Template) and SAFE (Simple Agreements for Future Equity) taken from Anglo-Saxon law, as mirrors in convertible securities used in our environment, but which permanently undergo updates as a result of the collaborative evolutionary effort of operators. In and of participation business and participative loans introduced in our Civil and Commercial Code are part of that unstoppable development that involves the incipient systematization of the organizational relationships.

614. Lastly, intangible assets, which today are those of greater value, are registered in the parent companies that channel the investment, so that all commercialization is proposed from those companies born under legal systems that present not just flexible conditions with respect to corporate and investment engineering, but also the due protection of intellectual property rights and the like. Then, in order to exploit these assets, the company enters different markets through commercialization contracts, either intercompany or with third parties.

Reinterpretation of the Elements of the Corporation Concept

615. It should be mentioned that, with the evolution of complex post-modern societies at a global level, the corporation concept, which can be summarized as follows: "common contributions to be destined to the entity that develops the organized economic activity and then to participate in its results" (contribution, management, control and participation of positive or negative results), cannot now be abstract and is affected by post-modernity. Thus, in these times, the corporate purpose is no longer limited to the resulting profit motive; the following must necessarily be observed: care for the environment; human rights; the social function; the evolution of the community of risk among the partners; the diversity of contributions; the autonomy of will as a destination and result of a broad organizational contractualism with the only limits of abuse of rights and duty not to harm; the flexibility of the bodies in terms of their competences; the 2030 UN agenda for sustainable development (end of poverty; zero hunger; gender equality; decent work and economic growth; industry and innovation; responsible production; peace justice and solid institutions; partnerships to achieve objectives, etc.).

616. We do not believe that the concept of corporation has become obsolete, but we do believe that an evolutionary re-interpretation of its elements is necessary. This is imperative as a consequence of some facts that have undoubtedly urged us to review the box of memories from the adoption of sole proprietorships by different regimes; the flexibility of the corporate types; the feasibility of the most diverse intangible contributions; the variation in the current functions of capital; the diversity of possible contributors according to the different activities to be financed; the unrestricted corporate purpose; the possible delegations of competences between bodies; the inexhaustible breadth of the terms profit and loss; the notion of individual and collective third parties; the emphasis on viability in connection with the assets (tangible or intangible) available and not on their amount. All within the limit of not disregarding the imperative rules that tend to prevent damage, and which are but a reflection of the principle of good faith.

The Digital Era

617. The digital age implies the dizziness of immediacy and the savings that a common language means in international business. Custom takes care of that.

Digitalization also allows for the possibility of streamlining processes and information, avoiding bureaucracy, and guaranteeing operators a considerable horizontal and democratic pluralism to assess all the elements involved in contracting, eliminating asymmetry in the information of all stakeholders.

618. In terms of records, not only has the digital era had an impact on their digitization as they emerge from public records, but it has also made them less public. Not only do real rights enjoy the ius persequendi and follow the thing as the shadow follows the body, but there are also digital tokenization mechanisms that certify the originality and ownership of the non-fungible digital object and even constitute a note of value and publicity thereof, as is the case with the NFT (Non-Fungible Token). The confidence that an NFT generates in the global market about the product with respect to its originality and ownership far exceeds that offered by a territorial state R.P.

619. However, the reception of cryptocurrencies in international and domestic markets is common knowledge, generating a formal means of parastatal payment with uncertain backings. All of this is the result of the exponential growth that has taken place with respect to all these symbolic events of global digitization.

620. With digitalization in the era of global integration, the importance of the place of residence of the parties or the place of conclusion and even the language of a given instrument has also been relativized, since the legal relationship will be governed by the provisions of the exercise of party autonomy (the language that prevails in the event of ambiguities, applicable law according to conflict autonomy, etc.) and only, residually, by the criteria prevailing in the rules of conventional or autonomous private international law (the place of performance of the characteristic performance, application of converging rights, etc.).

621. Next, it is worth highlighting cases that deserve special attention nowadays in view of the virtual environment, such as a virtual head office of an Argentine company or even a virtual branch (web page) hosted in an Argentine geographic domain of a company incorporated abroad, which makes section 118 of the LGS applicable, electronic addresses for the purpose of formal notifications, etc. It is time to wonder about the efficiency of notification versus electronic means of communication as compared to the Official Gazette.

622. Digitalization has also entered modern corporate law, allowing the incorporation of companies at a distance through entirely digital processes. This can be seen from the mere assessment of the state regimes of the United States of America, of the 2019/1151 directive of the European Union recently transposed by Spain by way of Law 11/2023, as well as in Argentina in the provisions of Law 27349. In the latter case, digitalization in simplified joint stock companies has not been limited to the mere incorporation of the entity but also to bookkeeping, etc., so the jurisdictional control agencies have provided technological tools for this purpose (platforms for bookkeeping, registry entries, etc.) and this has also been replicated for the rest of the private legal entities. It will perhaps be the end of the uncommon practices of the disappearance or destruction of books in corporate insolvency proceedings.

623. Lastly, a brief reference should be made to the possibility of incorporating a company by means of a smart contract. Blockchain technology is applied to various scenarios, including smart contracts. What are smart contracts? As we have indicated on another occasion and to put it simply, we could say that a smart contract is a computer program that executes an agreement between parties in a system not controlled by any of them in such a way that, when one of the conditions included in its contractual provisions is fulfilled, the program executes the corresponding contractual clause without the intervention of a human beings. There are different programs that draw up these contracts or forms, highlighting those that allow access to the code (visual code) and this is written in Viper language (a version of programming language understandable by non-programmers).

624. In adopting blockchain technology, the Forms in the form of Smart Contracts make the execution of the provisions traceable. Thus smart contracts respond in their automatic operation to events which, when they occur, trigger the notification that a condition considered in the contract/form has been fulfilled and execute the default response (partial termination, withdrawal rights and voluntary withdrawals; suspension of rights due to non-compliance; transfer of shares and impact on the share registers; etc., and why not the incorporation of a company to consolidate the organization that the parties wanted to ensure if the conditions they considered were met).

Arbitration Clause

625. Arbitration, today, is not just an alternative mechanism for dispute resolution at the international level, but also increasingly so at the domestic level. The speed, confidentiality, specialization, unappealability, international recognition of the award as a "parastatal" solution as a consequence of the New York Convention or other international agreements, and other features that characterize it, account for the frequent use of the institute.

626. In contrast to the first stage in which institutional arbitration found shelter in international institutions dealing with international commercial arbitration, specialized arbitration and investment arbitration (ICSID, ICC, WIPO, etc.), and which had a lukewarm domestic presence as a complement to ad hoc arbitration, which was also exceptional, today we can affirm that the reality has changed. In developed countries this is evident, but even in Argentina, it can be concluded that arbitration is growing rapidly and has been institutionalized not only by stock exchanges and chambers of commerce but also by bar associations and a number of other different institutions.

627. This vertiginous gap in our age difference does not prevent us from thinking of returning to the so-called old heart of commercial law, always renewed, in a double effort: a simpler substantive law, configuring what we call the "economy of law," with fewer but more effective rules, freeing behavior to autonomy of the will as long as it does not infringe or damage the social order, and achieving a quick solution to conflicts.

628. It must be understood that stability will not be achieved through "market" laws without arbiters, involved in mere short-term financial speculations, not supportive, that try to undermine nations. This can only be achieved by applying the legal system as the order of the intended social order. Of course, as we pointed out, it is necessary to provide legal certainty through the stability of the laws and the rapid resolution of conflicts.

629. To return to the old heart of commercial law, to that which propelled it in the ancient world, perceiving the requirements of post-modernity: to return to practices and customs such as business ethics, and to immediate justice, without prejudice, as part of that ethics, to the obligation to negotiate, incorporated into the General Conditions of Contract of the European Union and UNCITRAL.

630. Ole Lando, after highlighting the number of countries that have adopted arbitration laws on the basis of the 1985 UNCITRAL Model Law—whose Article 28.1 opens the applicability of the rules of the lex mercatoria chosen by the parties—succinctly invokes the rules of the French Code of Civil Procedure (Article 1496), the Dutch Code of Civil Procedure (Article 1054) and the Italian Code of Civil Procedure (Article 834) and the 1996 English Arbitration Act (Article 46.1.b), as well as decisions of the Austrian Supreme Courts (Article 46.1.b). 1496), The Netherlands (Article 1054) and Italy (Article 834) and the 1996 English Arbitration Act (Article 46.1.b), as well as decisions of the Supreme Courts of Austria and Norway, to show the expansion of the tendency to allow arbitrators to apply the lex mercatoria even if the parties have not chosen it.

631. Correlatively with this, immediate justice is necessary—absolutely indispensable—or at least more efficient justice.

632. Today, the law is an "unknown," transactions are largely carried out clandestinely and justice is not efficient—because it is slow—with "hyperguarantism" that generates mountains of paperwork that does not honor the rules of due process and does not encourage entrepreneurs and investors. We are facing a change.

633. Our union in this essay is like a premonition of openness to freedom, not forgetting the traditional mandates imposed by good faith, the duty not to harm and the barriers against any abuse in the exercise of rights.

634. Lastly, Law 27349 proposes arbitration as an alternative solution to corporate conflicts regarding simplified joint stock companies and we believe its inclusion is appropriate. We even think that for the greater benefit of the partners or whoever has rights over the shares, obligated to accessory benefits, usufructuaries, joint owners, exercise of minority rights, etc., the possibility of establishing a virtual arbitration contract (accelerated) of the open justice type (e.g., Jur, Kleros, etc.) can be proposed with certain audacity, with the certainty that the arbitration awards are 100% binding in the domestic sphere according to the provisions of the CCCN and the CPCCN and in the international sphere according to the New York Convention. These arbitrations, such as KLEROS, consist of automated processes based on game theory for fast, safe and economical decisions. These automated arbitrations have a jury evaluation system (subject to criteria of speed, coherence, etc.) consisting of a system of rewards and penalties, which encourages them to be correctly carried out. Almost like the arbiter of the Middle Ages who, in the face of a conflict over the quality of the merchandise, ensured that the merchandise was incorporated into the market and that the parties received fair compensation for the state of affairs. The grain did not rot in a warehouse, nor did it generate warehouse expenses.

§3. Information Records and Corporate Law. A Tech Guarantee that Revitalizes Efficiency

635. The possibility of automating pre-qualified processes through the use of new technologies is a window of opportunity to overcome the bureaucracy that continues to affect us. Today, the state must allocate its human resources to those issues where reason cannot be sidestepped to guarantee the due exercise of rights, but not squander them in maintaining rigid, slow-moving structures that should nowadays undoubtedly be replaced by platforms and their operation by automated computer processes. Also, computerization and automation of processes in state platforms not only make them efficient but also democratize their use by all those administered. The following are some ideas where computerization has had and, if it continues to be implemented, may have a total impact on the different institutes of corporate law.

Introduction

636. The luster of these new times summons legal operators to rethink the institutes offered by the system within the reality offered by the information society and their possible not-so-distant future applications.

637. Thus, if the pandemic has been of any use to us, it is to think and entertain us with intellectual "flights" (the material ones have been delayed and/or suspended) that allow us to propose new alternatives to the somewhat deficient reality we live in. Perhaps a good institute that corporate law presents us with is information on the organization of legal entities, as a basis for future negotiations, particularly with predisposed contracts not negotiated with third parties, determining the powers of organic representatives between debtor and creditors in order to save time and also to favor distance negotiations or to make contact with other companies for the background and registered specialties.

638. It is worth noting that the new trends in digital law, added to the FAST culture of these times, generate a scenario that is not very compatible with the traditional reality of local, non-national and unfriendly registries. Advances such as electronic files, online auctions and hearings have been made, as well as the case of "prometea," which applies artificial intelligence in the administration of justice, but we do not know when incorporating a company if there is homonymy (although thank God the trademark right has been protected for some time by cross-checking), not even when the local control body authorizes the registration. And the matter is further complicated by the increasingly intense activity of unregistered companies, authorized by section IV of the General Companies Law.

639. However, the aim is to ensure security and success at the lowest cost and in the shortest time, so the digitization and automation of registration processes must necessarily comply with these objectives. Fast and cheap but unsafe is of use to no one.

640. What is certain is that, if alternative digital methods of business practice are incorporated into the registry routine and can then be assembled with orthodox practices, we would be on the right track in a country where the public sector overflows in structure and the private sector that sustains it contracts and decreases in summary proceedings.

641. Lastly, these lines no doubt involve a starting point, a trigger, but there is no glimpse of the seagulls announcing proximity to the coast, but only sailing on the high seas enjoying the freedom in the fresh air that proposes alternatives to abandon the robust and parsimonious, without losing guarantees or security and, if possible, which is possible, even strengthening them.

642. Meanwhile, we will try to postulate how blockchain technology at the head of a Smart Contract can be useful when implemented in a registration process, not only for practical purposes but also for the security of third parties and partners themselves.

Blockchain Technology

643. In a simplified approach to Blockchain technology, we could say that it refers to a safe way of storing and processing information. Lately, we have been used to storing information in a single place, whether it was memory in the PC, or external complementary or on a web hosting site (mail, cloud, etc.). With the blockchain—or some similar electronic scheme—that information can be stored in one place—with simultaneous parallel backup—so that the information is validated and any future modifications are subject to validation in the backup.

Smart Contracts—Automatic Registration Forms

644. Blockchain technology applies in several scenarios, among which is that of Smart Contracts. What are Smart Contracts? Again, to put it simply, we could say that a smart contract is a computer program that executes an agreement between parties in a system not controlled by any of them in such a way that, when one of the conditions included in its contractual provisions is fulfilled, the program executes the corresponding contractual clause without the intervention of a human being. We think of this in the AFIP (the Argentinian tax revenue agency) form, which, once filled out by the company after the public agency grants the CUIT (tax registry number), certain information will automatically be recorded in the general registry of companies, with a notice to the provincial registries that will not be altered and could then automatically register its local authorizations in the national registry by way of the same system.

645. There are different programs that draw up these contracts or forms, highlighting those that allow access to the code (visual code) and this is written in Viper language, a version of programming language understandable by non-programmers—interesting considering the participation that we propose of an official agency, AFIP in our opinion.

646. In adopting blockchain technology, the Forms in the form of Smart Contracts, as explained, make the execution of the provisions traceable. Moreover, although the costs involved in the use of this technology are not minor and hence a possible obstacle to its widespread use, we propose it as Official Forms that would make it possible to assume low costs for the contribution of those interested in registering or in getting to know the registrations. In this sense, the networks where Smart Contracts are used may consist of public networks (e.g., "mainnet" and "ropsten"), which we propose, even though there are semi-public networks (e.g., "alastria" created by several companies); or a private network. For the case proposed here, an alternative could be the use of the AFIP platform or a judicial one in "semi-public" mode used and consulted only by extranet subjects (lawyers and registered interested parties) so that they can be reliably informed of the data.

647. Finally, in their automatic operation, Smart Contracts respond to events which, when they occur, trigger the notification that a condition foreseen in the Form has been fulfilled by communicating it to the registry, in this case to those with extranet access.

Registry of Shares

648. Let us keep on thinking. One topic being discussed is the possibility of electronic registration of share ownership. We have no doubt that this data could be integrated into the national registry that we have just imagined. But in no way could it currently replace the Share Register book of immediate consultation for the partners and interested parties, as an information obligation in charge of the representative body. However, given the constitutive nature of the registration with respect to the condition of shareholders, we believe it is inexorable, for the viability of the tokenization of shares, that digital share registers be implemented where they automatically impact share transfers. Otherwise, tokenization could only make the transfer of the right to the share feasible, but not the share itself, regardless of the fact spousal assents and preemptive rights, drag-along clauses, among others must first be observed. As the issue of tokenization is currently being considered, it is more appropriate to implement it as a scheme for the organization of equity rights in a share management trust, rather than for the transfer of the shares themselves.

Open Justice Arbitration Clause

649. Nor do we rule out, but rather advise the insertion of an arbitration clause in the Articles of Incorporation, whether registered or not, with the simplicity that it can be incorporated in a simple company. Law 27349 proposes arbitration as an alternative solution for corporate conflicts regarding simplified joint stock companies and we believe it has been a wise inclusion.

650. For the greater benefit of the partners or whoever has rights over the shares, obligated to accessory benefits, usufructuaries, joint owners, exercise of minority rights, the possibility of establishing a virtual arbitration (accelerated) of the open justice type (e.g., Jur, Kleros, etc.), may be considered in the contract, whose arbitration awards are 100% binding domestically in accordance with the provisions of the CCCN and the CPCCN as well as internationally under the New York Convention. These arbitrations, such as KLEROS, consist of automated processes based on game theory for fast, safe and economical decisions. As with Jur, Kleros also holds its token (we stake pnk by paying for the cost of the operation and for three main functions: juror incentives, attack protection and governance of the administration platform). Kleros also has a jury evaluation system (subject to criteria of speed, consistency, etc.) consisting of a system of rewards and penalties in pnk. Kleros and Jur are very similar, although they are hosted on different networks.

Displaying Balance Sheets, Reports and Alerts

651. Although it is not our intention to reiterate in excess what has already been stated by the doctrine, it is worth noting that it would be important to add the incorporation of balance sheets or tax information, annual reports and decisions related to the viability of the company to the proposed registry, in order to reduce information and security costs, as well as to try to reduce the risks of access to information.

Form and Freedom of Content

652. However, the digital signature speeds up the subscription of instruments to be registered observing the ritual assumptions of validity, and freedom of content in autonomy of will is perhaps a tempting window between so much public order required in excess by certain regional jurisdictions, although clearly, it must observe good faith, no abuse of rights or distortion of the real documentation.

Judiciary Platform and Process Automation

653. Continuing with the proposal, in addition to preparing the registration system, the same platform can establish the data hosting process necessary for registration, that is: (1) Name and domicile (real and electronic) of the company, and of the partner or partners, and purpose or purposes of the activity, duration if any and escape clauses; (2) Company's assets, contributions, ancillary services and any rights to tangible or intangible assets, partners' participation; (3) Agencies, representation and statutory clauses; (4) Rules considered for the provisions of the general corporate law; (5) The clause for the resolution of conflicts and any restrictions on the transfer of shares, whether inherited or contractual.

654. The whole process of incorporation of companies and subsequent acts can be fully achieved through a judiciary application or the corporate police or AFIP, as the latter is federal. A change in the form of notifications could also be provided. A system of alerts on an electronic board of the registry and linkage with the original entry, with automatic notification at the registered electronic addresses, could be envisaged in view of the dubious effectiveness of publishing edicts in the local jurisdiction. Finally, we say that this document constitutes a starting point to jointly think of solutions to automate those acts subject to being automated and, in this sense, to collaborate with the reduction of the state and to strengthen its function of facilitator of individual and collective development of the administered party, whether human or legal person.

Selected Bibliography

Abriani, N. et al., *Derecho Italiano de Sociedades,* ed. Tirant lo Blanch, Valencia, 2008.

Balbin, S., *Manual de Derecho Societario,* Abeledo Perrot, Bs As, 2015.

Boggiano, A., *Curso de Derecho Internacional Privado,* ed. Abeledo Perrot, Bs As, 2003.

Bottiglieri, M.G. & Zavatti de Rougier, A., El Derecho Internacional Privado Argentino, ed. Lex, Córdoba, 2016.

Corcos, L., *La Sociedad de Responsabilidad Limitada: Fallas, Omisiones y Observaciones a la actual Ley 11645, Su Corrección y Proyecto de Modificación a la Misma*, UBA, BS As, 1962.

Díaz Labrano, R., Globalización, el Derecho del Mercado y la Defensa de la Competencia en el Mercosur, en http://www.oas.org/es/sla/ddi/docs/publicaciones_digital_XXXI_curso_derecho_internacional_2004_Roberto_Ruiz_Diaz_Labrano.pdf (disponible al November 9, 2018).

Díaz Labrano, R., EL Mercosur, Marco Jurídico Institucional, Análisis y Perspectivas de sus normas derivadas, Ed. Continental, 1993.

Dobson, J.M., *El Abuso de la Personalidad Jurídica,* ed. Depalma, Bs As, 1985.

Dreyzin de Klor, A., *El Derecho Internacional Privado Actual,* Zavalía, Bs As, 2017.

Dreyzin de Klor, A., "Derecho Internacional Privado," Ed. Zavalía, Buenos Aires, 2015.

Escuti, I., "Sociedades," Astrea, Bs As, 2006.

Farina, J., Sociedades Comerciales, Zeus, Rosario, 1972.

Favier Dubois, E. (h), *Las Sociedades Constituidas en el Extranjero Frente a la Ley 19550,* ed. Errepar, Bs As.

Fernandez Rozas, J.C., *Ius mercatorum, Consejo Gral. Del notariado, Madrid,* 2003.

Fernandez Rozas, J.C., Arenas García, R. & De Miguel Asensio, P., *Derecho de los Negocios Internacionales,* ed. Iustel, Madrid, 2016.

Ferrara, F., Empresarios y Sociedades, ed. Revista de Derecho Privado, Madrid.

Ferro, H.R., Legislación de la Empresa, ed. Astrea, Bs As, 1979.

Garcimartín Alférez, F. La Sentencia "Centros" del Tribunal de Justicia de las Comunidades Europeas: una visión a través de los comentarios, en: file:///C:/Users/Jose/Downloads/nota_GARCIAMARTIN_FranciscoJ%20(2).pdf (disponible en internet al November 9, 2018).

Garo, F., *Sociedades Comerciales,* La Facultad SRL, Bs As, 1949.

Selected Bibliography

Gomez, N.A., Libertad de Establecimiento de las Sociedades en el Marco de la Integración, VIII Congreso Argentino de Derecho Societario, IV Congreso Iberoamericano de Derecho Societario y de la Empresa, Rosario, 2001. https://repositorio.uade.edu.ar/xmlui/bitstream/handle/123456789/2201/CDS08040099.pdf?sequence=1 (disponible al November 9, 2018).

Halperin, I., Sociedades Comerciales, Ed. Depalma, Bs As, 1964.

Machado de Villafañe, T., *Inaplicabilidad del Artículo 31 de la Ley de Sociedades a las Sociedades Extranjeras,* LL, Bs As, 1995.

Manovil, R., *Sociedades Multinacionales: Ley Aplicable a sus Formalidades de Constitución y Contralor de Funcionamiento,* LL, Bs As, 2005.

Mercado de Sala, M.C. (Dir.), et al., *Empresa y Sociedad*, ed. Lerner, Córdoba, 2018.

Molinari, I., *La Nueva Resolución de la IGJ: Un Paso Acertado en Relación a las Off Shore,* elDial.com-CC384.

Nissen, R., *Curso de Derecho Societario,* Ed. Hammurabi, Buenos Aires, 2015.

Nissen, R., *La Situación Legal de las Sociedades Extranjeras Integrantes de Sociedades Argentinas en Infracción a lo Dispuesto por el Artículo 123 de la ley 19950,* IV Jornadas de institutos de derecho comercial.

Orchansky, B.K., *Nuevos Enfoques Respecto de la Actuación en Nuestro País de las Sociedades Constituidas en el Extranjero, Advocatus,* Córdoba, 1996.

Otaegui, Julio C., La Sociedad desde la Ley 15 hasta el Proyecto de 1998 sobre Código Civil Unificado con el Código de Comercio, disponible al 20 de abril de 2019 en www.acaderc.org.ar.

Ramirez, A., "El Objeto Social en la Sociedad por Acciones Simplificadas," Tomo La Ley 2018-B, Bs As, fecha April 18, 2018.

Reyes Villamizar, F. Derecho Societario en Estados Unidos y la Unión Europea, ed. Legis, Bogotá, 2013.

Richard, E.H. & Muiño, O.M. "Derecho Societario," Astrea, Bs As, 1997.

Richard, E.H., Escuti, I. & Romero, J., "Manual de Derecho Societario," Astrea, Bs As, 1980.

Rodriguez Artigas, F. y otros, Revista Derecho de Sociedades, ed. Thomson Reuters, Madrid, 2010.

Roitman, H., Aguirre, H. & Chiavassa, E., cap. Las Sociedades—Proyecto de CCC-, Revista de Derecho Privado y Comunitario, Ed. Rubinzal Culzoni, 2013.

Roitman, H., Ley de Sociedades Comerciales Comentada y Anotada, ed. La Ley, Bs As, 2006.

Rovira, A., *Los Arts. 30, 31, 32, y 33 de la Ley de Sociedades Comerciales y su Aplicación a las Sociedades Constituidas en el Extranjero,* LL, Bs As, 1981.

Verón, A.V., *Sociedades Comerciales,* Ed. Astrea, Bs As, 2007.

Verón, A.V., *Tratado de los Conflictos Societarios, LL,* Bs As, 2006.

Vitolo, D.R., *Manual de Sociedades,* ed. Estudio, Bs As, 2016.

Zaldivar, E. & Rovira, A., *El artículo 123 de la Ley 19550. Una Polémica Concluida en Torno de su Alcance, Jurisprudencia Anotada,* Bs As, 1980.

Zunino, J.O., *Régimen de Sociedades,* ed. Astrea, Bs As, 2016.

Index

The numbers here refer to paragraph numbers.

Index

www.ingramcontent.com/pod-product-compliance
Lightning Source LLC
Chambersburg PA
CBHW071341230926
51846CB00002B/411
9789403532783